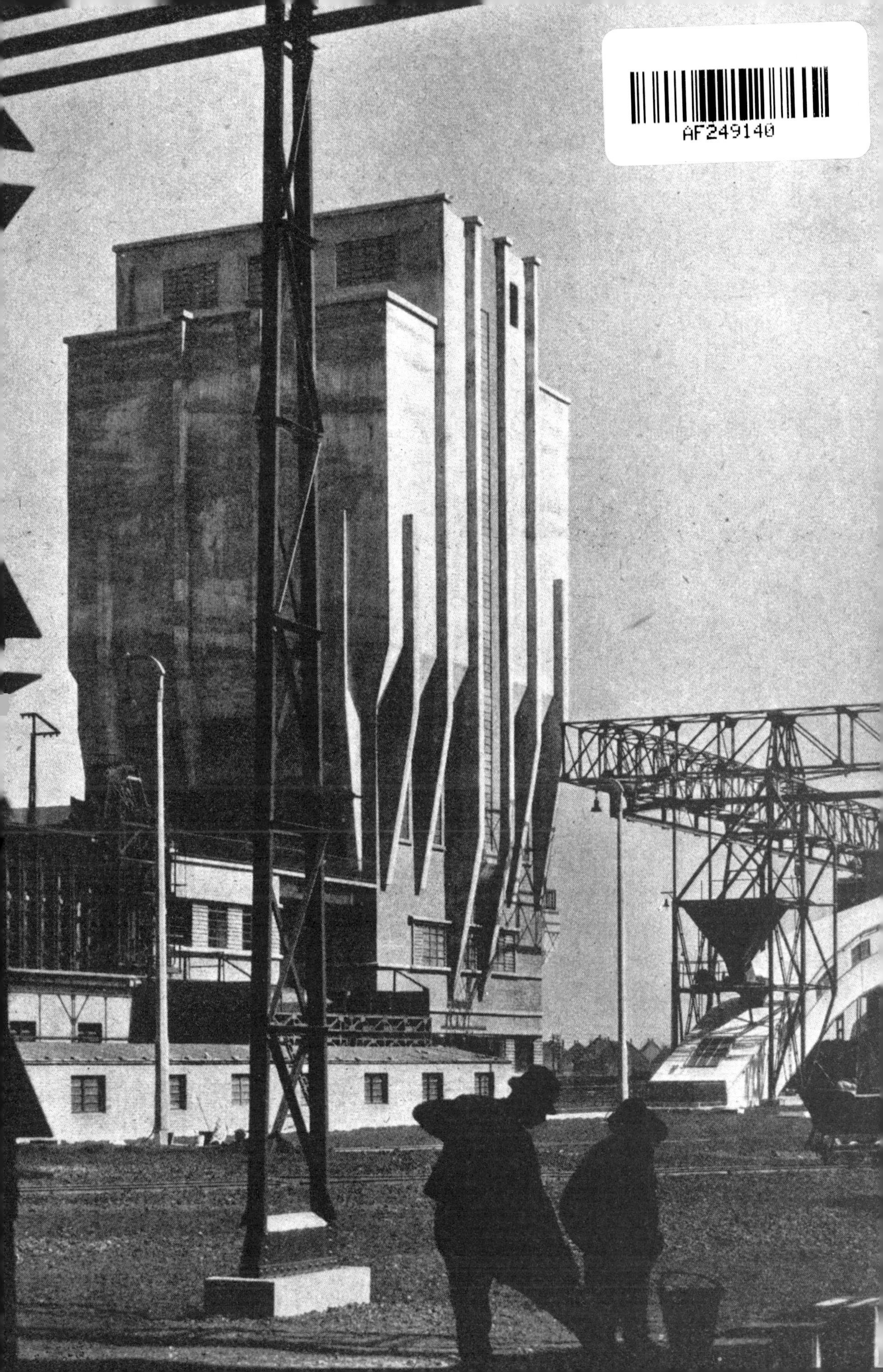
AF249140

The Victory of the New Building Style

Published by the Getty Research Institute

Walter Curt Behrendt

The Victory of the New Building Style

The Victory of the New Building Style

Walter Curt Behrendt

Introduction by Detlef Mertins

Translation by Harry Francis Mallgrave

Texts & Documents

The Getty Research Institute Publications and Exhibitions Program

Texts & Documents
Julia Bloomfield, Kurt W. Forster, Harry F. Mallgrave, Thomas F. Reese, Michael S. Roth, and Salvatore Settis, *Editors*

The Victory of the New Building Style
Christian Otto, *Editorial Consultant*
Steven Lindberg, *Manuscript Editor*

Translated from Walter Curt Behrendt, *Der Sieg des neuen Baustils*. Copyright 1927 by Akademischer Verlag Dr. Fr. Wedekind & Co., Stuttgart, succeeded by Karl Krämer Verlag, Stuttgart. Published by agreement with Karl Krämer Verlag

Published by the Getty Research Institute, Los Angeles, CA 90049-1688
© 2000 by the Getty Research Institute
All rights reserved. Published 2000
Printed in the United States of America

04 03 02 01 00   5 4 3 2 1

Cover: Alfred Fischer-Essen, Municipal offices, Hans-Sachs-Haus, Gelsenkirchen, North Rhine-Westphalia, Germany

Frontispiece: Alfred Fischer-Essen, Coal tower, Saxon mine, Hamm, North Rhine-Westphalia, Germany

Library of Congress Cataloging-in-Publication Data
Behrendt, Walter Curt, 1884–1945.
[Sieg des neuen Baustils. English]
The victory of the new building style / Walter Curt Behrendt;
introduction by Detlef Mertins; translation by Harry Francis Mallgrave.
p. cm. – (Texts & documents)
Includes bibliographical references and index.
ISBN 0-89236-563-3 (pbk.)
1. Architecture, Modern – 20th century – Germany. 2. Architecture – Germany.
3. Functionalism (Architecture) – Germany.
4. Architecture, Modern – 20th century – Philosophy.
I. Title. II. Series.
NA1068.B4513 2000
724'.6 – dc21   99-38321
                                                         CIP

Contents

Acknowledgments

I would like to express my appreciation to the editors of the Texts & Documents series for affording me the opportunity to contribute to this invaluable program of translations. I am grateful to Harry F. Mallgrave for his guidance and encouragement throughout the project and to Steven Lindberg for his careful editing and help on so many other fronts. The research was assisted in Berlin by Laurie Stein at the Werkbund-Archiv and by Kai Gutschow, who generously shared with me his compilation of book reviews along with many insights into Behrendt's work and the context of architectural criticism in Germany between the wars. Conversations with Fritz Neumeyer enriched my understanding of Behrendt's role in the competitive architectural scene in Berlin. Christian Otto provided insightful and helpful criticism of the introduction. Finally, my thanks to Sharon Brooks for her unwavering patience and support.

—Detlef Mertins

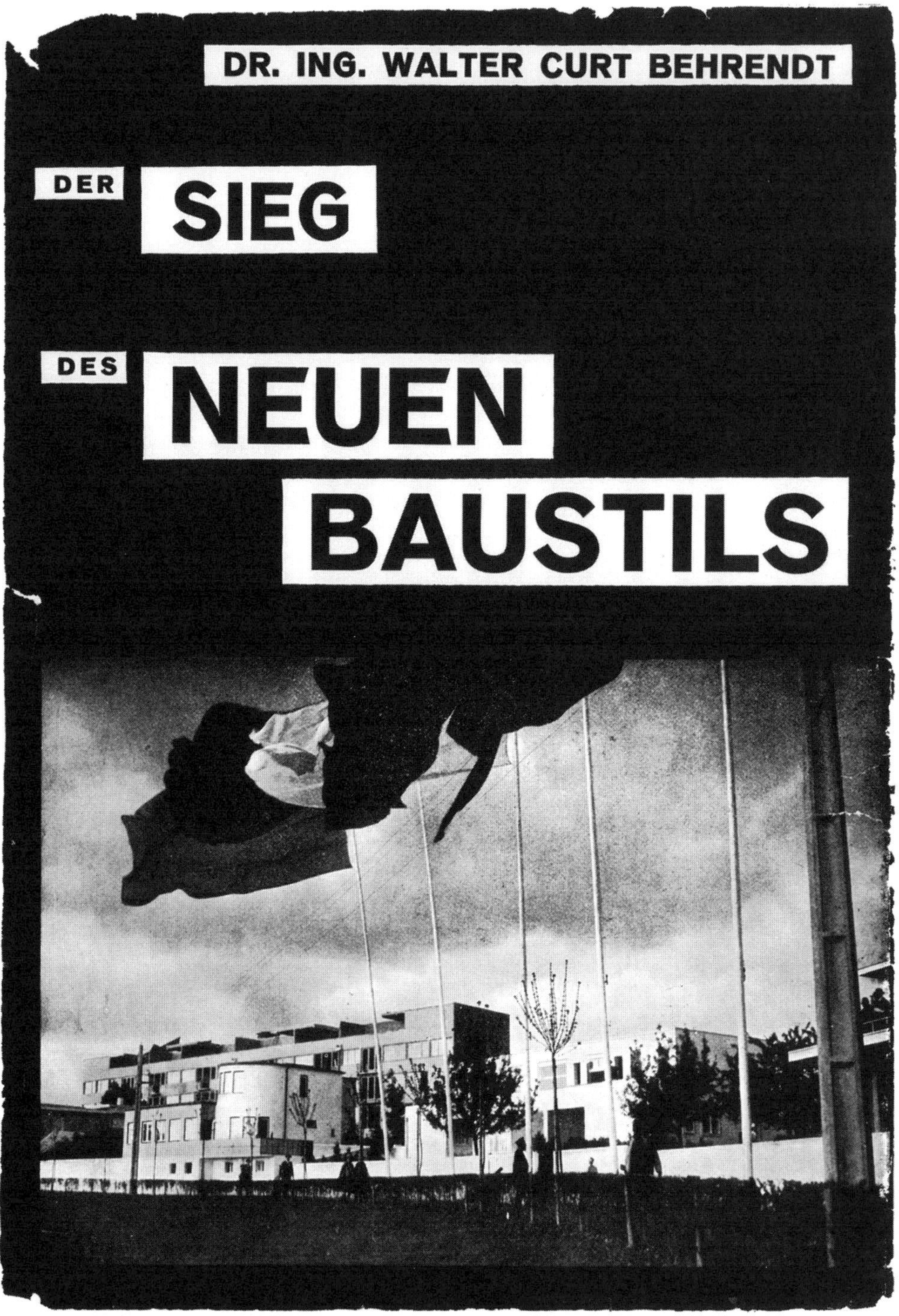

Fig. 1. *Der Sieg des neuen Baustils*
Cover design by Werner Gräff, using a photograph by Dr. Lossen & Co., Stuttgart-Feuerbach
From Walter Curt Behrendt, *Der Sieg des neuen Baustils* (Stuttgart: Fritz Wedekind & Co., 1927)

Introduction
Detlef Mertins

Image

In the annals of architectural history, Walter Curt Behrendt's *Der Sieg des neuen Baustils* (The victory of the new building style), 1927, has been remembered most often for its bold declaration that the battle for modern architecture had been won, that a new mode of cultural production had arisen which would, finally, be adequate to the modern age.[1] It has been remembered most, then, for its title, or more precisely for the combination of slogan and image that gave its cover the character of a graphic manifesto. Linking his cry of victory to a heroic publicity image of the newly opened Weissenhofsiedlung of the German Werkbund's *Die Wohnung* (The dwelling) exhibition in Stuttgart, Behrendt capitalized on the extensive publicity for the show and heralded its model housing estate (*Siedlung*) as demonstrative of a new unity between design and everyday life, not only in Germany but internationally. Photographed from below, on the slope of the hill, the *Siedlung* appears like an ocean liner looming on the horizon of history (fig. 1). From this vantage point, the open ensemble of buildings and gardens by sixteen different architects coheres into a rising mass of smooth surfaces perforated by expansive windows and terraces. A continuous, low wall ties the otherwise irregular profile into a unified front and catches the light as storm clouds pass overhead. A battery of flags, planted on the crest of the hill, fly vigorously in the wind, collapsing the protracted emergence of the new into the drama of a moment—the rush of battle suddenly turning into the nervous euphoria of the first, still tentative, declaration of victory.

This group of blocky buildings with unornamented surfaces, flat roofs, frameless windows, and airy terraces appeared to mark the crystallization of a new paradigm that had been desired and even projected by several generations of architects, albeit without durable success. Writing in 1860, for instance, the influential architect, theorist, and historian Gottfried Semper had invoked the image of nebulas, "glimmering … among the brilliant miracles of stars … between destruction and regeneration," to portray the new historical formation whose emergence he thought he was witnessing.[2] Contending, however, that expressing "the social structure of society and the conditions of the times … artistically and in a monumental way has always been the most eminent task of architecture,"[3] Semper suggested that a new architecture remained contingent on the prior emergence of a "new idea of universal historical importance."[4]

1

For the generation raised in the heady atmosphere of modernization and urbanization at the turn of the century, coming to maturity during the vast destruction of World War I and the equally vast reconstruction afterward, the widespread proliferation of new types of buildings seemed to confirm that new norms of everyday life had definitively emerged for mass society and that their legitimate architectural counterforms had arrived with them. The unprecedented forms of railway stations, department stores and arcades, exhibition buildings, factories, mass housing, theaters, and cinemas featured refined engineering structures and an expansive spatiality, all realized with mass-produced elements, synthetic materials, and industrialized modes of construction. The massive public-housing programs of cities such as Berlin and Frankfurt demonstrated that modest yet generous dwellings were finally achievable in a generalized way. The shift of political support in 1924 from the extremist parties to the centrist Sozialdemokratische Partei Deutschlands, the steady rise of the German mark and expansion of the economy following the Dawes Plan, the high level of public spending in the arts as well as housing, and the explosion of artistic innovation in new media, all contributed to the sense that a new historical formation was rising from the ashes of destruction and defeat.

The image of a phoenixlike rebirth of society through cultural work had been promoted vigorously by artists, writers, and architects during the suspended state between war and peace in 1918–1919.[5] In turn, these dreams of the "new man," "new society," and "new building" rearticulated the earlier hopes of Jugendstil, the Secession, and the German Werkbund prior to World War I, as well as youth and reform movements across the fine arts, decorative arts, education, everyday life, and urban design. From the "rebirth of German culture" at the artists' colony in Darmstadt and the "reform of life" (*Lebensreform*) in garden cities such as Hellerau[6] to the post–World War I provocations of artists' groups such as the Arbeitsrat für Kunst (Work council for the arts) and the Novembergruppe (November group),[7] artists and architects had been assigned leading roles in the comprehensive renewal of society under the adverse conditions of modern industrial capitalism.

The postwar mood of new beginnings was captured most comprehensively in a trilogy of 1918–1919, not by an artist or architect but by the industrialist, banker, intellectual, and politician Walther Rathenau. Having been a minister in the war cabinet as well as director of the giant German electrical company AEG (Allgemeine Elektricitäts-Gesellschaft), which was founded by his father, Emil (the patron of Peter Behrens), Walther Rathenau set out a vigorous polemic for a new socialist republic in a trilogy of works: *Die neue Wirtschaft* (The new economy), 1918; *Der neue Staat* (The new state), 1919; *Die neue Gesellschaft* (The new society), 1919.[8] The importance Rathenau assigned to cultural production centered on its capacity to provide a new image of society to which we could "adapt ourselves."[9] No longer was the work of culture taken to be the symbolic interpretation of preexisting social forms and conditions. Instead, Rathenau considered culture to be a productive force capable of generating these forms through education, new knowledge, and willful innovation. Acknowledging the challenge of rebuilding his country, he advocated that "the will to complete cultivation of the body, the intellect and the soul of the people must be so strong that all questions of convenience, of enjoyment, of prestige and of material interests must sink far into the background."[10] He projected a long period of toil and poverty, "of a penurious civilization and of a deeply-endangered culture"[11] and counseled, "Let us tread our path of suffering with a pride which disdains to be consoled by illusions."[12] He argued nevertheless that spiritual culture (*Kultur*) was central to social renewal, as both its goal and the means for passage beyond a purely materialist civilization (*Zivilisation*):[13]

> The conception of Culture as our true and unique faculty must be so profoundly grasped that in public life and legislation it must have the first word and the last. Though we become as poor as church-mice we must stake our last penny on this, and tune up our education and instruction, our models and outlook, our motives and claims, our achievement and our atmosphere, to so high a point that any one coming into Germany shall feel that he is entering into a new age.[14]

Among the artistic avant-garde, the topos of new beginnings continued to be reiterated in the years after World War I, among Expressionists and Dadaists alike, figured alternatively in terms of inner soulfulness, nihilism, and engineering—the last being valued for its combination of radical rationality and precise fantasy. At the same time, new emphasis on simple construction (*Bauen*) in architecture affirmed the break with the past and served as a rallying cry for new collaborations among the arts from which a new architecture was thought to emerge. Sharing the realist spirit of Rathenau's new poverty, avant-gardists and reformers alike were ready to ride the wave of reconstruction as Germany embarked on a comprehensive restructuring of its economic, technological, social, and urban matrix. Inspired by the example of De Stijl in Holland and Constructivism in the Soviet Union, the architectural scene in Berlin turned against its postwar celebration of craft and utopian fantasies in favor of concrete realizations of objective social ideals. At the same time, Berlin became a site of convergence for the European avant-garde and assumed an orientation more international and cosmopolitan than strictly nationalist. The Düsseldorf Congress of Progressive Artists and the Dada and Constructivist meeting in Weimar, both organized by Theo van Doesburg in 1922, helped establish a beachhead for a pan-European and pan-avant-garde Constructivist movement.

Similar efforts at consolidating European Constructivism were made in the magazines and exhibitions. Journals such as *De Stijl*, 1917–1932; *L'esprit nouveau*, 1920–1925; *Veshch' = Objet = Gegenstand*, 1922; *G: Material zur elementaren Gestaltung*, 1923–1926; *ABC*, 1924–1928; and *i 10*, 1927–1929, attempted to redefine architecture in relation to the larger, historical formation. All aimed at comprehensiveness, unity, and totality, albeit each from its own perspective. All were interdisciplinary. Gustav Friedrich Hartlaub's celebrated exhibition of 1925, *Neue Sachlichkeit: Nachexpressionistische Malerei* (New objectivity: Postexpressionist painting), and Franz Roh's concurrent publication, *Nach-Expressionismus: Magischer Realismus* (Postexpressionism: Magical realism), were among the best known of the efforts to define postexpressionist artistic production in Europe.[15] While some called the new direction a return to order and even a new classicism, Wilhelm Worringer recognized the bit of magic in Roh's "magic realism" as "the sediment from Expressionism grown cold." In this way, he pointed to the persistence of fantasy and mystery in objective realism and to the principle that outer appearances expressed inner purposes, spiritual forces, and mysterious wills that otherwise remained hidden.[16] Various names were offered for the new formation—Neues Bauen (New building), Neue Sachlichkeit, Rationalismus, Funktionalismus, Konstruktivismus—yet none proved fully adequate to subsuming the diverse theories and practices, aims and ideals proliferating in architecture, art, photography, and design.

In the sphere of architecture, Walter Gropius led the way in presenting the new paradigm to a general public with the Bauhaus exhibition of 1923, which included a survey of new international architecture that was followed by his picture book of 1925, *Internationale Architektur*.[17] This collection of images, focusing on the external forms of the new architecture, provided graphic evidence that a new spirit, international in scope and hence comparable to the Gothic, Baroque, and Renaissance, had already assumed a clear, identifiable corporeal form. Gropius's publication was the first in a series of Bauhaus books, edited by László Moholy-Nagy, which also served to draw the avant-gardists together.[18] Adolf Behne's publication of 1926, *Der moderne Zweckbau* (The modern functional building), extended the genre of the didactic picture book focusing on utilitarian buildings as the original locus of the new architecture and offered a more extensive theoretical exposition.[19] Heinrich de Fries's *Junge Baukunst in Deutschland* (Recent building-art in Germany), which also appeared in 1926, presented a diverse cross section of work by younger and lesser-known German architects as exemplary of a new way of thinking about building, related to the larger transformation of the world picture (*Weltbild*) and world feeling (*Weltgefühl*).[20] In the same year as Behrendt's *Sieg*, the first comprehensive and scholarly history of modern architecture appeared, also heavily illustrated: Gustav Platz's *Die Baukunst der neuesten Zeit* (Building-art of the latest period).[21] The production of popularizing documentations of the new architecture continued during the late 1920s and early 1930s, including Behne's *Neues Wohnen—Neues Bauen* (New living—new building), 1927; Ludwig Hilberseimer's *Internationale neue Baukunst* (New international building-art), 1927, and *Beton als Gestalter* (Concrete as designer), coauthored with Julius Vischer, 1928; Sigfried Giedion's animated history of iron and concrete, *Bauen in Frankreich, Bauen in Eisen, Bauen in Eisenbeton* (Building in France, building in iron, building in ferroconcrete), 1928; Walter Müller-Wulckow's series, *Deutsche Baukunst der Gegenwart*

(Contemporary German building-art), 1925–1929; and Arthur Korn's *Glas im Bau und als Gebrauchsgegenstand* (Glass in construction and as a utensil), circa 1929.[22] In English, Bruno Taut's *Modern Architecture* (simultaneously published in German under the title *Die neue Baukunst in Europa und Amerika*), 1929, and Henry-Russell Hitchcock's *Modern Architecture*, 1929, provided survey introductions, one by an architect-protagonist, the other by a historian.[23] Hitchcock and Philip Johnson's *The International Style: Architecture since 1922,* which followed their exhibition at the Museum of Modern Art in 1932, remains today the best-known example of this genre combining photographic documentation with theoretical-historical exposition.[24] As Werner Oechslin has observed, this genre attempted to exploit the power of the image to precipitate a new architectural mainstream and a new public.[25]

In 1919 the Werkbund resumed the full scope of its prewar activities, having continued the publication of the yearbook even into World War I. A new journal was launched in 1922 with Walter Riezler as editor.[26] Titled *Die Form: Monatsschrift für gestaltende Arbeit* (Form: Monthly journal for design work), the journal served a coalition of organizations and lasted only the one year.[27] The Werkbund's exhibition program resumed in 1923 with the show *Die Form ohne Ornament* (Form without ornament), accompanied by the catalog and texts by Wolfgang Pfleiderer and Walter Riezler. The show portrayed a middle road to modernity — moderate and bourgeois — conceived as a potentially generalizable new normativity in the production of household items, furniture, and applied arts.[28] It sought to isolate new types and constants that offered security in the rush and flux of change. The catalog launched a new book series that included Fritz Schopohl's *Deutsche Wiederaufbauarbeit* (German reconstruction work), 1925; Riezler's *Das deutsche Kunstgewerbe* (German crafts), 1926; and Ernst Kropp's *Wandlung der Form im 20. Jahrhundert* (Transformation of form in the twentieth century), 1926.

It was in this context that the Weissenhofsiedlung was initiated in 1925.[29] With the participation of leading Modernists from across Europe, it was promoted as the very image of a new, overarching environmental paradigm, operative at all scales from domestic fittings to city planning. It was to be the most definitive iteration yet of cultural renewal by means of a new domesticity adequate to mass society. And it was in this context that Behrendt proffered a portrait of a new collective formation in architecture, poised finally to supersede the historicism of the late nineteenth century. In his review of the show, Theo van Doesburg clarified the nature of the undertaking when he called it a "demonstrative exhibition" that "wanted to place the visitor within, instead of opposite, the new environment and make him 'experience' it, instead of 'looking at' it."[30] For van Doesburg, the exhibition was successful because it was already a piece of the new world achieved in advance of its fuller realization. The *Siedlung* made it possible to experience the internal cohesion of the "new entity," to see how all parts of the *Gesamtarbeit* (the total product) of furniture, color, and utensils were organically combined into "the unity of a collective stylistic purpose."[31] Van Doesburg gave credit for this idea to the younger generation grouped around Hans Richter's periodical *G,* and he commended one of its collaborators, Ludwig Mies van der Rohe, for having brought it to fruition as chief architect of the exhibition — "by far the strongest personality of the group of German constructivists."[32]

The image on the cover of Behrendt's book tied it to the Werkbund exhibition in a complex relationship. Having reactivated the Werkbund's journal, *Die Form* — he was editor from October 1925 to December 1926 — Behrendt had actively shaped the discursive field within which the exhibition took place.[33] Behrendt entered the architectural scene in Berlin just as the Werkbund was being founded, and his intellectual formation paralleled its trajectory. In his five previous books and numerous critical essays, as well as his editorial direction of several other journals, Behrendt too had hoped to articulate the terms for a new unity of cultural production under the sign of technology. Furthermore, it was Werner Gräff — artist, photographer, filmmaker, *and* director of public relations for the show — who designed Behrendt's cover. Gräff used the image again as the frontispiece of the two official publications of the show, which he edited: *Bau und Wohnung* (Building and dwelling), 1927, and *Innenräume* (Interiors), 1928 (fig. 2). Also published by the Akademischer Verlag Dr. Fritz Wedekind & Co. of Stuttgart, the continuities between *Sieg* and these other books lent it a quasi-official status with respect to the exhibition, aligned as much, perhaps more, with the principal organizers as with the Werkbund itself.[34] More directly associated with the Werkbund, Ludwig Hilberseimer's *Internationale neue Baukunst* resembled *Sieg* in its scope, while featuring examples that were more Constructivist and rationalist and providing only a brief text (fig. 3).[35]

As has often been noted, the opportunity of the exhibition brought to the fore tensions and rivalries within the Werkbund, which had, from its inception, been but a loose coalition of figures and ideologies. Drawn together by the common ambition of reforming German manufacturing in architecture and the applied arts, it was as prone to be drawn apart over disputes of principle as practice. Appointed by Mies as publicist for the Werkbund exhibition, Gräff maintained his loyalty throughout the battles over its planning, having already collaborated with Mies on *G.* Although Behrendt's affiliation with Mies and Gräff was less unequivocal and remained tempered by concurrent relationships with others in the Berlin architectural scene, he was a consistent promoter of Mies's work. In 1923 he had been responsible for the first American reception of Mies's Glass Skyscraper project.[36] During the early days of planning the Weissenhofsiedlung, he had even been considered for organizing it in conjunction with Mies and Hans Poelzig.[37] Later, in 1926, it was Behrendt who relayed Mies's invitation to Le Corbusier to participate in the exhibition.[38] And Behrendt featured three of Mies's seminal projects in *Sieg:* the Glass Skyscraper, the Concrete Office Building, and the Brick Country House.

Opposition to Mies's plan for the Weissenhofsiedlung formed along several fault lines within the Werkbund and among its sponsors. The geographic division between Berlin and Stuttgart — center and periphery, north and south —

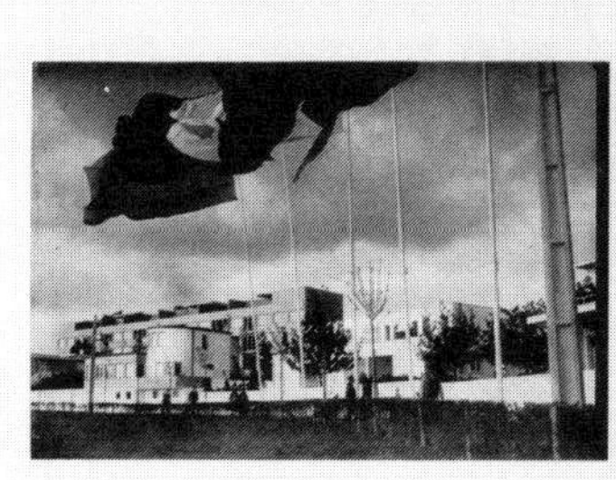

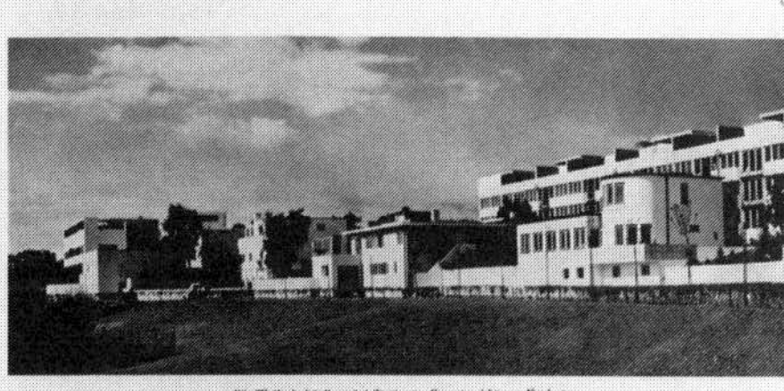

Die Weißenhofsiedlung bei Stuttgart. Gesamtansicht von Nordosten.

INTERNATIONALE NEUE BAUKUNST

Die Voraussetzungen und Grundlagen der neuen Baukunst sind verschiedenster Art. Die jeweiligen Benutzungsansprüche bestimmen den Zweckcharakter des Bauwerks. Material und Konstruktion sind die materiellen Mittel seines Aufbaues. Daneben üben Herstellungstechnik und Betriebsführung, wirtschaftliche und soziologische Momente einen erheblichen Einfluß aus. Über allem aber steht herrschend der schöpferische Wille des Architekten. Er bestimmt das Maß des Anteils der einzelnen Elemente. Bildet aus dem Nebeneinander die gestaltete Einheit des Bauwerks.

Die Art des Gestaltungsvorgangs bestimmt den Charakter der neuen Baukunst. Sie ist nicht auf äußerliche Dekorativität gestellt, sondern Ausdruck der geistigen Durchdringung aller Elemente. Das ästhetische Element ist daher nicht mehr übergeordnet, Selbstzweck, wie bei der den Bauorganismus ignorierenden Fassadenarchitektur, sondern ist gleich allen andern Elementen eingeordnet in das Ganze. Erhält erst im Zusammenhang mit diesem Ganzen seinen Wert, seine Bedeutung.

Überordnung eines Elements hat immer Störungen zur Folge. Daher erstrebt die neue Baukunst Gleichgewicht aller Elemente, Harmonie. Diese ist aber keine äußerliche, schematische, sondern eine für jede Aufgabe neue. Ihr liegt kein Stilschema zugrunde, sondern sie ist der jeweilige Ausdruck der gegenseitigen Durchdringung aller Elemente unter der Herrschaft eines gestaltenden Willens. Der neuen Baukunst liegen daher keine Stilprobleme, sondern Bauprobleme zugrunde.

So wird auch die überraschende Übereinstimmung der äußeren Erscheinungsform dieser internationalen neuen Baukunst verständlich. Sie ist keine modische Formenangelegenheit, wie vielfach angenommen wird, sondern elementarer Ausdruck einer neuen Baugesinnung. Zwar vielfach differenziert durch örtliche und nationale Sonderheiten und durch die Person des Gestalters, im ganzen aber das Produkt gleicher Voraussetzungen. Daher die Einheitlichkeit ihrer Erscheinungsform. Ihre geistige Verbundenheit über alle Grenzen hinweg.

Ludwig Hilberseimer.

Fig. 2. *Innenräume*
The photograph of the Weissenhofsiedlung on this title page also appeared on the cover that Gräff designed for Behrendt's *Sieg*
From Werner Gräff, *Innenräume* (Stuttgart: Fritz Wedekind & Co., 1928)

Fig. 3. *Internationale neue Baukunst*
This view of the Weissenhofsiedlung is similar to the one on the cover of Behrendt's *Sieg*, albeit from a slightly different angle
From Ludwig Hilberseimer, *Internationale neue Baukunst* (Stuttgart: Julius Hoffmann, 1927)

became the basis for an increasingly public polarization of the reform architects, in political as well as architectural terms. The organizers based in Berlin were mostly, like Behrendt, members of the newly formed lobby group Der Ring, advocates of Neues Bauen (German functionalism/Constructivism), politically "left wing," and internationalist in orientation.[39] In contrast, the Stuttgart school, led by Werkbund members Paul Bonatz and Paul Schmitthenner, was conservative and nationalist, both in architecture and politics. For them the only authentic architecture was rooted in the inheritance of the past and the character of the people, homeland, blood, and soil. For those hoping to secure for Stuttgart a public-housing program similar in scale to that of Berlin or Frankfurt, Mies's inclusion of so many individually designed villas also seemed inadequate. Even Richard Döcker, a young Stuttgart protégé of Bonatz who was nevertheless an advocate of Neues Bauen and was responsible for coordinating the construction, criticized Mies's plan, preferring repetition, orthogonality, and a more conventional approach to site planning. In Berlin, Mies was further challenged by his colleague Hugo Häring, who attempted to circumvent his authority in order to promote uniform results by imposing a design code.[40] By 1927 a general sense of expectancy had precipitated a host of competing efforts to set the terms, forms, and image of the immanent paradigm, with each protagonist accusing the other of false claims to authenticity and unity, often rehearsing oppositional tropes long familiar to architectural discourse, most notably the opposition of organism and mechanism.

In the opening segments of *Sieg*, Behrendt explicitly identified the opponents of the new building-art in a way that suggests his alignment with Mies, albeit on somewhat different terms. Behrendt isolated three types and ranked them in order of greatest danger: those who dismissed the new building-art as harmless artistic folly; then, the defenders of sanctified traditions, academic rules, and professional judgment who failed to recognize the vital role within tradition of the coincidence of life and death, growth and decay, construction and destruction; and, most importantly, those among the Modernists whom Behrendt called opportunists and profiteering imitators, whose slogan, "form without ornament," he said discredited the movement and raised the specter of "a new formalism" taking its place alongside earlier codifications.[41]

In statements made on the occasion of the opening of the show, Mies singled out only one target of criticism. But he threw the entire weight of the enterprise against it, against what Behrendt called the specter of a new formalism. This specter assumed a number of guises for Mies, whose primary concern was to break with all reliance on prior determinations and codifications irrespective of the categories through which they were made operational—whether style, tradition, form, construction, or standardization. It was against this reliance, among Modernists as well as traditionalists, that he sought to assert a new approach. He cautioned that standardization could not be treated as a generator of urban designs, just as building designs could not be generated from functions, materials, or methods of construction. Although

Mies appears to have struggled for some time over the Werkbund's pursuit of a new unity—he wrestled with the issue of a design code as well as the list of participating architects—his official statements reiterated the critique of formalism that he had first made in 1923. Rather than give the architects formal prescriptions, he asked them to confront freely the problem of building housing in their time.[42] The diversity of results at Weissenhof has often been overlooked in the wake of its successful self-promotion as an emblem of a uniform Modernism. A close look at the buildings, however, reveals that significant differences in structure, cladding, building type, spatial concept, windows, and even colors had unfolded within the framework of Mies's plan.

In the context of these various disputes and divisions, the photograph of the Weissenhofsiedlung on the cover of Behrendt's book achieved an image of unity that was sufficiently cohesive yet composite enough to address a range of aspirations, including Mies's own. The looming presence of Mies's apartment block, aligned with the villas and terraces but rising above them like a *Stadtkrone* (literally, city crown) might even have appeased some advocates of mass housing.[43] At the same time, the image is clearly a resolute response to Mies's critics, demonstrating how a new kind of urban unity could be achieved by providing an open framework within which the form of individual units could unfold in an organic process directed toward common goals and principles. A snapshot of reality in the making, the image captured a contingent configuration that could be experienced, analyzed, and refined. It bears witness to a new conception of wholeness whose image was not preconceived, but rather the product of purposive unity and free relations struggling to assert themselves. These regulative ideals were thought to guarantee unity regardless of how much the results diverged in outward appearance.

Historians who have linked Behrendt's book to the Weissenhofsiedlung and the appearance of a new uniform architecture[44] have tended to miss the gap between the image on the cover and the body of the book in which Behrendt mentioned neither the Weissenhofsiedlung nor the Werkbund, although he did point to the internationalism of what he called the new style movement. In fact, the scope of the book was different from the theme of the show: It was broader in embracing machine design, city planning, education, and patronage, but also narrower in its exclusion of the applied arts. Nevertheless, its rhetoric and theoretical framework overlap sufficiently with those of the exhibition and its protagonists to reveal Behrendt's intention to intervene in the debates that surrounded it. Where Mies sought to articulate subtle distinctions between his own views and those of others, Behrendt offered a model of cultural production that would, like the cover photograph, speak to all parties and claim the middle ground of a new, organic normativity. Yet, Behrendt did not want to neutralize or deny oppositions. Rather, following Friedrich Schiller, whom he had cited in earlier writings, Behrendt saw opposing forces as the tools for a new synthesis.[45] His approach converged with Mies's in the search for a milieu in which a true architecture could grow, capable of reconciling individual and collective, order and becoming. Where

Mies developed a new strategic kind of site planning in order to safeguard the as-yet-unformed by focusing on the moment and the art of building, Behrendt recast the theory of style into a performative, dynamic, and constructional model of creative work whose definitive achievement of unity he nevertheless deferred to the future—however close that future sometimes appeared to be.

The architectonic core of Behrendt's theory of the new building style is contained in his section on new problems of form. Describing the new system of construction that had emerged with new materials and methods of fabrication, he presented his own version of the now well-known conception of Modernism in terms of a new constructional system. Pointing to two buildings by Erich Mendelsohn, he suggested that the relationship between load and support had been radically altered with the development of cantilevered construction. The function of the wall had also changed, albeit in two different directions. First, precast concrete had replaced brick construction with large uniform plates, as in Ernst May's *Siedlungen* in Frankfurt. At the same time, the structural frame made possible the separation of enclosing membrane from support, transforming the wall into an outer protective skin that could be made entirely of glass or could be used for both wall and roof at the same time. These were the constituent elements of a new architectonic system. Behrendt called them "new aesthetic elements" capable of bringing the "inner tensions of the spatial organism...into a pure and harmonious relationship."[46]

Notwithstanding Behrendt's efforts to articulate his openness to heterogeneity, singularity, and difference, the examples that illustrate *Sieg* appear formally consistent, even homogeneous. But the precise nature of this consistency needs to be specified. Its locus was in what Behrendt called "aesthetic elements"—we might say constructional elements—rather than complete forms. With the exception of two projects by Häring and Mies's Glass Skyscraper, all the buildings cited as exemplary are orthogonal, asymmetrical compositions of articulated and dynamic cubic masses and overlapping planes, often in brick or stucco. While the photographs generally feature only the exterior forms of the buildings, the consistent compositional sensibility suggests that the specific configuration of elements has, in each case, been generated by arranging the interior spaces and functions according to the open plan and open section developed by Frank Lloyd Wright and De Stijl. Certainly, Behrendt had held Wright in great esteem for a long time and had been one of the few Europeans to review the edition of Wright's work published by Wasmuth in 1911.[47] In *Sieg,* he still called Wright the "ur-father" of the new architecture, despite concerns then being raised that modern architecture in Europe was coming dangerously close to a Wrightian formalism.[48] While Werner Gräff's publication *Bau und Wohnung* documented the Weissenhofsiedlung in such a way that the differences among the buildings register clearly, the ensemble of images in *Sieg* presented a new constructional system in action. Approaching each new building task with elementarized means and a flexible logistics of spatial relations allowed the architect to shape space to suit the specific functions, needs, desires, and relationships—to create unique, differentiated spatial organisms that would nevertheless be systemically linked. Considered through the lens of this architectonic system, the image on the cover of Behrendt's book depicted the result of a new mode of production, one that bridged the industrial, organic, and artistic and combined fixity and fluidity, universality and uniqueness, system and freedom.[49]

Critic

Born in Metz, Germany, Walter Curt Behrendt (1884–1945) belonged to the same generation as Walter Gropius (1883–1969), Ludwig Mies van der Rohe (1886–1969), Le Corbusier (1887–1965), Sigfried Giedion (1888–1968), and Adolf Behne (1884–1948).[50] Like Behne, he was well known on the German architectural scene during the interwar period as an indefatigable critic, polemicist, and editor. Like Behne, too, he died in the 1940s, considerably earlier than his more celebrated and remembered colleagues. His relative obscurity today also owes something to the fact that he was more a reformer than an avant-gardist, although *Sieg* sought to bridge these two orientations—approaching the union of art and society from opposite directions. A man in and of the middle in more ways than one, Behrendt occupied a place that by 1927 had become a focus of contestation as architects—Modernists and traditionalists alike—attempted to secure support from the German middle class.

The son of a government official, Behrendt studied at the Technische Universität in Berlin and the Technische Universität of Munich. He started writing as an architectural critic in 1907 and had already published fifty articles and reviews by 1910. Behrendt completed his doctorate in architecture at the Technische Universität of Dresden in 1911 with a dissertation on urban design titled *Die einheitliche Blockfront als Raumelement im Stadtbau: Ein Beitrag zur Stadtbaukunst der Gegenwart* (The street wall as unified spatial element in city building: A contribution to contemporary urban design; fig. 4). That same year he wrote a monograph on Alfred Messel, one of the leaders of the older generation who had recently died (fig. 5). With *Blockfront* and *Alfred Messel,* both published by Bruno Cassirer in Berlin, Behrendt inaugurated themes that continued to occupy his entire career: the longing for a new form of city and a new conception of architectural style, both of which would constitute forms of organic cultural unity capable of resolving the problematic conditions of modernization and metropolitanization inherited from the nineteenth century. His books entailed narratives of loss, portraits of a conflictive present, and forecasts of unity regained in the imminent future, this time in full consciousness, synthetically.

Behrendt's early writings were, moreover, strongly influenced by the dualistic conception of the modern movement presented by the critic Karl Scheffler in his *Moderne Baukunst* (Modern building-art) of 1907.[51] One direction, Scheffler suggested, was led by Henry van de Velde with Hermann Obrist, Bernhard Pankok, and August Endell; Peter Behrens was the key figure of the other, which included Bruno Paul, "the Viennese [architects]," Paul Schultze-

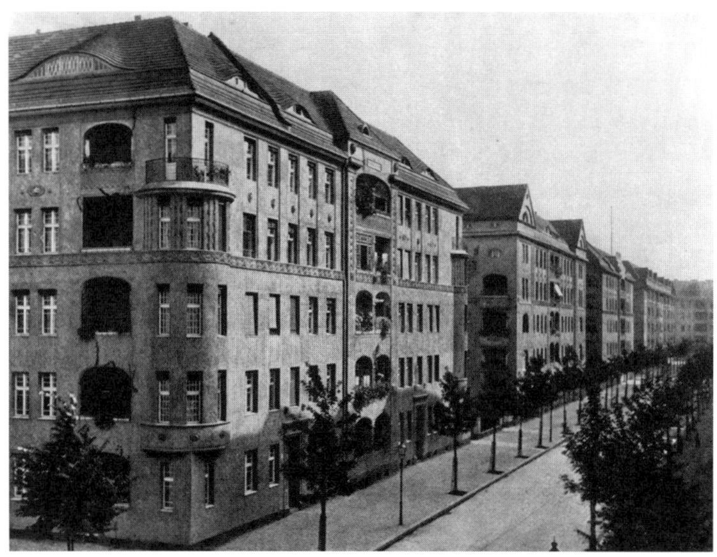

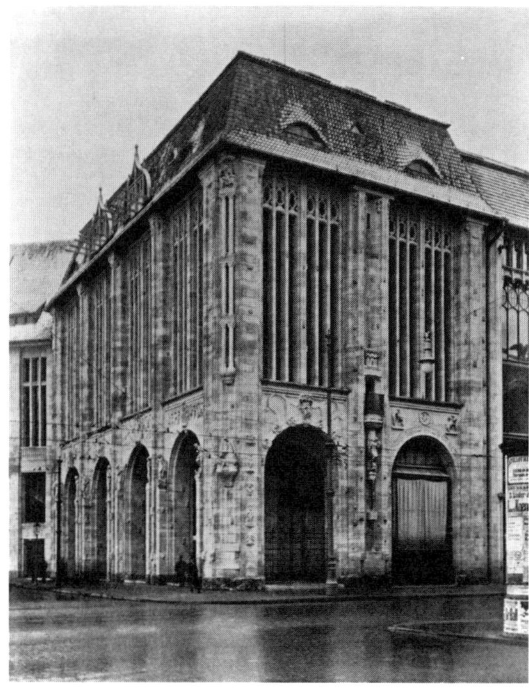

Fig. 4. Paul Mebes, architect
Housing block, Berlin-Charlottenburg
The architectonic treatment of this project was exemplary
for Behrendt in its ability to give form and character to
urban space
From Walter Curt Behrendt, *Die einheitliche Blockfront als
Raumelement im Stadtbau* (Berlin: Bruno Cassirer, 1911)

Fig. 5. Alfred Messel, architect
Wertheim Department Store on Leipzigerplatz, Berlin, 1904
Behrendt presented the Wertheim store, celebrated by
many for its modernity, as but a document of a great
searching effort to find a vital and durably effective form
From Walter Curt Behrendt, *Alfred Messel* (Berlin: Bruno
Cassirer, 1911)

Naumburg, and Emil Rudolf Weiss. The first group took the decorative arts and functional buildings as points of departure, while the second attempted to work through the academic science of style toward a new universal. Where the one was revolutionary—great talents and independent, creative personalities—the other was conservative and intellectual, moving deductively from ideals to realizations. The first stream was natural, direct, and intuitive; the other was mathematical, logical, and unnatural. For one, forms arose from below, from a mysterious unconscious life force; for the other, they existed a priori and were imposed on matter from above. Where one focused on singularities, the other emphasized totality. Yet, Scheffler contended, the distinction could never be pure, and both elements—the revolutionary and the conservative—may be united in the same person, as in the case of Messel. Since both had limitations, "in the end it can never be about a fight for or against one of these 'directions.'"[52] Ultimately, he concluded, the two directions needed to be united. If the building-art was to be "the most mature and beautiful of the fruits of culture," Scheffler observed, "all of the forces working in combination must be satiated by health and a will for the future."[53] Nevertheless, setting in motion the logic of Behrendt's later deferrals, he suggested that "it is not yet possible to say anything conclusive about this great and wide-ranging movement," nor could one expect conclusive results from the two points of departure for a long time. Rather, one had to be satisfied for the moment with simply witnessing the contest between "the strongest architectonic force[s] of the present." Nevertheless, the task for architects with life and vitality was "to give in, completely and confidently, to this will that has been suddenly aroused and is struggling fiercely."[54]

Electing not to pursue private practice, Behrendt followed his father into the public service in 1912, working first in the Prussian Ministerium für öffentliche Arbeiten (Ministry of public works). According to the American critic and historian Lewis Mumford (1895–1990), whose personal and intellectual friendship with Behrendt began in 1925, "his highly developed critical sense" made Behrendt "aware of a lack of creativeness in his own designs" and led him to decide "courageously" to "devote himself to the administrative problems connected with architecture."[55] Following war duty as a private in the German army, he resumed this position, transferring later to the Ministerium für Gesundheitswesen (Ministry of public health). In 1927 he became architectural advisor to the minister of finance, who was responsible for reviewing all public buildings in Prussia. In that capacity he was involved in regional projects for greater Hamburg, the Ruhr region, and central Germany, as well as for public policy on housing and urban development. With Hitler's consolidation of power in 1933, Behrendt—a nonpracticing Jew married to a Christian, the concert pianist Lydia Hoffmann[56]—was attacked by the Kampfbund für Deutsche Kultur and then discharged from his government post.[57] In the following years, with only a modest government pension, he concentrated almost exclusively on his second, parallel career as a writer and editor while exploring opportunities to emigrate to the United States.

Unfortunately, little more is known of Behrendt's work in the civil service. In contrast, he left an extensive archive as a writer and editor. As a young man, he entered the Berlin architectural scene around 1907 and quickly became active in it. His early writings were published mostly in *Neudeutsche Bauzeitung*, which he edited during 1910, but also in *Deutsche Bauhütte*, *Berliner Architekturwelt*, *Moderne Bauformen*, *Bauwelt*, *Der Profanbau*, *Architektonische Rundschau*, *Kunst und Künstler*, *Wasmuths Monatshefte für Baukunst*, and *Zentralblatt der Bauverwaltung*. It was apparently Karl Scheffler's writings from 1905 to 1906[58] that won Behrendt over to the cause of Modernism, and the older critic became a mentor and lifelong friend.[59] Certainly his affiliation with Scheffler's *Kunst und Künstler*, arguably the most intellectually sophisticated venue for art in Germany, was the most durable of his relationships with the journals, lasting from 1910 until 1932.[60] Scheffler may have helped him find a publisher for his first books, which appeared the year after Behrendt started writing for him. *Blockfront* was dedicated to Scheffler, who, in turn, contributed the introduction to Behrendt's book on Messel. Although Behrendt wrote fluidly and philosophically, his orientation remained more architectural, urban, and practical than Scheffler's. Scheffler's breadth of learning and critical refinement, as well as his optimistic conception of metropolitan architecture and culture, informed Behrendt's views and their interests continued to be aligned.

Behrendt's first extensive historical assessment of Modernism, which he began prior to World War I, was only finished afterward and published in 1920 (figs. 6a,b): *Der Kampf um den Stil im Kunstgewerbe und in der Architektur* (The battle for style in the decorative arts and architecture).[61] In 1919 Behrendt helped found the Arbeitsrat für Kunst (Work council for the arts), or AfK, together with a group of like-minded reform architects: Paul Schmitthenner (architect of the Gartenstadt Staaken, 1914–1917), Paul Mebes (architect and author of *Um 1800* [Around 1800] of 1908), and Otto Bartning. When the leadership of the AfK was taken over by Bruno Taut, Walter Gropius, and Adolf Behne, whose utopianism and radical politics came to shape the association's public profile, Behrendt's group — more moderate, practical, and less engaged in Postcubist art — founded the journal *Die Volkswohnung: Zeitschrift für Wohnungsbau und Siedlungswesen* (fig. 7). With Behrendt as editor, the journal was produced from January 1919 until December 1923, at which point its name was changed to *Der Neubau: Halbmonatsschrift für Baukunst*. Behrendt continued as editor until May 1925. Whereas Taut's *Frühlicht* became the first new organ of the avant-garde in Berlin after World War I, *Die Volkswohnung* promoted the revitalization of a vernacular, land-based tradition of building. According to Behrendt, the journal was dedicated to "rebuilding the spiritual and economic life" of the country by promoting practical reforms in the planning, design, and construction of *Siedlungen*. It encompassed everything from small housing estates to garden suburbs and garden cities.[62] Similarly, while the AfK used the phrase *Neues Bauen* as the title for an exhibition of Expressionist architecture, Erwin Gutkind also used the phrase for the title of a

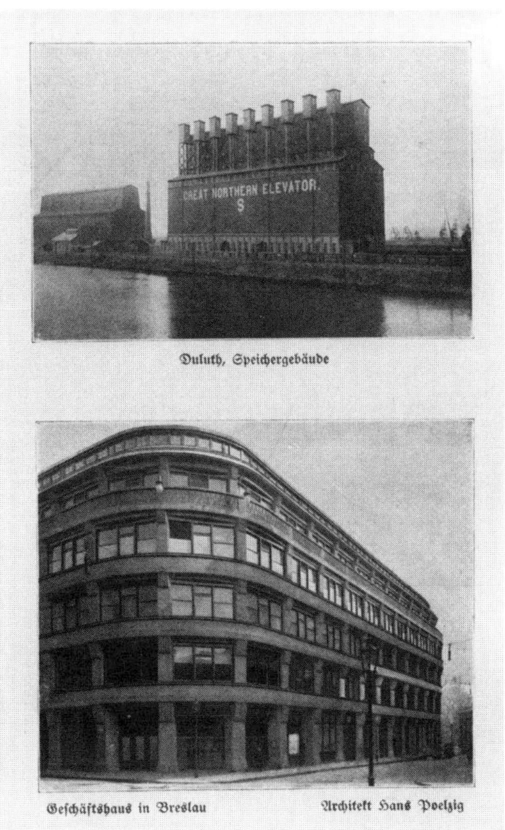

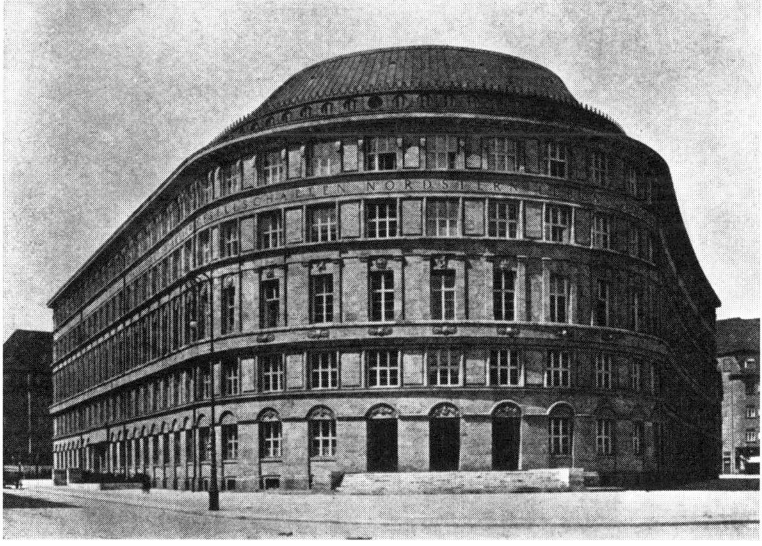

Figs. 6a,b. Hans Poelzig and Paul Mebes, architects
Behrendt showed office buildings by Poelzig and Mebes together with an American grain
silo, increasingly invoked at this time to demonstrate how outer form could be the direct
expression of inner purpose, plan, or function
From Walter Curt Behrendt, *Der Kampf um den Stil im Kunstgewerbe und in der Architektur*
(Stuttgart: Deutsche Verlags-Anstalt, 1920)

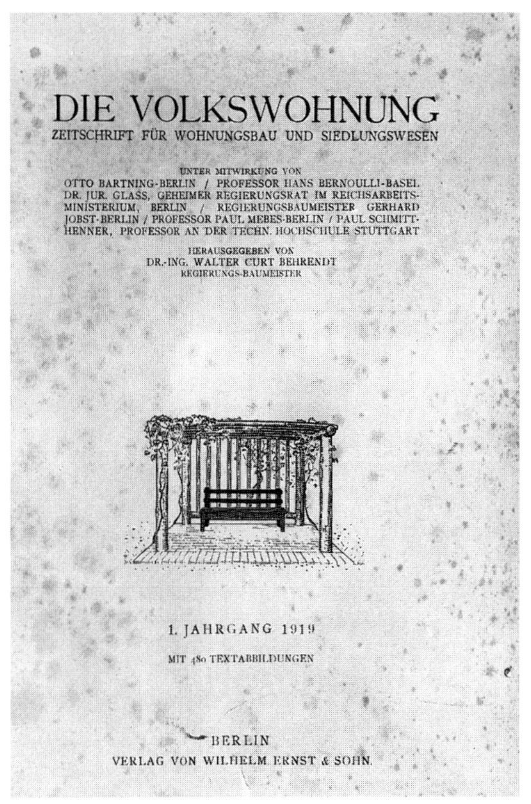

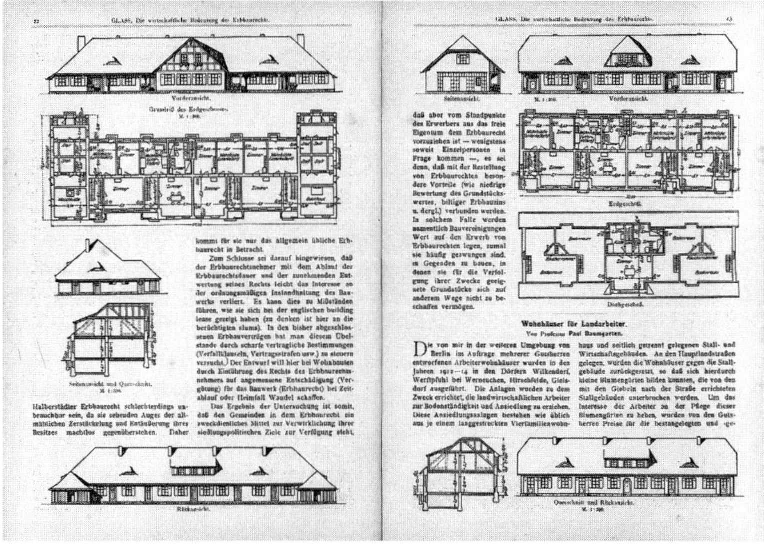

Fig. 7. *Die Volkswohnung*
The title page of the cumulative volume for 1919 of *Die Volkswohnung,* a journal edited by Walter Curt Behrendt from 1919 to 1923, featured a drawing by Heinrich Tessenow

Fig. 8. Paul Baumgarten, architect
Housing project for worker families in the country
From *Die Volkswohnung* 1, no. 2 (24 January 1919)

publication promoting *Siedlungsreform,* to which Behrendt contributed along with several members of his editorial board.[63] In addition to Bartning, Mebes, and Schmitthenner, the editorial group included the Swiss architect Hans Bernoulli and Berlin-based state officials Gerhard Jobst and Otto Glass. Articles and projects were published by Adolf Rading, Paul Baumgarten, Hermann Jansen, Bruno Taut, Heinrich Tessenow, Erwin Gutkind, Heinrich de Fries, Ernst May, Martin Wagner, Walter Gropius, Otto Salvisberg, and Fritz Schumacher, among many others (fig. 8). Sketches by Tessenow were featured on the covers of the annual volumes.

Volkswohnung (literally, "people's dwelling") was intended to refer not only to the home as the locus for nourishing society, but in the widest sense to the dwelling place of humanity.[64] The journal embraced the total environment of the *Siedlung,* including gardens, as well as areas for sports and play. Articles covered a wide range of topics in considerable detail, focusing on site planning, financing, building regulations, construction materials and techniques, exemplary designs for housing complete with construction drawings, furnishings, and annual statistics on the performance of the industry. Socialist in its politics, the journal promoted the socialization of the construction and development industry. It also contributed to the movement for land reform (*Bodenreform*), which sought to win back for the majority of people a direct share in the land.[65] And it lobbied for greater standardization of building components — *Normalisierung* and *Typisierung*[66] — in order to achieve economies of scale while providing architects with elements flexible enough for varied and creative uses. As Bartning put it, the journal pulled together the sciences, technics, politics, problematics, and systematics of small settlements in order to support the comprehensive restructuring of housing design and production.[67] Promoting economy, simplicity, and collectivization not only served to address the housing crisis, but at the same time to instill a new ethos and way of life for urbanized German people.

In 1922 Behrendt reoriented the journal's mandate to develop a new order of work (*Arbeitsordnung*), around which, he suggested, all the various economic and social struggles of the day circled. While the machine and industrialization had brought many benefits, they had also led to the economic domination of the spirit of human community. Work had become "a source of discontent and discord." Behrendt observed that a struggle for a new order of work, through which the "human soul tries to save itself," had been set in motion everywhere. Although humanity was "ready to give form" to such an order, Behrendt, in a characteristic gesture, held that one could only guess at what it would look like.[68] Nevertheless, it was already clear that it would entail a new form of cohesion that, without inhibiting the unfolding of the singular, would expand the powers of the whole. Much of the spirit of the Middle Ages would be revived, along with a similar flowering of the arts and the self-determination of the design disciplines. For Behrendt, this new social order would allow new needs and habits to establish themselves, for which the building-art would create new forms of expression. Citing the nineteenth-century social historian

Wilhelm Riehl, he suggested that the German people had always had an especially high conception of the idea and moral value of work.[69] Merging nationalist and internationalist outlooks, he contended that it would be their destiny to fashion a new ideal that would serve the whole of humanity.

In his opening editorial for *Der Neubau* in 1924, Behrendt changed direction once again. He expanded the scope of the journal to embrace architecture, the applied arts, and urban planning more fully and at the same time to focus once again on achieving artistic quality. To do this, he now sought to renew, articulate, and disseminate the elementary concepts of *Gestaltung* (form creation) in the building-art—"to reawaken understanding of the most original tasks of constructional *Gestaltung*." Leaving behind his earlier goal of reanimating old building traditions, he suggested that the inheritances of the past could now only weaken the creative forces and lead to a lifeless academic formalism. Once again, Behrendt concluded, it was not yet possible to say much about the new form, for that would be "the work of genius, spirit, and creative force." Instead, the journal addressed itself to the problems generated by history. Clarifying these problems would, he hoped, "prepare the ground for the becoming and growth of the new form."[70]

Like Scheffler, Behrendt became a close observer of the American scene. Having recognized the importance of Wright as early as 1913,[71] Behrendt was by 1923 in contact with Charles Whitaker, under whose editorial direction the *Journal of the American Institute of Architects* (*JAIA*) promoted both modern architecture and the garden city movement in America. Behrendt's article in the *JAIA* on the competition of 1921–1922 for a skyscraper at the Friedrichstrasse train station in Berlin included the first American publication of Mies's entry, along with those of Hans Soeder and Hans Poelzig. Responses by two American architects launched a transatlantic exchange on metropolitan architecture and urbanism whose consequence for Behrendt would only increase.[72] In 1924 he published in *Der Neubau* a report on American urbanism by the Committee on Community Planning of the American Institute of Architects, headed by Clarence Stein.[73] Following in the footsteps of Adolf Rading,[74] Behrendt traveled to America in 1925, sent by the Ministry of Finance to attend the Congress of the International Federation for Town and Country Planning and Garden Cities in New York (20–25 April) and to study firsthand the conditions and forces of American urbanism. His tour took him throughout the East Coast and inland to Chicago and Pittsburgh. Criticisms of the overcrowding and congestion of the American metropolis by Whitaker, Mumford, Stein, and others involved in regional planning dampened Behrendt's enthusiasm for the skyscraper city, if not for the skyscraper itself. His report on this trip, *Städtebau und Wohnungswesen in den Vereinigten Staaten: Bericht über eine Studienreise* (Urban planning and housing in the United States: Report of a study trip), 1926, was a comprehensive critique of metropolitan urbanism (figs. 9a,b).[75] Behrendt's experience in America reinforced his commitment to decentralizing the metropolis by resettling urban populations in garden suburbs.

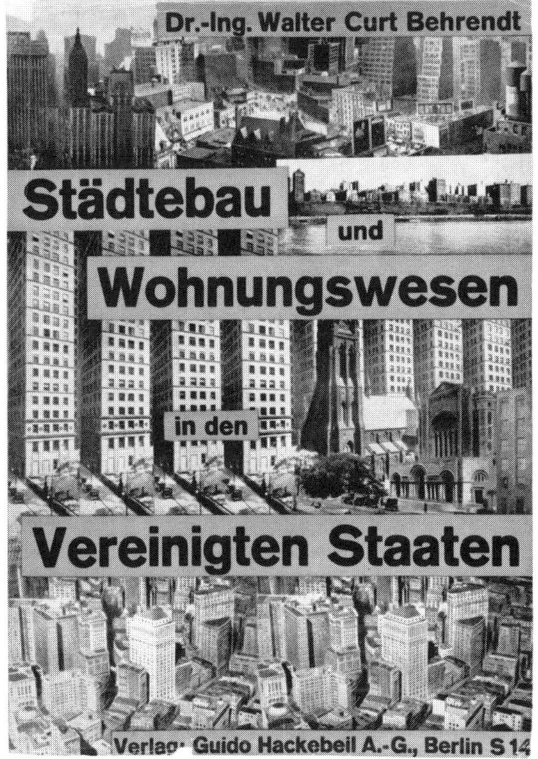

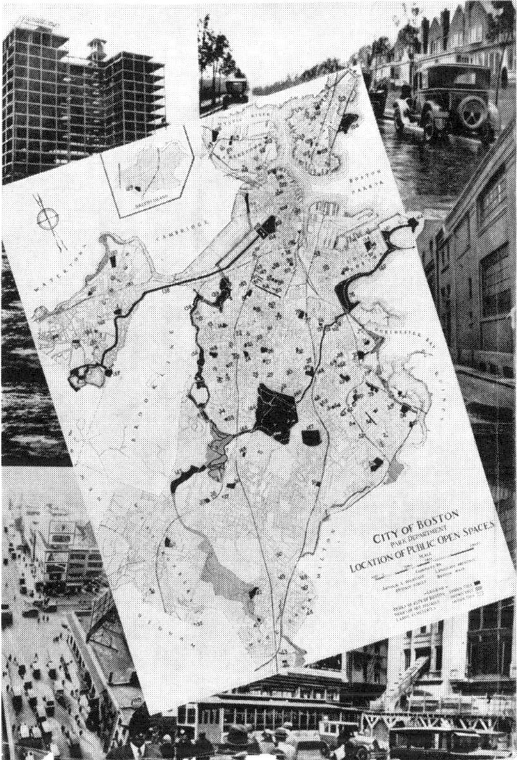

Figs. 9a,b. *Städtebau und Wohnungswesen in den Vereinigten Staaten*
Front and back covers of Behrendt, *Städtebau und Wohnungswesen in den Vereinigten Staaten,*
2d ed. (Berlin: Verlag Guido Hackebeil, 1927)
Photo: Collection Centre Canadien d'Architecture/Canadian Centre for Architecture, Montreal

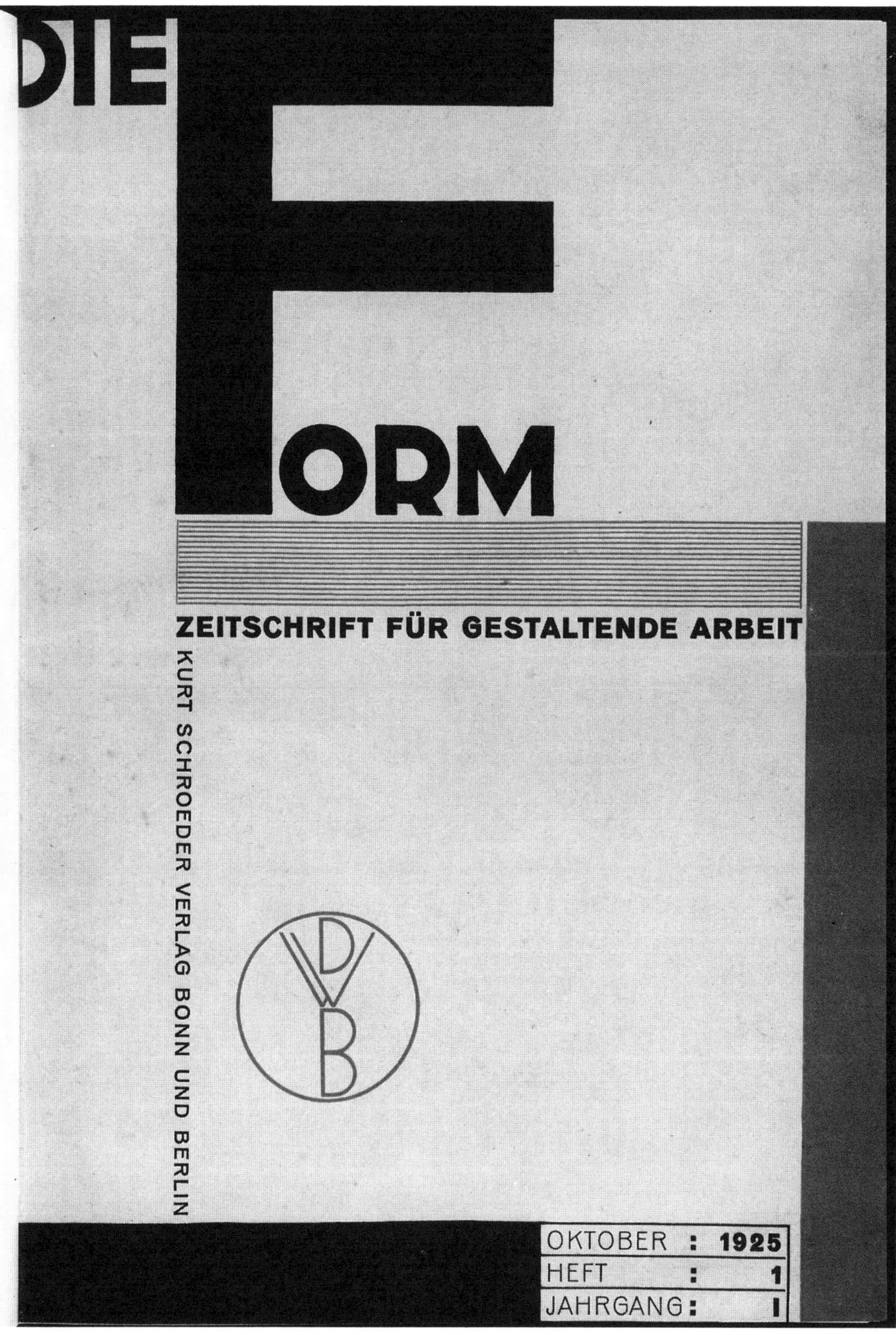

Fig. 10. *Die Form*
Cover of the journal Behrendt edited from 1925 to 1926
From *Die Form: Zeitschrift für gestaltende Arbeit* 1, no. 1
(October 1925)

Returning from America, Behrendt launched the second incarnation of *Die Form* (fig. 10). He used the opportunity to adjust his sails once again, turning to the emergence of what, in *Sieg,* he would call the *"technical* style."[76] With articles focused on the exemplarity of machine design and industrial architecture — articles by Gropius on airplanes, Gräff on cars (fig. 11), and Behrendt on utilitarian structure — the journal mapped the outlines and principles of a building style adequate to industrial society (fig. 12). Where Rudolf von Delius charted a course for the convergence of art forms and natural forms using Goethe as his guide, Kurt Ewald rehearsed the terms for the new beauty of machines.[77] The impetus for this rather substantial change in orientation, from which *Sieg* was to emerge, may also have come from Behrendt's American experience. For while Mumford and his circle reinforced Behrendt's skepticism about mechanization and the metropolis, they also introduced him to the ideas of Patrick Geddes, the Scottish biologist, sociologist, and urbanist whose influence extended throughout the international garden city movement. For Mumford, following Geddes's theory of cultural evolution, the present found itself on the threshold of a technological revolution that raised great hopes. Moving from steam energy to electricity meant leaving the "paleotechnic" era of exploitative and reductive industrialization to enter the "neotechnic" era of clean energy, easy transportation, empowering machines, functional (organic) architecture, and garden cities. In his popular study of American architecture and civilization, *Sticks and Stones* of 1924, Mumford argued that it was time to reconcile humanity and its machines, touching themes familiar to German architectural theory albeit through American examples.[78]

Behrendt was so taken by Mumford's critical vision that he immediately solicited contributions to *Die Form.* He published three articles in 1925 and 1926[79] (fig. 13) and arranged to have *Sticks and Stones* translated into German.[80] It must surely have been an extraordinary moment for Behrendt to find so many resonances in the eloquent writings of this American, who was an avid reader of German and admired equally the architecture of Wright and the "new German school" which, he noted, had been influenced by the Chicago Modernists. Having already met Erich Mendelsohn and Ernst May,[81] Mumford went so far as to refer to the key German word *bauen* (to build) in a pun on two senses of *bauen* ("to build" and "to farm"): "Architecture begins historically when the 'Bauer' who plants becomes the 'Bauer' who builds; and if our architecture is to have a substantial foundation, it is in a refreshed countryside that we will perhaps find it."[82] Emphasizing the relationship between architecture and the changing system of production — "the whole [technological, economic, and social] complex out of which architect, builder, and patron spring, and into which the finished building … is set"[83] — Mumford suggested contriving new elements with which to "alter once more the profounder contours of our civilization."[84] For Behrendt, what Mumford offered was a way to negotiate between social reform and the polemics of the German avant-garde, to forge a unified conception of Neues Bauen as an

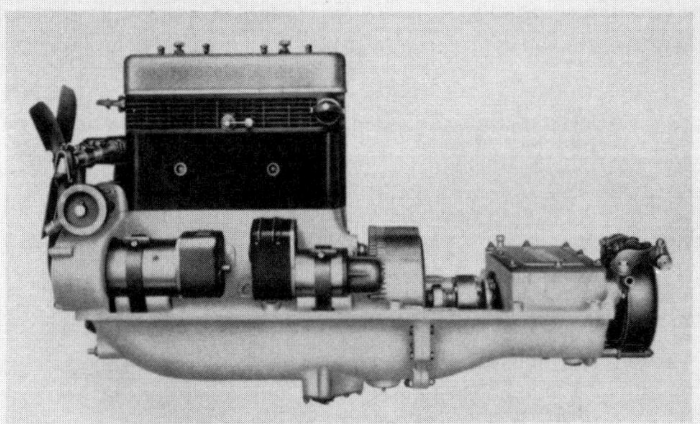

Motor und Getriebe zum 6/24 PS Wanderer   Wanderer-Werke, Schönau b. Chemnitz

Zur Form des Automobils

VON WERNER GRÄFF, ORANIENBURG

I.

Wir Europäer tun uns ein wenig darauf zugute, daß wir Henry Ford enttäuschten, indem wir seine Wagen trotz ihrer außerordentlichen Billigkeit und Zuverlässigkeit nicht so allgemein annahmen, wie er es erwartete, und daß wir ihn dadurch bestimmen konnten, neuerdings auch auf die *Form* zu achten. Wir wissen, daß er seinen Wagen seit 1907, achtzehn Jahre hindurch, kaum geändert hat. Und der war damals schon geschmacklos. Inzwischen sah er obendrein noch völlig veraltet aus. Ford selbst gibt zu, oder vielmehr: bildet sich etwas darauf ein, daß er nie Wert auf das Äußere seines Fahrzeugs gelegt hat, sondern stets nur seine Verbilligung und technische Verbesserung im Auge hatte. Und seine Amerikaner stimmten ihm bei, denn sie kauften „Fords" millionenweis. Jetzt sind aber tatsächlich die europäischen Fordmodelle 1926 unvergleichlich hübscher und bequemer als die bekannten alten amerikanischen: eine bedeutsame Wandlung.

Gewiß ist ein Automobil auch in Europa in allererster Linie Verkehrsmittel — nicht Schmuckstück. Und wenn es nicht anders ginge, so wollten wir uns gern in die scheußlichsten Fahrzeuge setzen, wenn sie uns nur gut beförderten. Aber wir wissen seit 15 Jahren, *daß* es anders geht. Daß ein schönes Auto keineswegs schlechter fährt als ein häßliches. Ja, noch mehr: daß der Herstellungspreis für ein Fahrzeug von anständiger Form prinzipiell gar

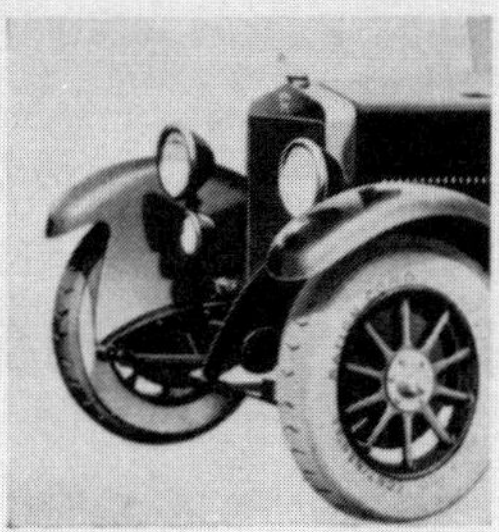

Kühler eines Horchwagens
Horch-Werke A.G., Berlin

195

Fig. 11. Werner Gräff, "Zur Form des Automobils"
From *Die Form* 1, no. 9 (June 1926)

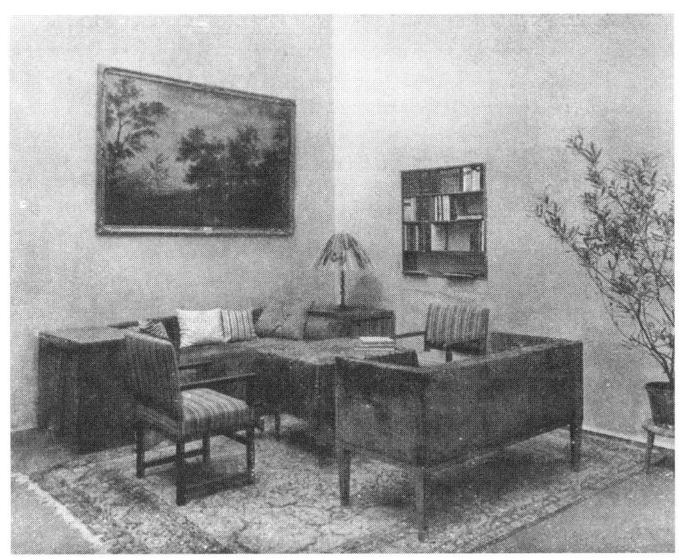

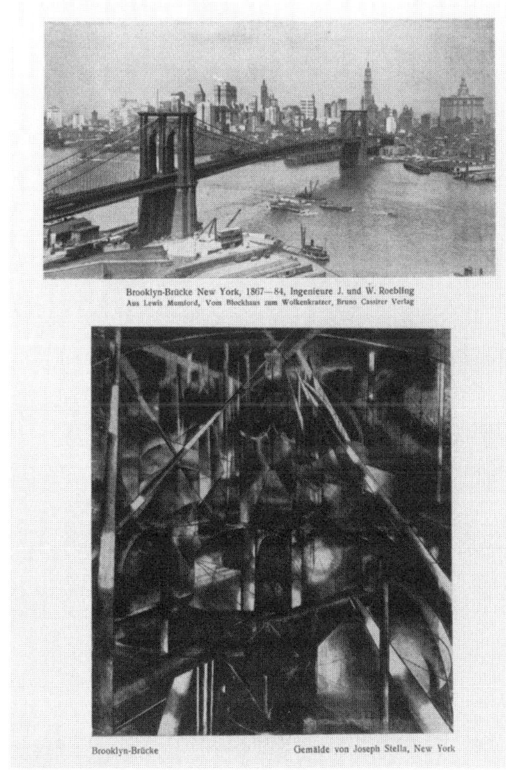

Fig. 12. Heinrich Tessenow, architect
A living room in Dresden
From Walter Curt Behrendt, "Die Situation des Kunst-
gewerbes," *Die Form* 1, no. 2 (November 1925)

**Fig. 13. Photograph of the Brooklyn Bridge and painting
of it by Joseph Stella**
From Lewis Mumford, "Die Form in der amerikanischen
Zivilisation," in *Die Form* 1, no. 2 (November 1925)

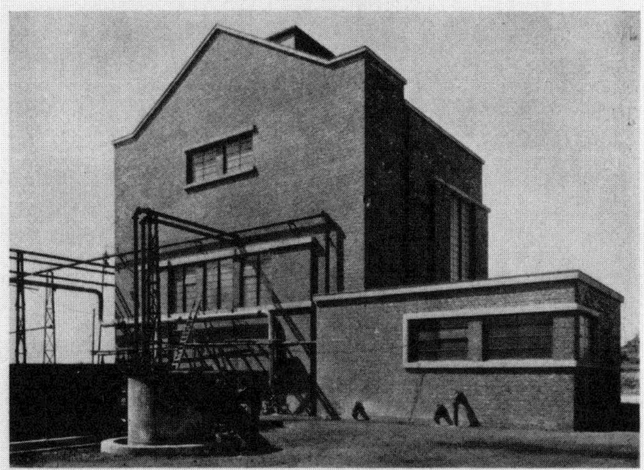

Zeche Sachsen, Hamm i. W., Benzolfabrik, 1926   Arch. Prof. Alfred Fischer-Essen

ZUM FORMPROBLEM DER ZEIT

VON WALTER CURT BEHRENDT, BERLIN

Die nachstehenden Sätze, die einer größeren Arbeit über den neuen Baustil entnommen sind, bringen wir hier zum Abdruck als Beitrag zu dem Thema, das die bevorstehende Jahresversammlung des Deutschen Werkbunds beschäftigen wird. Sie bilden zugleich eine Paraphrase zu den Arbeiten des Architekten Prof. *Alfred Fischer*-Essen, die in eindrucksvoller Weise den Anteil der Großindustrie an der Formung unserer Zeit an einer Reihe praktischer Beispiele anschaulich machen.
Die Schriftleitung.

Auf allen Gebieten gestaltender Arbeit, die mit Kunst nichts zu tun haben, die vielmehr dem unmittelbaren Einfluß und dem Zugriff der Kunst entzogen sind, will sagen, auf allen Gebieten der *technischen Gestaltung*, ist heute eine formbildende Kraft am Werke, die eine ganze Welt von neuen, bisher unbekannten Formen geschaffen hat. Der Reichtum dieser neuen Formenwelt ist unermeßlich, und die Fülle und Mannigfaltigkeit der neuen Gebilde straft diejenigen Lügen, die bei jedem Anlaß in bewegliche Klagen ausbrechen über die Gestaltungsarmut unserer Zeit und unsern Mangel an formbildender Kraft. Zugleich aber bestätigt der Reichtum eben dieser neuen Formenwelt, die wir in den Gebieten der technischen Gestaltung rings um uns entstehen sehen, in sinnfälliger Weise das denkwürdige Wort Konrad Fiedlers, wonach nicht alle Zeiten das *Beste*, was sie zu sagen haben, gerade in der *Kunst* ausdrücken. Die Formkraft unserer Zeit — das wird man angesichts ihrer unzähligen neuartigen Schöpfungen nicht bestreiten können — ist gewiß nicht geringer oder schwächer als die vergangener Zeiten. Aber ihr Gestaltungsvermögen hat sich bisher am stärksten und reinsten nicht in der Kunst, sondern in den Gebieten der technischen und industriellen Produktion offenbart.

Alle diese mannigfachen Formen der technischen Gestaltungsarbeit, unsere Maschinen und Apparate, unsere Instrumente und Gebrauchsgeräte, unsere modernen Fahrzeuge, Schiffe, Flugzeuge, Automobile usw.

187

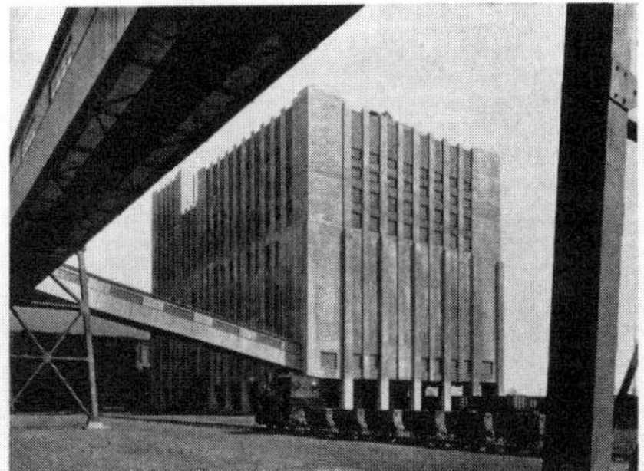

Zeche Sachsen, Hamm i. W., Kohlenwäsche, 1910/11 Arch. Prof. Alfred Fischer-Essen
Größte europäische Kohlenwäsche in Eisenbeton mit sparsamer Ziegelsteinausmauerung, die Betonaußenflächen
unverputzt, die Vertikalteilung entspricht der Rahmenkonstruktion

sind *Zweckformen*. Sie sind geschaffen im Hinblick auf einen bestimmten Leistungsanspruch, mit dem Ziel auf vollkommenste Zweckerfüllung. Dieses Ziel wurde nicht mit einem Male, nicht beim ersten Wurf erreicht. Ganz allmählich, über einen langen Weg, wurden diese Formen in schrittweisem Vorrücken auf das gegebene Ziel — von Versuch zu Versuch, von Ergebnis zu Ergebnis fortschreitend — herausgeschält, herausgebildet, herausgeformt,

in immer schärferer und genauerer Anpassung an die neuen Produktionsverfahren, an die maschinellen Arbeitsmethoden, an die konkreten Bedingungen des Materials und der Konstruktion,

in immer schärferer Erkenntnis und klarerer Durchdringung aber auch des Leistungsanspruchs.

An den einzelnen Stadien, die die Formfindung in dieser Weise durchläuft, läßt sich deutlich verfolgen, wie mit der fortschreitenden Erkenntnis des Leistungsanspruchs sich gleichzeitig auch das Formgefühl vervollkommnet und verfeinert. Die Formentwicklung der Lokomotiven, der Flugzeuge, der Automobile usw., die wir ja als Augenzeugen miterleben, gibt dafür anschauliche Beispiele.

*

Alle diese Formen sind, wie gesagt, *Zweckgebilde*. Die Formfindung ist hier nicht ein ästhetisches, sondern ein konstruktives Problem. Gleichwohl enthalten diese neuen Formen eine ganze Reihe von ästhetischen Elementen: in der knappen Prägnanz ihrer Linienführung, in der vollendeten Reinheit ihrer Proportionen, in der straffen Gespanntheit ihrer ebenen und geschwungenen Flächen, in der leuchtenden Farbigkeit ihrer Anstriche und Lacke, in dem spiegelnden Glanz ihrer Polituren usw. Solche ästhetischen Elemente sind in all diesen Gebilden so viele vorhanden, daß bezeichnenderweise die schnittige Karosserie eines modernen Luxusautos, wie in diesen Blättern schon bei früherem Anlaß erwähnt wurde, gelegentlich als kunstgewerbliche Leistung unserer Zeit in Vergleich gesetzt wird mit einer Prunkkarosse Friedrichs des Großen.

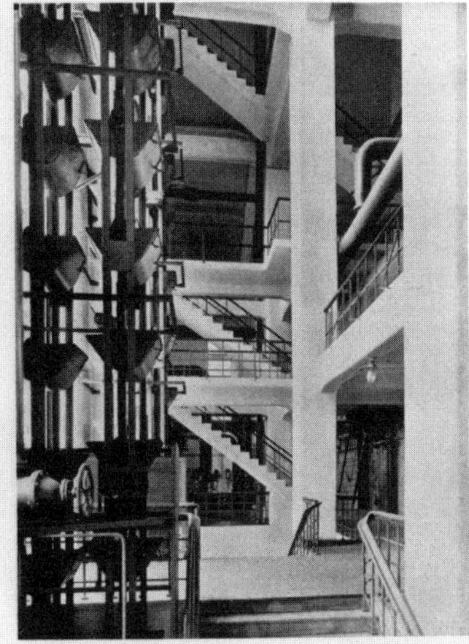

Zeche Königsborn, Unna i. W., Treppenhaus mit Kohlentransportanlage, 1925 Arch. Prof. Alfred Fischer-Essen

Und diese ästhetischen Elemente dürfen, wenn nicht selbst etwa schon als Elemente eines neuen Stils, so doch als Fermente und Anknüpfungspunkte für die Bildung eines solchen angesehen werden.

*

Wenn nun die *Baukunst* — und sie ist ja selbst zu überwiegenden Teilen ein Gebiet technischer Gestaltung — sich heute an diesen Methoden der technischen Formfindung neu zu orientieren versucht, wenn sie bei diesem Orientierungsversuch anknüpft an jene ästhetischen Elemente, die in den Gebilden der technischen Gestaltung zutage treten, so geschieht das nicht in einem äußerlich formalen Sinn: etwa indem sie diese

Figs. 14a–c. Alfred Fischer-Essen, architect

Photographs of industrial buildings by Fischer-Essen accompanied Behrendt's "Zum Formproblem der Zeit," the first iteration of *Der Sieg des neuen Baustils*
From Walter Curt Behrendt, "Zum Formproblem der Zeit," *Die Form* 1, no. 9 (June 1926)

industrial urban material culture, or "modern vernacular," to use the term suggested by David Samson and Francesco Passanti.[85]

Throughout the 1920s Behrendt wrote regularly for the *Zentralblatt der Bauverwaltung, Kunst und Künstler,* and the *Frankfurter Zeitung,* as well as his own journals. At the same time he contributed to numerous others, including *Die Woche, Das Werk, Bauwelt, Moderne Bauformen,* and *Die Gartenkunst.* His book *Der Sieg des neuen Baustils* grew out of his work on *Die Form,* where he published a first iteration, accompanied by extraordinary photographs of industrial structures by Alfred Fischer-Essen (figs. 14a–c).[86] In 1928 he published his second book focused on the city, this time extolling the virtues of historic Dutch cities, their integration with the land and unity of social expression through consistency of ordinary types (fig. 15).[87] From 1930 to 1933 he worked on the manuscript for a book on the modern house, assembling between 350 and 400 photographs of Neues Bauen from around the world.[88] Publication was unfortunately curtailed in 1934, when the publisher withdrew from the project because of the political conditions in Germany.[89]

On emigrating to America in 1934, Behrendt worked primarily as a teacher, lecturing on housing and city planning at Dartmouth College in Hanover, New Hampshire, initially from 1934 to 1937 and then as full professor from 1941 to 1945, and at the University of Buffalo from 1937 to 1941.[90] During his time in Buffalo, he also served as technical director of the local City Planning Association, in which capacity he prepared a master plan for the city.[91] Reginald Isaacs described him as "an exacting teacher...[who] broadened the understanding and appreciation of contemporary architecture for all who listened."[92] His friends encouraged and helped Behrendt write another book. Mumford even helped him see it through the press at his own publisher in New York.[93] Published in 1937 under the title *Modern Building*—a close but somewhat flat approximation of Neues Bauen—it proved to be Behrendt's most extensive and engaging history and became a popular textbook for modern architecture at midcentury (figs. 16a,b). When he died at the age of sixty, the *New York Times* carried an obituary that recognized him as an authority on architecture (fig. 17), city planning, and housing.[94] Several years later, still mourning the loss of his friend, Mumford singled out Behrendt as a critic who combined "professional training, practical experience, and mature critical judgement, based on the widest sort of humanistic study." Moreover, he noted that even in hailing the modern movement, Behrendt remained "a judicious and discerning critic of the actual performances of modern architects." Mumford considered *Modern Building* the best book on the modern movement, "at once succinct and comprehensive, with historical perspective and a rich insight into the nature of our age and its social as well as its architectural problems." He regretted that, with Behrendt's early death, "America lost a rare citizen, who loved her land and her folkways, and who demanded the best of his students, so that they might serve her well."[95]

In acknowledging Behrendt's contributions as a critic, Mumford alluded to his conception of the critic's role as a discerning guide and regulative judge

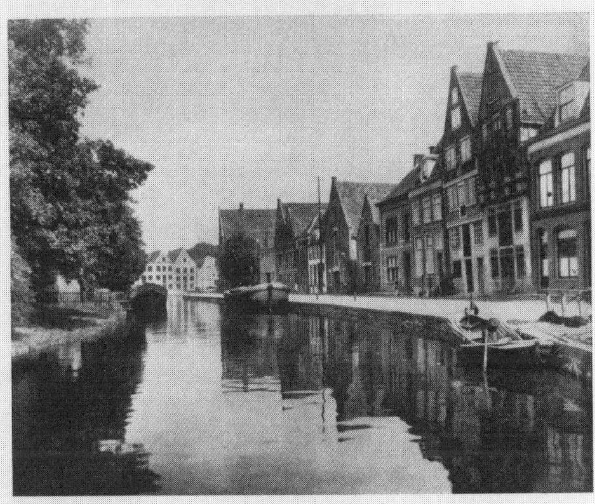

Fig. 15. *Die holländische Stadt*
Behrendt admired Dutch towns for their vital unity
From Walter Curt Behrendt, *Die holländische Stadt*
(Berlin: Bruno Cassirer, 1928)

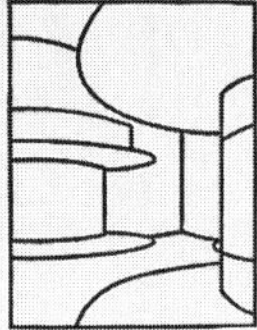

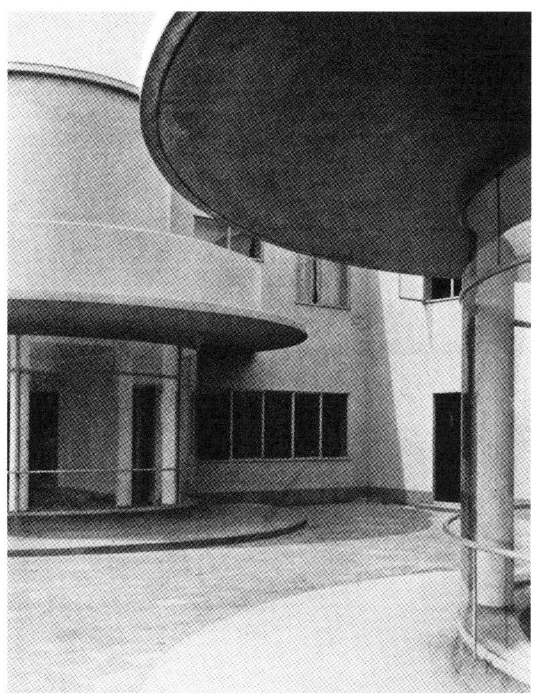

Figs. 16a,b. *Modern Building*
Title page, designed by Robert Josephy, and the plate featuring the photograph of
J. J. P. Oud's housing estate in Hoek van Holland on which the diagram was based
From Walter Curt Behrendt, *Modern Building: Its Nature, Problems, and Forms* (New York:
Harcourt, Brace and Co., 1937)

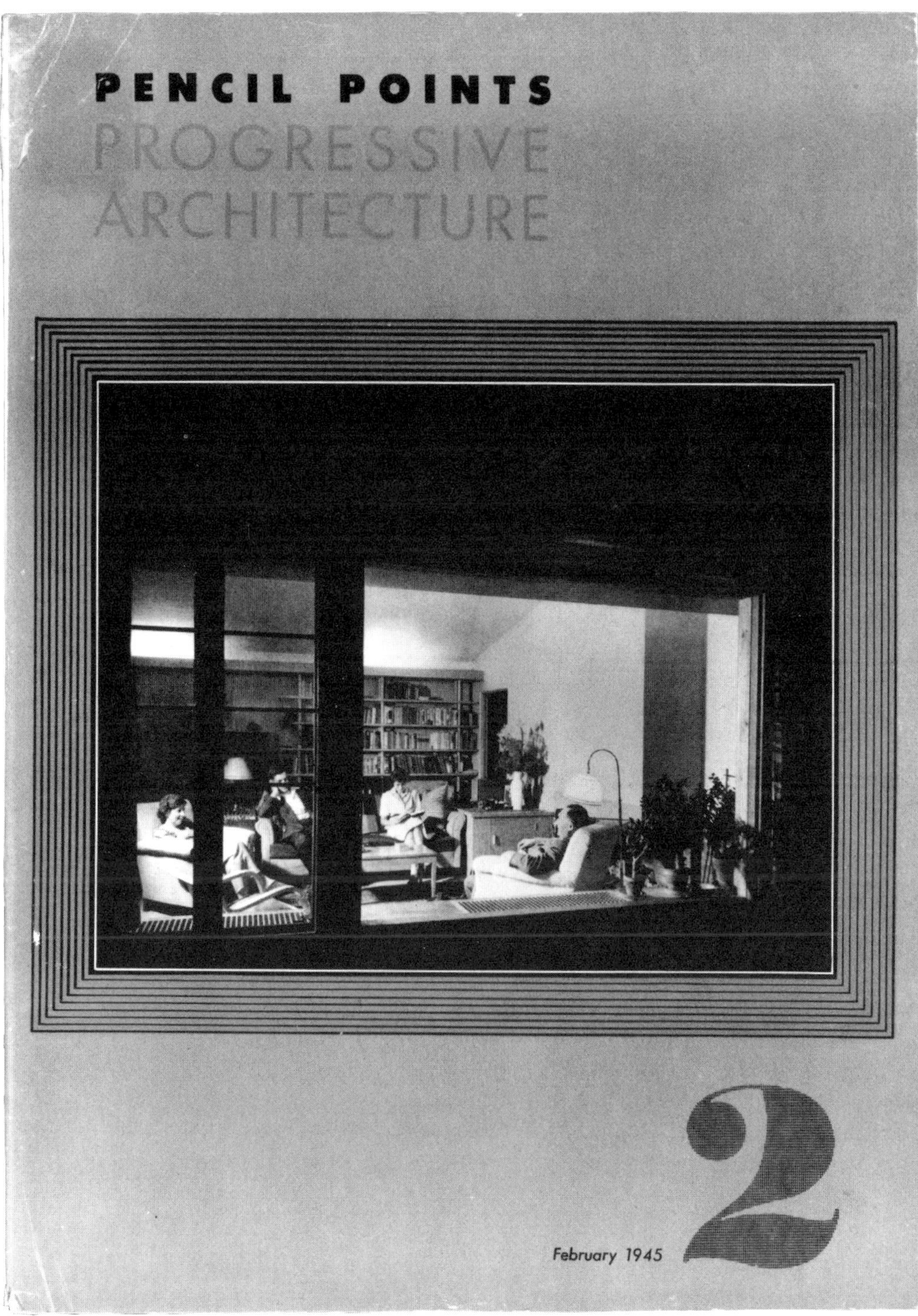

Fig. 17. Walter Curt Behrendt, architect, with John Speath, Jr.
Cover features the view through the picture window of the
Behrendt house in Norwich, Vermont. This modest wood-frame
house exemplified Behrendt's quest for a modern vernacular
From *Pencil Points (Progressive Architecture)* 26, no. 2
(February 1945)

for history in the making. For both Mumford and Behrendt, humanity, like other natural species, was evolving. They understood the present as a period of transition between two stages in the development of industrial society—an especially difficult period, full of turmoil, exploitation, and confusion, yet also full of promise. For Behrendt, the aim of criticism was to read the social and the formal together in order to help his readers understand the present and act appropriately, ethically, in relation to it. He considered architecture a social artifact, an index of collective well-being. Judging architecture could no longer be divorced from assessing the conditions and needs from which it arose, or its place in context and in time. This demanded another kind of history and another kind of criticism. Instead of assessing new work by the standards of masterpieces, historical precedent, or compositional rules, Behrendt, like many of his contemporaries, looked to metaphors of nature and organic processes as regulative principles, for throughout his writings the goal of historical development was always a new state of organicity. What that meant, how organic unity was figured—how the route to it was conceived—varied from book to book as Behrendt's thinking unfolded in relation to changing discursive formations, historical conditions, and opportunities. In many ways, it also stayed the same, continuing to search for the terms of a new system while inflecting to absorb criticism, new knowledge, and new directions. He consistently relied on a performative conception of style as a category for such unity, linked to society, political economy, and increasingly to the industrial mode of production and engineering. What would make the style of the modern era distinctive from all previous ones were the new means, materials, and methods of construction generated by engineering and industry to meet the needs of mass society. He did not, however, take these to be adequate in themselves for the purposes of cultural work. Rather, they provided the material basis for an elemental architectonic system with which to attain organic cultural expressions. The clarification of this system was the task to which he dedicated his critical enterprise.

Against Style

In America, the idea of modern architecture as a style remains strongly indebted to revisionist interpretations promoted by Philip Johnson, first in 1932 in cocurating the *International Style* exhibition and again in the 1950s in speaking against the functionalist teachings of Walter Gropius at Harvard, insisting that only architecture can, after all, beget architecture.[96] For Modernism had quickly become equated with functionalism, or more precisely with the slogan "form follows function," which entailed a critique not only of formalism—especially the reiteration of historical styles—but also of the very idea of style. Even Hitchcock's earlier history, *Modern Architecture* of 1929, had avoided the concept of style, relying instead on the seemingly dated notion of a "new tradition" to characterize what was paradigmatic in Modernism. What then are we to make of the fact that in *Sieg*—an apparently exemplary treatise of German functionalism—Behrendt continued to mobilize the category of style where most Modernists of his generation eschewed it altogether in favor of the regulative ideal of expression and its architectural counterparts, *bauen* ("to build" or "construct") and *Gestaltung* (form creation)? The term *Gestaltung* has multiple connotations that are not adequately registered by translating it as *design*. It refers both to form and to the process of formation or shaping, and it retains traces of the vital, creative energy of becoming in the concreteness of the resultant form. It also implies a figure or configuration that is a clear and individuated totality. In psychology, a gestalt is an organized whole whose parts belong together and are not simply juxtaposed or randomly distributed; it is understood to be perceived as such because human experience has the same structure as the underlying brain processes. The following sections of this essay examine how Behrendt's commitment to articulating the terms of a new holistic model of culture led him to revise, rather than reject, the term *style* by revaluing and redefining *Baustil* (building style). Frequently used for architectural periodization in the nineteenth century, *Baustil* came to designate, for Behrendt, a totality of architectural production based not on the (mechanical) imitation of appearances, forms, or a canon of works, but on the (organic) principle of expression and its biological counterpart, self-generation.

The ground for a conception of style based on the theory of expression, rather than imitation or representation, had been prepared at the turn of the century. At that time critics attempted to provide the theoretical basis for decorative artists, architects, and manufacturers struggling with the problems engendered by mechanizing manufacturing and competing on the international market. Other European countries had achieved power and prosperity on the basis of colonization, but the lateness of German unification in 1871 precluded that; instead, it was generally understood that industrialization would be the key to national wealth and international prestige.[97] However, German thought was so deeply invested in the opposition between *Kultur* and *Zivilisation* — artistic culture and material civilization, high and low, spirit and nature — that this fateful acceptance of industrialization required the construction of new bridges between these divided domains. The theory of architectural representation established in the 1840s by Carl Bötticher, which linked *Kernform* (technical form) and *Kunstform* (art form), no longer appeared adequate by the turn of the century. Although Bötticher had acknowledged the validity of new advances in technology, he had required that they be assimilated into existing systems of representation.[98] For Alfred Gotthold Meyer, a historian of engineered structures writing at the turn of the century, technology was already capable of producing its own beauty: the new steely, dematerializing, and sublime beauty of the Bridge over the Firth of Forth, the Crystal Palace, and the Eiffel Tower. Bötticher's technical form, born of a mysterious source in the human unconscious, no longer needed the mediation of prior formal conventions.[99] By contrast, Friedrich Naumann, a leading voice in the early Werkbund, still distinguished between the present as a transition period and the future potential of an industrial art (*Industriekunst*) that would be the modern successor to handcrafted art. The present artless state of mechanically reproduced work remained too narrow for him; it still needed to be refined, just as the machine had yet to be spiritualized. But, he forecast, it might not take long for the "language of the machine" to become so supple that there will be no limits to its possibilities.[100] In the meantime, Naumann concluded, the machine's promotion of simplification served to reeducate public taste.

In the years during which Behrendt entered the architectural discourse, a variety of propositions were being offered to achieve what Naumann called the "spiritualization of the machine," which was itself linked to the reception of technology as a natural expression of life. The crisis of artistic value engendered by the mechanization and commodification of the applied arts — artless utilitarianism and replicas — led to the pursuit of "quality" as the substitute for lost spiritual and cultural value, especially among members of the Werkbund.[101] For Peter Behrens, appointed by the AEG in 1907 as the first comprehensive designer for a corporation, technology was to be ennobled by applying a priori forms, which were presumed to have eternal aesthetic value — the pure forms of elementary geometry considered as autonomous things-in-themselves.[102] Hendrik Petrus Berlage and Hermann Muthesius each put forward a case for pure practicality and objectivity as the guarantor of beauty, functionality, economy, and (for Muthesius) marketability. In contrast to both pure form and pure sobriety, Henry van de Velde proffered an ethos of pure presence under the sign of a dynamic functionalism for which all forms were the unique result of a constellation of forces given material presence by the artist, provided, of course, the artist employed rational means toward rational ends.

At this time, architectural theory also drew on expression-based conceptions of style and historical process developed in the new social science of art history. Heinrich Wölfflin, August Schmarsow, Alois Riegl, and others posited the existence of an underlying form of vision, imagination, and spatiality specific to a given culture or historical period. They developed techniques of comparative analysis for discerning the attributes and biases of these underlying forms, which not only mediated the expression of individual works but were themselves expressions of the epoch. Riegl coined the term *Kunstwollen* (will to art), as an alternative to the idea of style, to designate the unconscious and fundamentally unknowable, mysterious formative will, desire, or feeling specific to a given historical period.[103] The universality inherent in the concept of *Kunstwollen* suggested an even more inclusive model of cultural production that went beyond the fine arts, for which Riegl introduced the notion of art industries (*Kunstindustrien*). Building on Semper's contention that style originated in the crafts, it was a short step from Riegl's analysis of the art industries of the late Roman period to those of the modern age, often already characterized as the age of machines.

Like Riegl, Muthesius sought to avoid the concept of style entirely, which he considered compromised by the inauthentic cult of styles, mechanically reproduced in industry and by the growing legions of designers catering to bourgeois society, all of which had led to the commodification of style as fashion. With his *Stilarchitektur und Baukunst* (Style-architecture and building-art), 1902, Muthesius helped inscribe a further distinction into the discourse on culture and technology, one that qualified the quest for a new style by a critique of style as such.[104] As the title of the book announced, he established an opposition between an architecture based on codified style(s) and a building-art that responded straightforwardly and objectively to the material tasks and conditions at hand. Muthesius gave the long-standing critique of imitation—mimesis having become suspect with the Enlightenment imperative to reground the authority of art in nature and sensibility—a new target in industrially produced copies, which he called surrogates. While hardly the first to use the term *Baukunst,* Muthesius helped popularize it as a substitute for *Architektur.* He thereby established the template for the later opposition between function and style, as well as the oppositional logic of the debates it engendered. In turn, setting the pursuit of authentic form against formalism recapitulated the problematic relation of inner essences to outward appearances—content to form—so thoroughly inscribed into the history of Western art.[105]

Rather than using "style" as the regulative idea for his model of historical formation, Muthesius referred to a practical and scientific attitude, a new (yet originary) way of designing oriented to simplicity and directness, but also to life in the modern world. "The world," he wrote,

> lies under the spell of the phantom "style-architecture." It is hardly possible for people today to grasp that the true values in the building-art are totally independent of the question of style, indeed that a proper approach to a work of architecture has absolutely nothing to do with "style."[106]

To free architecture from its ossification and alienation from life, he recommended that "[w]herever possible we should for now ban completely the notion of style." And rehearsing the later emphasis on problems, embarking on the right path, and developing toward a goal whose end remained indeterminate, he suggested that "when the master builder clearly refrains from any style and emphasizes that which is required of him by the particular type of problem, we will be on the correct path to a ... truly new style no longer so distant."[107] Although this appeared to open the door to a new conception of style commensurate with a living building-art, Muthesius nevertheless insisted that architecture be freed from the "stylistic chains in which she has lain bound for a century" so that "the rays of a new artistic life" could emanate from her once again.[108] He reiterated this rejection a few years later, writing that the goal of "creating works of impressive artistic value on the basis of absolutely independent *Gestaltung*" was unconcerned with the idea of establishing a modern style.[109]

Just as, in *Sieg,* Behrendt criticized formalism creeping into the new style movement through its increasing fashionability, so Muthesius, more than two decades earlier, had criticized Jugendstil for allowing itself to be appropriated by fashion and thereby transformed into a new formalism.[110] He criticized van de Velde for pursuing a new style through purely outward appearances, in contrast to the Arts and Crafts movement in England. While Muthesius considered the hankering after so-called new forms "once again basically the old miseries of style and ornament,"[111] he took this to be symptomatic of the transitional nature of the present, which he considered "a teething period through which an ascending, truly new conception of art is about to unfold."[112] Rehearsing much of the later meaning of *Gestaltung,* he characterized this new conception as "a free and unfettered shaping of form [*Gestaltung*], which takes account of every special circumstance, which fluently adapts to every need, tacks down the inner essence of the problem, and seeks to express everything outwardly."[113] Rather than a pedantic academic approach to design, he saw this as individualizing it. Moreover, it already "expressed a victory of the contemporary spirit that the movement embodies."[114] For him, the most important change in the present condition of art was precisely this "movement" of spirit, which marked "the beginning of a new perspective on the question of style."[115] Its various strains needed to be integrated to achieve a clearer awareness of their center of gravity.[116]

To bridge the gap between art and modern life, Muthesius suggested looking to railway terminals and exhibition buildings, large bridges, steamships, railway cars, and bicycles for demonstrations of design that embody truly modern ideas and new principles of *Sachlichkeit:* "a rigorous, one might say scientific objectivity, an abstention from all superficial forms of decoration, a design strictly following the purpose that the work should serve."[117] He described machines as improved tools and machine forms as exemplary for architecture and the applied arts:[118]

> While Mother Architecture found herself on a wrong path, life never rested but went on to create forms from the innovations it had produced, the simple forms of pure practicality. It created our machines, vehicles, implements, iron bridges, and glass halls. It led the way soberly in that it proceeded practically—one would like to say purely scientifically.[119]

At the same time, Muthesius held that architecture would succeed once again in being a vernacular—an art of everyday life[120]—only with the reform of domesticity.[121] Since the gap that separated ordinary people from specialists made them vulnerable to the illusions of style-architecture and fleeting fashions,[122] a focus on the house as the strategic vehicle for reform—pursued later by Behrendt in *Die Volkswohnung* and the Werkbund in its exhibitions of the late 1920s—promised to bring the building-art once again into the realm of general public understanding as the "genuine art" of a "genuine people."[123]

Many of the subsequent efforts to redeem industry also sought to absorb it into an expanded definition of culture whose first extensive treatment was in Paul Schultze-Naumburg's widely read book series *Kulturarbeiten* (Cultural works), published sequentially beginning in 1901.[124] In this set of nine books, ranging in topic from houses to gardens, villages, cities, and industrial landscapes, Schultze-Naumburg mapped the "culture of the visible" and its transformations in order to intervene in it. Heavily illustrated with photographs — 2,500 in all, placed one per page, often staging comparisons between good and bad examples on opposing pages — these books aimed to expand the audience for the critique of cultural decline, long-standing among the educated class. Schultze-Naumburg described the problem as "the disfiguration of the physiognomy of our land" wrought by industrialization. To "work against the terrible destruction of our land,"[125] he popularized a new model of culture as the production of *Gestalten* (forms) capable of "conferring reality on the Idea,"[126] of giving it external form as a culture of the visible. For him, "the culture of the visible embraces not only houses and monuments, bridges and streets, but also clothes and forms of sociability, forests and livestock, machines and national defense."[127] This expanded definition allowed him to account for "the transformation of the entire surface of the earth through human hands," to which everyone contributes, "the farmer and the engineer, the shopkeeper and the gardener, the sailor and the soldier, the forester and the builder." For "truly all kinds of *Gestalten* belong to the same family."[128]

Schultze-Naumburg explained, however, that the *vital* concept of *Gestalten* had been lost, for "only when it is a *Gestaltung* of the Idea does it have cultural value, only when it serves its purpose [*Zweck*] perfectly and at the same time expresses this perfection in its outer form."[129] The highest form of *Gestaltung* arises when the purpose is an ethical one, for then "the individual will make the harmony of an ethical world picture visible."[130] A power was ethical when it was able to put a higher purpose in order organically. Schultze-Naumburg reiterated the link between perfection and beauty, suggesting that only form that serves a good purpose and expresses it with the simplest and most perfect of means can achieve beauty. "Beauty is closely related to ethics in that it takes what is 'good' in the broadest sense for humankind, makes it visible as 'beautiful,' and teaches us to love it."[131] Harmony was to be possible again once people grasped this link. Despite his regret at the waning of premodern society, Schultze-Naumburg, like other reformers of his generation, was open to the possibility that, in the new era, a new kind of beauty and harmony would be ushered in by fulfilling rather than denying the telos of technology. According to the present "feeling for life" (*Lebensgefühl*), even a locomotive, he suggested, was beautiful. "Could there be any stronger expression of humanly harnessed natural forces," he asked, "when, with glowing eyes, the monster approaches along the curve of the tracks, arrives in the station coughing and blowing, barely able to breathe, and accepts its new load with a deep groan?"[132] While the locomotive still had some imperfections, overall, he concluded, it was beautiful, for its powerful function had already been brought to perfection. Moreover, the railway need not have destroyed the landscape that it traversed and could still be integrated with it. Industrial complexes too had the potential to be better and more beautiful *Gestalten* than they usually were. In fact, history itself could have taken another course; it need not have resulted in degradation and could still be redressed by stressing simplicity, directness, the elimination of ornament and false motifs, and the proper placement of houses in their environment (*Umwelt*). While he sought to avoid the use of historical styles, he held that the age of Goethe was the last exemplary period.

The idea that industrial society could take an alternative course was extended beyond the preservation and renewal programs of *Heimatschutz* and *Heimatstil* in the final three volumes of Schultze-Naumburg's series: *Die Gestaltung der Landschaft durch den Menschen* (The formation of the landscape by people), 1916–1917. Here he turned to the problems and opportunities of industry itself, presenting good and bad examples of industrial sites, structures, and landscapes. Critical of the short-term exploitation of the land for profit, he suggested that this was neither the necessary nor the only expression of the new age. He sought to examine humanity's activity in transforming the earth's crust in terms of its economic and ethical value. In a country like Germany, he explained, where the land had been largely subjugated to human control, everyone worked on the overall *Gestaltung* of the environment and was responsible for its appearance. Using words and images he sought to win over the ordinary people, farmers, and workers whose daily activities served to maintain and transform the face of the land.

Several decades prior to Schultze-Naumburg's *Kulturarbeiten*—during the 1870s and 1880s—the aesthetician Conrad Fiedler had put forward an idealist conception of art as a form of cognition—visual cognition (pure visibility) made operational through free artistic creativity.[133] Following the philosopher Johann Friedrich Herbart, Fiedler held that vision had its universal form—timeless, constant, and abstract—just as knowledge had its a priori form for Kant. It was the unique role of art to produce works that embodied artistic vision, understood as a higher, clearer, and purer form than is given by nature. Once captured in material presence, it was then seen to be accessible to others who, observing a work of art, were thought to reexperience the moment of vital artistic creation. Schultze-Naumburg's "culture of the visible" effectively broadened Fiedler's interrelated concepts of form, artistic activity, and visibility beyond the fine arts and even beyond technology into an all-encompassing cultural anthropology. As Behrendt's references to Fiedler in *Kampf um den Stil* imply, the idea of *Gestaltung* in the architectural discourse of the 1920s remained indebted to Fiedler's theories, first popularized by Adolf von Hildebrand and Hermann Konnerth and then elaborated by others.

Fiedler presented this empathetic model of art in his book *Über die Beurteilung von Werken der bildenden Kunst* (On judging works of visual art), 1876. "Artistic activity," he wrote, "is neither slavish imitation nor arbitrary feeling; rather, it is free creative Gestalt-formation [*Gestaltung*]."[134] Like science, it creates a humanly comprehended world that is simultaneously an investigation and a *Gestaltung*. But this is not, Fiedler emphasized, a second world alongside a world that is independent of art. What art creates is "the world made by and for the artistic consciousness."[135] The fantasy of the artist is nothing more than the imaginative power that all humanity needs in order to grasp the world as one of visible appearances, as something simpler, clearer, more intelligible and pleasurable than the endless proliferation and vacillating confusion that the abundance of life presents. Artistic activity begins for Fiedler when humanity confronts the visible world as "something immensely enigmatical" — "when, driven by an inner necessity and applying the powers of his mind, [the artist] grapples with the twisted mass of the visible which presses in upon him and gives it creative form."[136] Although winning the forms of a higher, pure vision from nature entails a struggle against it — because the activity of art flows from necessity and is governed by law — it also defines what is natural and originary within humanity. Just as nature was thought to possess an inexhaustible creativity, so too artistic activity was understood as an endless, continuous, and incessant working of the mind "to bring one's consciousness of the visible world to an ever richer development, to a Gestalt-formation [*Gestaltung*] ever more nearly complete."[137] So it is that, for Fiedler, art had nothing to do with forms already made, already possessed by human consciousness; rather, art began and ended in the creation of forms that attain existence only through it and thereby enrich the mental possessions of humanity. "What excites artistic activity," Fiedler declared, "is that which is as yet untouched by the human mind.... Art does not start from abstract thought in order to arrive at forms; rather, it climbs up from the formless to the formed, and in this process is found its entire cognitive meaning."[138] Yet, as the artist permits form after form to emerge into consciousness, the shapeless mass from which it comes still remains inexhaustible: "The realm of appearance develops infinitely before him because it grows out of his ceaseless activity."[139]

Fiedler's theory of art foresaw a significant change for the role of criticism and, less explicitly, for art history.[140] If appearances are, in fact, images constituted by the mind and the eye with the assistance of experience; if the function of the artist is to add to or subtract from appearances in order to gain clearer and stronger images of form; and if these images are valued for what new knowledge of form they generate, then assessing art by the standards of preexisting works was no longer relevant. Nor was it appropriate for theory to dictate to artistic activity, to impose formulas, laws, and prior conceptions. Rather, Fiedler suggested, the work of the critic should follow that of the artist and, entering a posteriori into the realm of artistic process, should aspire to decipher works as documents or traces of life. While the work of art is, in the final instance, fully alive only in the moment of its creation, it provides the attuned critic with a visible, durable, and memorable record of artistic consciousness — an inexhaustible source of inquiry and cognition through which to see the world anew.

Although Behrendt had already used the notion of *Gestaltung* at several strategic points in *Kampf um den Stil,* in *Sieg* it became central. He introduced it first in the context of technical and machine design, then developed it with respect to buildings and spaces (*Raumgestaltung*). It served to designate a principle of creative formation and a new approach to design capable of achieving for its products — be they objects, buildings, or cities — the integral and integrated attributes of organisms. For Behrendt, *Gestaltung* designated an orientation toward solving problems through construction, specifically the life problems of the age. "'To construct' [*konstruieren*]," he explained, "derives from the Latin verb *construere,* meaning 'to invent, to deduce, to shape, to form, to *design* [*gestalten*].'"[141] Unless otherwise impeded by the "influence and intervention of art," the activity of *Gestaltung* was driven by the "formative powers" and "formal energy" of the time — spiritual forces that were visible and knowable only through this activity. Aligned with immaterial formative forces, it became the designer's role to actualize them in forms that were as pure and clear as possible. For this, technical forms, considered pure rational creations without prior conceptions, became exemplary. They were functional constructs arising from necessity and guided by analysis and calculation toward the goal of perfection for their inner purpose or plan. This process was figured as a path of formal evolution and natural selection. For Behrendt, the form world generated by technology was a world of perfected physiologies, each differentiated and unique. It was a world filled with immeasurable wealth, richness, and diversity. While the problems of form that they addressed were constructional and not aesthetic, the results contained what he called "aesthetic elements" — "clean and precise lines, the consummate purity of their proportions, the taut tension of their flat and curved surfaces, the colorfulness of their paints and varnishes, and the sparkling sheen of their finishes."[142] These elements, he suggested, "may be seen, if not already in themselves as the elements of a new style, then as the yeasts or starting points for the formation of such."[143]

Although Fiedler himself had not extended his theory of artistic activity and pure visibility to the design of machines, Behrendt cited him explicitly in this context for having suggested that "not all times express the *best* of what they have to say in *art.*"[144] Similarly, in *Kampf um den Stil,* he quoted the sculptor and theorist Adolf von Hildebrand that, in following the path of natural creativity, an artist also hastens the decline of inauthentic expressions as a secondary side effect.[145] That this reference to Hildebrand — whose own widely read *Das Problem der Form in der bildenden Kunst* (The problem of form in the fine arts), 1893,[146] had extended and popularized the theory delineated by Fiedler — should appear in a discussion about the artistic task of industrial architecture and the exemplarity of American grain silos for achieving both functional and architectonic form, suggests that Fiedler's theory had by then been extrapolated — rather deliberately even — into the realm of technology. It had become a generalized principle of creative work in modern technological society. As a regulative idea it cut across opposing categories and helped reconcile art and industry, art and nature, art and life, individual and collective, process and form. As a universally valid principle, it served to guarantee unity of formal expression across the entire field of human culture, considered in the broadest sense. It had become, in other words, the operative key to a new synthetic, integrated, and unified system of material culture. If one started afresh and worked independently, constructionally, formatively, and creatively as nature did, then "[o]ne and the same driving force produces forms and proportions altogether integrated, a characteristic that Jacob Burckhardt has described as the most distinctive sign of all original and organic styles."[147]

An essay by Muthesius from 1913 demonstrates how Fiedlerian aesthetic theory had already been transposed into the reception of engineering among theorists seeking to incorporate industrial works into an expanded definition of culture.[148] To address the question of whether engineering constructions can, should, or must have the aesthetic effect of beauty, he invoked aesthetic propositions focused on the controlling judgment of the eye guided by an instinct for form and formal perfection. Without intending to make usability the sole tendency of *Gestaltung,* he cited examples from tailored clothing to cigars and domestic interiors as evidence that an unconscious aesthetic feeling was always at work in determining good form. "With all visible *Gestalten*… [o]ur eye is continually controlling everything we make that is visible, whereby we fashion, judge, and handle form in accordance with laws planted in our mind."[149] He insisted, in fact, that conscious artistic intention could not create forms of aesthetic effect. "Beauty is concerned with a problem of form and nothing else, utility with the naked fulfillment of a task.… To fuse the beautiful with the functional, to meet both their claims to complete fulfillment, is actually the purpose of architecture."[150] Functionality and beauty worked together from the beginning. The apparent self-generation of engineering constructions, free of the masking devices of architects, demonstrated that clarification toward good form could take place in this sphere as in art:

> The same tendencies of *Gestaltung* appear with the artist, the architect, the engineer, the machinist, the tailor, the housekeeper, the craftworker, the mother that makes her children clothes. These always concern the same things: good proportions, agreement of colors, effective construction, rhythm, expressive form.[151]

Since these tendencies, he concluded, are at work in all those who create (*alle Gestalter*), there can be no distinction between architecture and engineering. The point of departure for *Gestaltung* in both cases was necessarily the fulfillment of a program of functions, uses, or purposes.

While Muthesius's emphasis on the interrelation of vision and form may indeed have been influenced by Fiedler's and Hildebrand's conceptions of "the problem of form," what he achieved in this essay is something more than the simple transfer of values from art form to technical form.[152] Rather, he carefully rearticulated theoretical propositions for the applied arts and architecture that he had developed over many years in order to fuse *sachlich* functionality and the aesthetic judgment of beautiful form. The basis for this fusion lay in his discovery that these tendencies were structural—of "a general, so to say cosmic sort"—already "immanent to our brain activity."[153]

Among Behrendt's own generation, Walter Gropius was one of the first to employ the notion of *Gestaltung,* namely, in his essay on the value of industrial building forms for the development of style.[154] "The urge to design [*Gestalten*] in our time," he wrote, "is carried with originary freshness by the development of industrial forms."[155] For Gropius, engineers produced with a naïveté that architects should strive to emulate. Drawing not only on Muthesius's putative theory of good form but also on Riegl's *Kunstwollen,* he contended that, "As long as the intellectual conceptions of the age are uncertain and lacking a firm goal, art lacks the potential to develop style, that is, to draw the will to *Gestaltung* of the many together in *one* thought."[156]

For Style

Concurrent with the inauguration of Schultze-Naumburg's *Kulturarbeiten,* Scheffler launched another trajectory within reform thought, one that would come into open conflict with Schultze-Naumburg's nationalist, land-based, and increasingly racist conception of culture. In an essay of 1901, "Die Volkskunst," Scheffler revised the concept of folk art in the direction of a metropolitan culture, which he later developed in his books on Berlin and the architecture of the metropolis.[157] Scheffler deplored those nostalgic for the folk art of the past and insisted instead on reckoning with the iron realities of the industrial state and metropolis. Only by aligning art with the vitality of the present would a new folk art emerge. Scheffler's theory of metropolitan culture helped build a platform from which to develop the positive potentials of modernization. At the same time, the philosopher and social critic Georg Simmel suggested that the anonymity of the metropolis was the germ of a new form of sociability that was more cosmopolitan—open to change and difference—than the ideal of the uniform culture of the village advocated by theorists of community, notably Ferdinand Tönnies.[158] Similarly, August Endell presented a theory of a new kind of beauty latent in the metropolis.[159] He promoted a new way of seeing the metropolitan landscape, one that fused his earlier empathetic theory of art as an abstract world of soul-shattering forms with the impressionist's efforts to capture the eternal in the degraded and transitory conditions of the industrial city. Scheffler's interpretation of van de Velde also belonged to this impressionist reading of a metropolitan culture seeking to find a new redemptive world latent within it. In his book of 1913 on van de Velde, Scheffler praised him as "a great organizer of vital forces."[160] He considered what van de Velde promoted as the new style to be an idea of the formative will of the age and suggested that, through him, it had achieved form. In a talk given in 1913 at the Nietzsche-Archiv on the occasion of van de Velde's fiftieth birthday, Scheffler described the designer's program for a new style as building a bridge toward a new "classically regulated future."[161] For projecting a new total culture (*Gesamtkultur*), Scheffler called him a realist utopian (*Realutopist*). However, he also felt obliged to distance himself from van de Velde's built work, still so firmly associated with Jugendstil.[162] In similar terms, Behrendt continued to cite van de Velde as founder of the new dynamic and functionalist style movement, which in 1920 he too characterized as a utopia.

Behrendt's *Der Kampf um den Stil im Kunstgewerbe und in der Architektur* (The battle for style in the decorative arts and architecture) is marked by the intensified spirit of social reform and revolutionary new beginnings that characterized the architectural discourse in Berlin in the period immediately following World War I—seeking to sever ties with the past in order to reunite art and life. Broadening and radicalizing the themes of his earlier writings in the direction of Scheffler's metropolitan vision, this work was Behrendt's most extensive historical and theoretical exposition, and thus it deserves to be reviewed in detail. Here he sought to portray, for the first time, the emergence, rather than merely the potential, of an entirely new mode of cultural production as the direct expression of modern life, or more precisely of changing life forces, life feelings, and life-forms. While he still called it a "new style," struggling to realize itself from within the old, he now considered the concept of style itself a utopia. As the circle of artists and architects around Bruno Taut proclaimed the need to reunite art and society under the sign of a glass utopia, and as the Arbeitsrat für Kunst called for dismantling the ossified institutions of the Wilhelmian period to clear a space for new artistic vitality, Behrendt too argued that art and architecture should be seen in relation to the changing social order. The applied arts were for him formal expressions of the general will and spirit of the age (*Zeitgeist*), symbols of the purpose of life (*Lebensidee*). Although he credited socialism for having awakened a new collective consciousness, he held that social change that produced peace and calm in everyday life was more important to artistic change than activist politics. The struggle for style was the struggle for a total culture (*Gesamtkultur*) within the constellation of forces defining the historical moment. By emphasizing the generative capacity of life and making the new style in art dependent on a new style of life, Behrendt's utopia of integrated self-fashioning was to arise naturally as the transformation of consciousness embraced new means and creative possibilities.

Having established these programmatic propositions, Behrendt dedicated his book to providing a historical portrait of the situation in which cultural production then found itself. He characterized the situation in terms of social crises, conflicts, and the antagonism of forces arising from the ongoing dissolution of premodern society under the onslaught of modernization and the unrelenting struggle between social groups that had begun in the nineteenth century. Because the process of historical formation remained unresolved, Behrendt set out to follow the traces of its becoming, to develop a picture of the future from what was already at hand.[163] Paraphrasing Nietzsche, as many in the Berlin avant-garde were then doing, Behrendt suggested that in order to make the past useful for life it was necessary to learn how to grasp what was alive in the present, to find its creative forces and once again turn new events into history.[164] Yet, where the AfK would foreground extraordinary sculptural and graphic images thought to be drawn directly from the creative unconscious, Behrendt undertook to write a history of architecture and the decorative arts, hoping to reanimate the Berlin building tradition by developing a new, unified collective system of cultural production that would be simple, direct, economical, flexible, and generalizable.[165]

The origins of the new historical formation, Behrendt explained, lay in the ideas of democratic self-governance unleashed by the French Revolution, the spread of education, and the transformation of the economy into an industrial system. He characterized the nineteenth century as a time of questioning and dissolving previous social orders, blurring the boundaries between social groups, displacing craft by the mass production of goods in factories, and enlarging the boundaries of work through improved transportation and development of the global market economy. He alluded to the sweeping relocation of populations from the country to the swelling ranks of the metropolis, a shift in which the people (*das Volk*) were recast as work-seeking laborers. He depicted the emerging proletarian mass as the soulless instruments of industrialization, producing commodities for generalized consumption. This process, he explained, had occurred so fast that it was initially impossible to understand its causes and to respond to the changes. Under capitalism, the order and calm of premodern society was displaced by uninhibited economic competition, which set everyone against everyone else. This process generated two new social groups — the industrialists and the workers — who remained locked in conflict for hegemony in the new social order. Endemic to this new conflictive condition was a change in the nature of work as the intervention of industrialists, and the culture of publicity and fashion that they spawned, alienated makers from those who used what they made.

Parallel to these changes in political economy, Behrendt suggested, art had been displaced by science and instrumental rationality. Creative forces (*Schaffenskräfte*) were replaced by education (*Bildung*), contemplation (*Anschauung*) by thinking, and sensuousness by law and theory. Extending once more the distinction made by Schiller between "naive" and "sentimental" literature, he suggested that the artist could no longer work naively or unconsciously, but rather needed to work artificially to produce unified works in full consciousness. Moreover, Behrendt contended, in order for a new social life to find its form and a new period of society to unfold, a free play of forces needed to replace the old principle of *Gebundenheit* (togetherness).[166] He cited Karl Friedrich Schinkel as a transition figure whose early works were still products of creative will, sensuously materialized revaluations of antique precedent. Schinkel's later works did not, for Behrendt, evoke the same corporeal solidity and sensuous perception. Behrendt suggested that as the artists of Schinkel's overeducated generation became overburdened with historical precedent, their work became unproductive, placing a higher value on achieving perfect likenesses of ancient sources than on artistic force and inner, natural originality (*Ursprünglichkeit*). By midcentury the same was true in the decorative arts, which came to be seen exclusively in terms of style and surface and the possibility of imitation through the most unsensuous industrial reproduction.

To Behrendt this characterized the nature of the new *Zeitgeist.* Despite its higher standard of material living, the creative force of the nineteenth century remained, for him, impoverished, lacking any feeling toward culture, inwardly empty, and without emotion. Herein lay, for Behrendt, the problem of the commodity, which needed to be addressed by a renewal of art and creative force.[167] The metropolis was to be the locus of the fight *for* the new style and *against* the transformation of art into a luxury commodity.

Behrendt attributed the striving for a new style and the origins of the new movement in the decorative arts to Gottfried Semper's critique of art as a product of education (*Bildung*) — of the intellectualized approach ascribed to the late Schinkel, which had led, in Semper's time, to an art of industrially manufactured surrogates. Noting that a new holistic consciousness was awakened in socialism, with which all the leading artists and architects of the nineteenth century had been affiliated, he went on to admire the ethical and pedagogical aims of the Arts and Crafts movement in England. Notwithstanding the inspirational effect of these reformers, Behrendt held that the critical stand against industrialization taken by John Ruskin and William Morris limited the movement's potential to create a new style. For that he turned to their continental counterparts, focusing on the Belgian school led by van de Velde. What van de Velde had achieved was the formulation of a new program based on "a new 'realistic' principle of *Gestaltung,* according to which form was to be derived organically from its function, as the artistic symbol of its tectonic purpose."[168] Beginning each task again at the beginning, the artist was to be guided in expressive activity by three key spiritual principles: functionality or purposiveness (*Zweckmässigkeit*), the logic of construction (*Konstruktionslogik*), and the proper handling of materials (*Materialbehandlung*). This new orientation to the task of architecture in the context of the ceaseless transformation of society engendered by industrialization was encapsulated in van de Velde's catchphrase, "the line is a force." Behrendt continued to cite this, even in *Sieg,* as the first statement of the dynamic and functional conception of architecture — the regulative principle of all *Gestaltung* and of the new movement itself.

Behrendt described the continental reform movement in the decorative arts as marking a new attitude toward the *Kunstwollen* of the age, aspiring to a style that would be the natural outer result of the inner content of the times. By invoking Riegl's term *Kunstwollen,* Behrendt positioned the movement in relation to the broadly felt desire for an art that would be the valid expression of a universal, yet unconscious, desire and feeling specific to the modern period. Both *Gestaltung* and *Kunstwollen* refer to an unconscious productivity or, more precisely, to the productivity of the unconscious or spirit, the mysterious (godly) origin of humanity's creativity. Where *Gestaltung* considered this productivity in relation to specific forms and configurations (*Gestalten*), *Kunstwollen* and its various derivatives in art discourse — *Wollen, Wille, Kunstwille,* and *Formwille* — were invoked in relation to the totality of art. Behrendt cited Fiedler to the effect that it was sometimes necessary to discard the entire past in order to renew a people's feeling for truth and naturalness. Waving a nationalist flag, he contended that this was the mission of the German movement.

Despite, or perhaps because of, its willfulness, Behrendt contended that the initial attempt at a new will to form failed because it could not be generalized. The turn from Jugendstil to schematic Neoclassicism and neo-Biedermeier around 1904 represented, for Behrendt, more than a change of fashion. For the turn to *Sachlichkeit,* simplification and the systematic elimination of ornament, together with experiments in technique and material, aimed at new foundational forms that could be understood as classical. It marked the renewal of a way of working that was capable of achieving unity at all scales, linking the decorative arts with architecture and even cities. And it did so while distancing itself from the eclectic play of ornament and reasserting the primacy of inner necessity and lawfulness. In this context, Behrendt acknowledged the effectiveness of Schultze-Naumburg's *Kulturarbeiten* for having developed a preference for simplicity of form among the general public. Nevertheless, he remained critical of this return to classicism in the work of Schultze-Naumburg, Behrens, Bruno Paul, and others, because it still excluded society at large; it remained cut off from the life forces of the time. Similarly, he criticized reforms in education, particularly those initiated in Vienna, for having made this approach academic in a new formalism that was still isolated from the real economic problem of art and quality. With the industrialization of the decorative arts, Behrendt reiterated, emphasis was no longer on the originality and artistic merit of the singular work of a creative personality but on competitiveness in the international market. With the focus on the new problem of quality in the work of the decorative arts as the basis for Germany's market share, the decorative arts had arrived at its final question: the exploration of its economic function in the relationship between art and merchant.

The key instrument in the battle for new style as utopia was the principle of direct, unmediated, and unimpeded organic expression operative at the level of material means and life functions and at the higher level of spirit. Its signs were "good form" — self-identical and self-determined, the outer expression of inner formative forces — and "quality," that elusive ideal of the Werkbund to restore the spiritual effect of the craft object under the conditions of mechanical reproduction. Embracing packaging and marketing, as well as the design and production of objects, good design became the guarantor of quality. All this was incorporated in the idea of *Gestaltung,* at once form, formation, form creation, and configuration — verb as well as noun, process as well as product, force as well as form. *Gestaltung* was the form-generating activity of all organic beings[169] and of life itself.[170] It was the process of actualizing forces, *Gestaltungskräfte.*[171] As such, *Gestaltung* was the form of activity through which style, organicity, and unity were to be achieved in a struggle against the conflictive nature of the present period of transition. Moreover, the activity of *Gestaltung* promised to resolve the antinomies of modernity, for it was the principle of nature's own self-fashioning creativity, as well as the regulative principle in art *and* technology.[172] In art, it served to spiritualize living substance (*lebender Stoff*).[173] It marked the activity of life itself understood as ceaseless self-generation.[174] Offered as the antithesis of imitation, it reestablished mimesis in terms of process rather than form.

Turning from the decorative arts to architecture itself, Behrendt traced four lines of development: the transposition of engineering principles into architecture, the acceptance of new building types (from apartment buildings to museums and train stations) as problems needing new architectonic forms, the potential of new materials (notably iron) for new systems of construction and structural forms, and the betterment of the metropolis through its dissolution, decentralization, and resettlement in *Siedlungen*. These were the constituents of what he now called the new building style (*Baustil*), distinguished from style by its orientation to the creation of form from itself, rather than for itself. Behrendt presented the distinctive achievement of engineers as having developed a way of working that put aside the decorative as a principle of formation. Their simple utilitarian buildings—as well as their wide-spanning bridges and glass halls, gasometers, water towers, and cranes—had achieved monumental effect by themselves, without the transposition of a canon of forms. The renewal of the constructional spirit had awakened and given life to the yearning for new forms of expression.[175] The rise of engineering in the nineteenth century had opened up a division between the art of architecture and technologies of construction, which relegated the architect to a decorator, and even the new movement remained divided along parallel lines. Reiterating Scheffler's dualist interpretation of Modernism, whose resolution remained blocked by the antagonism of forces, Behrendt argued that all future development was contingent on overcoming the divisions between academy and life, form and function, art and technic.[176] Classicist formalism remained divorced from the vital will to *Gestaltung* of the age:

> The spirit of the age is a spirit of constant movement and restless activity. It knows neither completion nor conclusion, but only the unending striving for a better and more perfect solution. It knows neither ripeness nor harmony, but only constant change and all the dissonance of becoming.[177]

For Behrendt, it was imperative that architects learn the new constructional spirit and marry it with the architectonic spirit:

> Only when the architects find the will and the capacity to reject the academically transmitted decoration schema and to become masters once more of the engineers, the technicians, and artisans..., only then might the hope of a new independent style of building-art be fulfilled.[178]

The battle for style was at once critical and positive, a struggle *against* the dead weight of received conventions, practices, and habits of thought and *in favor* of redeeming commodified cultural production through spiritualization, as evidenced by "good form" and "quality," from objects to apartment buildings and urban precincts. The new style was offered as a systemic conception of cultural work—artistic, technical, and social—capable of transforming the system of production under industrial capitalism into a dynamic mode of unending organic productivity.[179]

In 1920 Behrendt also contributed an introduction for a new edition of Paul Mebes's book *Um 1800,* which had been one of the key texts in the Biedermeier and Neoclassical revival before World War I.[180] While Behrendt did not, on this occasion, discuss the role of new technologies in the new style, he did present his case for a new generalizable architectonic system in perhaps its most concise form. Once again distancing himself from the imitation of classicism, a category for which Schultze-Naumburg continued to be his key example, Behrendt took pains to explain that the value of Mebes's book, and of Biedermeier itself, was in showing what richness of appearance and harmony is possible using the simplest of means. For this was again the challenge inherent in the present-day task of constructing *Siedlungen* economically using simple building forms. He was critical of the striving among young architects (implying the avant-garde) for new forms of expression that he characterized as ecstatic and anticlassical. Leery of formalism on the one hand and social inadequacy on the other, he steered a course toward a new normativity of organic form creation (*Gestaltung*) using uniform means for structuring differentiated building bodies and spaces. Renewing the convictions of Neoclassicism, rather than its forms, offered the possibility that pure expression could become a new universal—a metropolitan style, a world style, and world language whose character he described as cosmopolitan. In a word, it offered the possibility of a mediating system for free and organic constructional activity.

"Gestaltung"

Allow me to return once more to those pivotal years following the destruction and defeat of World War I, which many considered an opportunity for beginning again at the beginning. Four years of unprecedented devastation and loss of life had interrupted the continuity of history to such an extent that nothing, it seemed, could possibly be the same again; the past had literally become rubble. Just as the constitution for the newly declared Republic was written on a blank page of German history, so too the new art, architecture, and urbanism was to be conceived and executed on an empty drawing board. After decades of theorizing and experimenting, reconstruction finally offered a condition under which new building tasks, it was hoped, would lead to a new reality. The anticipated immediacy of this constructional activity—this *Bauen,* answering broadly to the needs of the people without the distortion of old institutions, practices, and prejudices—generated utopian expectations. The "mighty drama of a sweeping transformation" was, as Behrendt would later put it in *Sieg,* "taking place before our eyes."[181] Prior to World War I Scheffler and Behrendt had recognized the utopian implications of the new style, but now utopia appeared to be generating itself as part of a comprehensive historical unfolding in which architects, along with so many others, saw themselves to be both witnesses and agents. At this historical juncture, the interweaving of fate and utopia — the acceptance of given realities as the basis for a redemptive future, which animated so much of German social theory in the late nineteenth and early twentieth century — played itself out in the sphere of lived experience.[182]

To describe the process of organic historical formation, the avant-garde invoked the expression of spirit, will, or desire, and spoke of realization, actualization, and crystallization — all in conjunction with a new emphasis on the activity of building (*Bauen*). Behne considered building to be the creative work of fantasy (*Phantasie*) and the expression of forces figured alternatively as *Ausdruckskraft, Schaffenskraft, Lebenskraft,* and *Gestaltungskraft.*[183] Van Doesburg spoke of "formation" (*Bildung*), Hermann Finsterlin of "plasticity," and El Lissitzky of "construction." To make architecture once more "the crystalline expression of humanity's noblest thoughts, ardor, faith, and religion," Gropius insisted in 1919 that "all of us become builders [*Bauende*] again," whose goal should be "the creative conception of the cathedral of the future, which will be once again in *one Gestalt* architecture *and* sculpture *and* painting."[184] By 1922–1923 the word *Gestaltung* had been added to the arsenal of Modernist polemics and came to subsume all of the above meanings. Where in 1918 the first manifesto of De Stijl spoke of "bringing to the light" and "realizing new consciousness in the outer world,"[185] by 1922 van Doesburg had given his programmatic essay "The Will to Style" ("Der Wille zum Stil") the subtitle "Reshaping Life, Art, and Technology" ("Neugestaltung von Leben, Kunst und Technik").[186] By 1923 *"neue Gestaltung"* was used as the term for Neoplasticism in a German translation of an essay by Piet Mondrian.[187] Not only was *Gestaltung,* for van Doesburg citing Goethe, paradigmatic of direct primary expression — the opposite of imitation — but it designated the "total expression [*Gesamtausdruck*] of a people" and the "physiognomy of an art period."[188] Speaking through Riegl, van Doesburg referred artistic production not only to a new universal *Stilwollen,* but also to an international *Gestaltungswille,* and even *Gestaltungswünsche.* Subsumed within "the problem of the economic reconstruction [*Neugestaltung*] of Europe,"[189] the new *Kunstgestaltung,* with its elementary means of expression (*Gestaltungselemente*), was aligned with the parallel fulfillment of technology. "The machine," he wrote, "is the phenomenon of spiritual discipline par excellence."[190] While the new spirit had already generated a new machine aesthetic, he suggested that "[t]he new spiritual view of art does not experience the machine in terms of beauty alone, but also recognizes in it a boundless potential for artistic expression."[191]

Able to designate the operative activity of both artistic creation and technical design, the notion of *Gestaltung* served to resolve the division between these two domains during a period of unprecedented construction. It guaranteed the much-longed-for unity in several interrelated ways: first, as a principle common to art, technology, and nature it resolved antinomies between culture and civilization, spirit and nature, art and technology, art and society, and artifice and nature; second, as the governing principle of production for all creative activity—from industrial design to clothing, buildings, and cities—it established the unity of the arts as well as the unity of art and life; third, it delineated a common ground among competing figures and groups in the Berlin avant-garde with whom Behrendt associated.

Werner Lindner's *Die Ingenieurbauten in ihrer guten Gestaltung* (Engineering constructions in their good form) of 1923 was perhaps the most direct extension of the prewar pursuit of quality, good form, and perfected types capable of restoring cultural value under the conditions of serial production.[192] Published under the auspices of the German Werkbund and the Deutscher Bund Heimatschutz, in collaboration with two associations of engineers, it drew on Gropius's photographic survey of industrial structures of 1911[193] as well as the final volumes of Schultze-Naumburg's *Kulturarbeiten,* dedicated to waterworks, bridges, industrial complexes, sheds, and railway structures. Expanding the range of these earlier publications, Lindner's portfolio presented exemplary structures from all times and all cultures. Forgoing Schultze-Naumburg's device of the counterexample, Lindner emphasized the potential of a timeless and universally valid world immanent to technology, as its telos and nature. The book proceeds from the most elemental building bodies (*Baukörper*)—cubes, cylinders, pyramids, and spheres—to the choice of materials, architectonic division, and the rhythmic composition of similar forms of bodies. Using a typological format, Lindner presented churches, old fortifications, wind and water mills, old cranes, gasometers, airplane hangars, cooling towers, warehouses, silos, great halls for exhibitions and manufacturing, industrial complexes, smokestacks, electrical poles and pylons, bridges, industrial cranes, waterworks, canals, dams, and lighthouses—in short, the entire landscape of good industrial forms, both functional and beautiful, modern and classic. In his introductory essay, Lindner declared that "in addition to their other achievements, examples of the modern art of engineering are worthy of wonder as few other human works have been," for they had achieved a new height of technical perfection.[194] He quoted Semper to explain that, as in nature so too in industry, repetition reveals norms and types under the surface of differentiated appearances. Unchanging laws of function, rhythm, and force are given visible expression within the manifold variety of these structures, which he called natural building bodies (*Baukörper*) and unified, vital building organisms (*Bauorganismen*). In good forms, the corporeal formation of the exterior depended on the clear, organic, and harmonious spatial formation of the interior. Lindner's emphasis on physiognomic as well as constructional expression led to a preference for clear, closed forms—regular, symmetrical, and well proportioned—as well as the regular repetition of elements in frame structures.

Excerpts and illustrations from Lindner's book were included in the second issue of the avant-garde magazine *G: Material zur elementaren Gestaltung* in

September 1923. Produced by the studios of Hans Richter (the principal editor) and Mies van der Rohe, the magazine sought to assemble evidence of an emerging elementarist culture. Bridging a diverse array of postexpressionist artistic research, cutting across disciplines in the natural and human sciences, and breaking the barrier between art, engineering, and industrial design, the magazine presented documents that would, it hoped, "clarify" and not merely express "the general situation of art and life,"[195] seen to be coming together in the reconstruction of Europe. "The striving for pure monumental *Gestaltung*," as Theo van Doesburg had already suggested in 1922, was making itself evident "in music, as well as sculpture and architecture, literature, jazz, and cinema, and above all in purely utilitarian works."[196] The journal hoped to assist creative workers, be they technicians, theorists, ideologues, economists, or pedagogues, to bring "inner order to our being." Six issues appeared between 1923 and 1926, shifting emphasis from technology to the arts and ending with a double issue devoted to film. The title *G* had been suggested by El Lissitzky as a shortened form of *Gestaltung*. The original circle included Richter and Viking Eggeling, van Doesburg, Hans Arp, Tristan Tzara, and Ludwig Hilberseimer, and it quickly expanded to incorporate Mies, El Lissitzky, Gräff, Raoul Hausmann, Naum Gabo, Antoine Pevsner, Frederick Kiesler, Georg Grosz, Man Ray, and Walter Benjamin—embracing Dadaists and Neoplasticists, Constructivists and Surrealists.[197]

The lead editorial of the first issue, by Richter and Gräff, echoed the proposition, familiar from pre–World War I architectural discourse, that elementary form creation was to be guided by economy, a pure relationship between force and material, elementary means, order, and lawfulness. Van Doesburg, for whom a square was included in the masthead as an homage, also reiterated tropes from architectural theory in his call for a new *"gestaltende"* monumentality whose objectivity would constitute the definitive alternative to decoration, tradition, dogma, and subjectivity. Recalibrating the union of the arts through the principle of autonomy, he suggested, "The new form creation [*Gestaltung*] grows out of elementary means. In them, the different arts become related in such a way that they are able to unfold the maximum force of expression."[198] Richter's reprise of van Doesburg's attack against imitation emphasized that the new forms were demonstrations of reality itself, rather than symbols or analogies. The first issue also included the "Realist Manifesto" by Naum Gabo and Antoine Pevsner of 1920, which declared that art was to give form to the expressions of life in space and time; El Lissitzky's Proun Room from the Berlin art exhibition of 1923; Gräff's characterization of a new generation of engineers as capable of advancing beyond mechanism by thinking and creating elementally; and Mies's project for a concrete office building of 1923, accompanied by his celebrated manifesto for a building-art of pure presence:

> Every aesthetic speculation, every doctrine and every formalism we reject. Building-art is the spatially grasped will of the time. Alive. Changing. New. Neither that

which was yesterday nor that which will be tomorrow can be given form, but only that which is today. Only this is created by building. Create the form out of the nature of the task with the means of our time. That is our work.[199]

Propositions such as these pushed aspects of prewar architectural theory to extreme formulations, while simultaneously broadening their purview to encompass the (re)construction of reality as a whole. Where De Stijl called for "a world war against individualism," El Lissitzky announced the scope of "world reconstruction" through Suprematism as "a new cosmic creation" that has become reality in the world, "a creativity from within ourselves which pervades our consciousness."[200]

The newness of this world was marked by its floating and moving character, beyond an image in the old sense, "beyond the frontier of the all-seeing eye and the all-hearing ear." Lissitzky's Proun series rendered the new reality of the world concrete by means of constructions through which material receives plastic form and through which emptiness, chaos, and the unnatural become space, order, and certainty. For Lissitzky, "Proun goes beyond painting and the artist on the one hand and the machine and engineer on the other, and advances to the construction of space" and a new body, creating "a new, many-faceted unity as a formal representation of our nature."[201] Several years later, this new spatial paradigm was theorized by László Moholy-Nagy and Sigfried Giedion in terms of *Raumgestaltung,* the interweaving of subject and object in the creation of fluid and dynamic idealist spatiality.[202]

Richter's editorial in the third issue confirmed the relational character of *Gestaltung.* In promoting the clarification of the emergent condition, he too absorbed Fiedler's theory of pure visibility into a materialist anthropology, but, unlike Schultze-Naumburg's, his was an anthropology of metropolitan, not rural, life. Reiterating the German ambivalence toward material civilization—described as "the hopeless chaos of our days" and "the dissolution of the ground"—Richter affirmed his optimism for the possibility of culture. In turn, he referred culture to "the general problem of existence" and the "play of life forces" directed toward a whole. The materials he sought to collect were to be "documents of a unified life drive."[203] This orientation to a vitalist conception of life, shared by all the key contributors, was stated most emphatically and esoterically by Raoul Hausmann in a manifesto for a biocentric, integrative, monistic conception of creative work, applicable equally to humans, animals, and plants. He suggested that every form was a frozen moment-image of becoming within the creative aura or atmosphere (*Fluidum*) that constitutes the universe. A new culture, oriented toward the movement and fecundity of biotechnic or biocosmotechnic creation, will no longer be concerned with causality or three-dimensionality. Since the universe is fluid, there can be no origin, only becoming. The task at hand, he explained, was to create forms appropriate to humanity and its universal consciousness, aligned with the creative atmosphere of the universe, but never the aura itself—forms that "show us the depth of our capacity for remembrance." Unconcerned with the ideal of harmonizing with surroundings, he insisted, "We can and must transform the biocenosis, if we genuinely hope to transport the resulting act and actuality into the milieu, into the overall region of shared experience, or, better, to work out from it."[204]

The magazine *G* provides evidence of a convergence among the avant-garde around a common desire to steer the self-generation of the new material culture. That they seized the notion of *Gestaltung* as a slogan reveals the extent to which process had become more important than product in the comprehensive restructuring of the economic, technological, social, and urban matrix. That *Gestaltung* assumed the connotations of world reconstruction points to a general recognition that the new formation would never be static but rather would continue to be a fluid, dynamic, and creative state of history in the making. This open-endedness was itself a sign of organicity. At the same time, the implications of *Gestaltung* as transcendent clarification lent the scope of reconstruction the character of an aesthetic utopia.

G was not the only instance of the impulse toward convergence. Reactivating *Die Form* in 1925, Behrendt's opening editorial reads like a distillation of the avant-garde discourse of *Gestaltung*, albeit less strident and more concrete, grounded in everyday life rather than floating in space:

> The journal will be concerned with the tasks of *Gestaltung* in all areas of applied and artistic creation.
>
> All creative work finds its end and its visible expression in form. Form is order.
>
> The new world of work that has arisen around us, however, has not yet found its order. The foundations of creative work have experienced a complete transformation.... We are aware that the problems of form with which the journal is concerned can only be addressed in conjunction with those higher-order problems that lead to the *Gestaltung* of a new order of work and the development [*Bildung*] of new life-forms.... [F]or us, form is less a problem of aesthetics than of construction. We are concerned here less with finished form and its critical evaluation according to inherited concepts of beauty. We will concern ourselves much more with the process of *Gestaltung*, the way to form, and the becoming of form [*Formwerdung*]. We will show the methods of *Gestaltung* that have led to new and often unfamiliar forms in every area of manufactured and artistic production.[205]

Like *G*, but without the emphasis on the visual arts, *Die Form* aspired to a comprehensiveness that embraced the decorative arts, graphics, book design, and clothing as well as domestic objects, interiors, buildings of all kinds, industrial structures, machines, and city planning.

The goal of achieving a new synthesis or fusion was also central to Gropius. In addition to marshaling photographic evidence with which to herald once again "a universal will to *Gestaltung* of a fundamentally new kind,"[206] his text in *Internationale Architektur* (1925) drew together assumptions and propositions current at the time, deftly weaving the disparate threads of architectural theory into a synthetic tapestry of unconscious wills and forces, objectivities, unities, and physiognomic expressions. Echoing the call for simplification reiterated by the Werkbund as well as the Biedermeier revivalists, he characterized buildings as bodies that would be improved if all ornament were removed to unmask their absolute *Gestalt*. Reiterating Riegl's *Kunstwollen* and van Doesburg's *Stilwille,* he wrote,

> A fundamentally new attitude to the building-art is emerging in all countries simultaneously. The realization is growing that a living will to *Gestaltung,* rooted in the life of society as a whole, embraces every aspect of human *Gestaltung* in a single goal, which begins and ends with building.... [T]he new spirit of *Gestaltung*... returns to the heart of things: when you want to form a thing so that it functions properly—a piece of furniture, a house—you first have to analyze its nature.... [T]he will to develop a *unified* worldview, which will characterize our time, presupposes the desire to free spiritual values from the confines of individuality and to work toward an *objective validity.* The unity of external *Gestaltungen,* which leads to culture, would then follow of its own accord.[207]

In moving the Bauhaus to Dessau, Gropius reinforced the shift from "crystalline expression" to *Gestaltung* in a new subtitle, "Hochschule für Gestaltung" (Institute for design). Although this use of the term helped make it synonymous with *design,* the word *design* fails to connote the broad range of meanings for *Gestaltung,* especially its implication of self-generation, idealist aesthetics, and world building. It is ironic that, as Bauhaus theory was disseminated, the creative and clarifying character of *gestaltende* activity was reduced to a formulaic "design aesthetic" or "style."[208]

"Baustil"

In his first issue of *Die Form* in 1925, Behrendt published a programmatic text by his friend Hugo Häring, titled "Wege zur Form," which updated Scheffler's dualism between formalists (Behrens) and functionalists (van de Velde) to the more overtly organicist discourse of the mid-1920s.[209] For Häring, things created by human beings were the result of efforts pulling in two directions: the first toward the fulfillment of functions, the second toward expression. He spoke of a struggle for the form of things between demands that were *sachlich* and *dinglich* (objective, real) and those that were spiritual, a struggle for which matter was the medium. The former, he explained, have a natural origin and arise organically and anonymously; the latter emerge through the expression of spirit, the subjective human psyche. Where the things created to meet the first demand are timeless and universal, those of the second kind are indeterminable and tied to blood, time, and place. For him, the past decades had, however, witnessed a fundamental transformation in the claim to spiritual expression. Under the rule of geometric culture, such claims had been diverted to conformance to law, which operated against the living, against becoming, movement, and nature. For Häring, a new stage in the history of form-becoming (*Formwerdung*) began with the discovery that humanity had become accustomed to the expression of machines, boats, cars, and other instruments. In nature, he explained, *Gestalt* was "the result of an ordering of many singularities in space which looked to an unfolding of life and the fulfillment of effort that applied as much to the singular as to the whole."[210] However, in the world of geometric culture the *Gestalt* of things was given through the imposition of geometric rules. Häring suggested that if we try to discover form, rather than constrain or impose it, we will find ourselves in consonance with nature, no longer working against it but within it. He wrote that the concept of the plan was being transformed from the ways of geometry to the ways of nature, to an organlike plan formation, to nature's own constructional and creative means and methods. To give order according to plan in this sense meant that the form of an outside corresponded to its inner form-becoming. Moreover, when individuality unfolded according to inner plan it served the life of the whole at the same time. Without postulating a category for totality, Häring contended that "the whole is the *Gestalt* of life."[211]

Häring concluded by taking issue with Le Corbusier, whose powerful polemics in favor of the "engineer's aesthetic" and "machines for living" quickly gave him a reputation as the leading advocate of rationalism if not mechanism. In Häring's view, Le Corbusier was wrong to refer objects back to geometric or crystalline *Grundfiguren,* which were not ur-forms or *Urgestalten* as some claimed, but rather merely abstractions, derived laws. Any unity achieved through them was merely an imposed uniformism, not the unity of life and vitality. "A polished metal sphere certainly provides an opportunity for our spirit, but a blossom is an experience [*Erlebnis*]." To impose geometric figures on objects was to homogenize and mechanize. Häring insisted that "we do not want to mechanize objects but only their production.... To mechanize production is to gain life."[212] Careful to oppose not Le Corbusier himself but only his principle, Häring argued that while the *Gestalt* of things in nature may sometimes assume a geometrical figure—as in the case of crystals—the geometric figure was never the content or origin of the *Gestalt;* it remained a human abstraction. And, attempting to avoid anthropomorphism himself, he concluded that it was not humanity's own individuality that had to be given form, but that of objects, whose expression was to be identical with themselves.[213]

Where Häring asserted the radical incommensurability of organism and mechanism, of a posteriori and a priori conceptions of autonomy, Adolf Behne concluded that this opposition needed to be overcome if a new style was to be achieved. Having dedicated much of *Der moderne Zweckbau* to dividing the architecture of the mid-1920s into two streams—organic functionalists such as Häring and rationalist formalists such as Le Corbusier—Behne argued, despite his bias in favor of rationalism, that German architecture should stop swinging between these poles. It needed to fuse form and function in order to "stabilize the strong dynamic tensions that living architecture must absorb."[214] Citing Kurt Schwitters, he described "style" as a compromise between the individual and the collective. Citing Paul Tillich, he suggested that the interpenetration of function and form "makes the building a living, concrete *Gestalt*."[215] And citing Alfred Vierkandt, he contended that "human beings are closely attached to two worlds: the world of biological necessity, a dark natural bedrock full of hardships, and a spiritual world with specific content and substance."[216] Not surprisingly, Behne also invoked van Doesburg and Mondrian, whose theories of Neoplasticism had made the resolution of dualities its primary goal. A building's "concrete form," wrote Behne, "is a compromise between individual (function) and society (form).... Its pure form is living equilibrium, realization of a behavior that plays to many sides, open and yet determined."[217]

Having previously subscribed to Scheffler's dualism, in *Sieg* Behrendt too attempted to reconcile or, more precisely, to subsume this duality within a model of cultural production — a revisionist theory of style — that gave equal emphasis to form and function, *Gestalt* and *Gestaltung,* typicality and singularity, being and becoming, collective and individual, mediation and immediacy. Behrendt was at once a fellow traveler of Häring, Mies, *and* Le Corbusier.[218] He sought to combine the fixity of type with the openness and vitalism of "Immaculate Conception." And while he insisted on singularity, the book overflows with examples of similarly cubic, or more precisely Cubist, buildings.[219] Despite, or perhaps precisely because of, these apparent contradictions, *Sieg* was well received by the critic Behne. In his short review, Behne called the book, "A spirited and knowledgeable interpretation of the new will to build [*Bauwille*], reinforced by an especially rich selection of illustrations."[220]

Both polemical and systematic, Behrendt's book achieved an equilibrium of tensions under the sign of "building style." Although *Baustil* was a commonly used term for *architecture* both before and after World War I, Behrendt had previously employed the term *style* to designate the comprehensive and unified framework capable of subsuming the variety of artistic production in a given period, including an emergent modern one. Redefining his style concept as "building style," he provided the discourse of Neues Bauen with a category of totality that minimized the connotations of formal codification, stressing instead *bauen* or the elementary constructional process.[221] Behrendt was careful to absorb the critiques of historicism and stylistic formalism, and he qualified his confidence in the emerging new order by insisting that it had not yet fully arrived. Instead, he emphasized the movement toward a new style and the spiritual atmosphere in which this movement was growing. He focused on "[w]hat supports and drives the new movement"[222] — the motive impulses and shaping forces that manifested themselves in unfamiliar and unassimilated forms; and he concentrated on contemporary problems of form, rather than on solutions, hoping to demonstrate "the legitimacy of this new way of designing."[223] By addressing tasks and problems that architecture had yet to accept fully, Behrendt located the activity of building at a site of unformed forces and needs. The orientation toward problems served to define the new building style as an activity or, more precisely, a mode of work — no longer a collection of formal motifs to be composed, but a performative system, an architectonic system of elements and relational logics for inventing, constructing, and producing. Taken over from engineering, this system and approach was, nevertheless, directed toward the visual cognition of art applied to the production of a new world, a world in which the machinic, the organic, and the artistic intersected. Having entered "the path that all original creations follow," he cautioned that it was essential to continue along it guided by "the principles of all original and organic creation."[224]

For Behrendt, the movement toward an organic building style was marked by a striving for origins, not a literal return but a new classicism in the sense of the vitalist classicism promoted by J. J. P. Oud in the mid-1920s and by van de Velde prior to World War I.[225] Behrendt's *Sieg* incorporated two apparently incongruous orientations: first, "the will to return to basic principles and elementary rules of building and once again to build exactly as the ancients did," and second, "the desire to come to terms with the new realities of the time and the new life they entail."[226] Reformulating the double moment of impressionist *modernité*—Charles Baudelaire's search for the eternal within the fleeting fashions of modern life—this longing, desire, and instinct for origins was understood to be mediated by the realities of the time. What made a return to origins (or *of* origins)[227] possible in the modern age was the precedent set in the paradigmatic sphere of technical design and mass production, where unselfconscious originality (*Ursprünglichkeit*) and elementarism had, for Behrendt, already come to define "the face of our time."[228] The spiritual wellspring that gave birth to the new world of forms was both timeless and yet located in historical time, both classic and modern.

Like many of his contemporaries, Behrendt employed analogies between buildings and bodies to underscore the organic character of the new building style.[229] In the opening pages of *Sieg,* he asked the reader to focus "superficially"—for a moment—on the external features of modern buildings. Behrendt described them as simple bodies of functionally disposed masses, naked and unadorned, composed of similarly elemental parts: walls, windows, floors, and roofs. He did not refer to a taxonomy of pure geometric forms or ur-forms as Lindner and Le Corbusier had, but rather cited building elements and features such as smoothness, straight profiles, and lack of ornament. Nor did he make universalizing and essentialist claims for the shapes of these building bodies. While replying to the notion of physiognomy and the theory of expression that underpinned it, what the exterior form of buildings expressed was not presented here as something comparable to the character of a person or particular race. Rather, the outer form could be read for signs of the inner disposition of spaces and relationships among parts whose meaning did not extend beyond the particular building. Having called the architectonic system of Neoclassicism "cosmopolitan," Behrendt directed his notion of building style toward originality, differentiation, and a rich new world of forms. He circumscribed that world with his selection of demonstrative works, whose commonalities and differences help render more explicit Behrendt's understanding of the reconciliation of system and freedom that the new paradigm offered. Works by each of the "ur-fathers" — Wright, van de Velde, and Adolf Loos — bear little similarity of form, although they consistently deployed a fluid and open spatiality. Works by Mies, Mendelsohn, Willem Marinus Dudok, J. J. P. Oud, Leendert Cornelis van der Vlugt, Ernst May, Gropius, Bruno Taut, Max Taut, Alfred Fischer-Essen, Josef Frank, Johannes Göderitz, Le Corbusier, and Häring mark the range of the new architectonic system — alternatively more planar or volumetric, opaque or transparent, simple or complex, blocky or asymmetrical, open or closed, rectilinear or curvilinear, De Stijl or Constructivist. Even Behrens made an appearance with a factory of interpenetrating volumes.

More central to Behrendt's concept of building style than physiognomy was the metaphor of the organism considered in both its own terms and in relation to its (shifting) environment (*Umwelt*). In the main body of the book, Behrendt emphasized the inner workings and relational principles on which external form depended — on a construction system that sought to emulate those found in nature. In this context, he described buildings and cities as spatial organisms, which he specified further as unified and organized forms.[230] Buildings and cities attained the status of organisms when autonomous elements were brought into purposeful, functional, and cohesive relationships, bound together in a spatial structure without compromising their integrity or freedom. What Behrendt called a new binding principle or idea defined a structure of relationships consistent with the theory of montage or assemblage underpinning technical design as well as the constructed image in art and the open construct in architecture. Updating the principle of organic unity in the relation of parts and wholes, Behrendt suggested that their "individual parts entail each other and are held in tension."[231] While Behrendt did not refer to specific biological theories or apply constructional principles from the life sciences in a literal way, his descriptions of functionally designed buildings evoke figures of animals and the self-generation of multicellular organisms.[232] In describing a floor plan for a house by Hugo Häring, for instance, he wrote, "the rooms of the house wrap themselves around an undulating staircase as around a spinal column, so that the individual needs of the household operations are most carefully accommodated."[233] In comparison, the plan of Mies's brick country house showed a "freer" development of rooms that "almost completely dissolve their borders by flowing into one another," yet are at the same time "also bound to one another by the dynamics of their internal tensions [*Spannungen*]."[234] Both plans could be interpreted using the theory of self-generation, which considered that each form was shaped anew by the interaction of living internal material and its external environment.[235] Parallels could be drawn as well with the theory of cell formation and growth, considered by scientists as analogous with the inorganic process of crystallization. As the nucleus grows, a cell forms and a surrounding membrane appears, setting it off as a new cell.[236]

A dynamic concept of formation also underlies Behrendt's characterization of the city as a living organism, carrying out the functions of dwelling, traffic, and recreation "with continuous interplay."[237] The city, he suggested in a way that approaches a structural conception of urbanism, "should now be conceived for what it really is—namely, *a living organism* whose supporting framework [*Gerüst*] and structure [*Aufbau*] are to be designed in such a way that they may unfold the many *functions of life,* which they have to fulfill, as perfectly and frictionlessly as possible, to the highest level of performance."[238] For him, these living spaces were set in motion and "related to one another according to their internal interactions and reciprocal tensions."[239] As demonstrated by the expansion plan for Magdeburg of 1923 by Konrad Rühl and Bruno Taut, the city as organism was to hold the forces of the human environment in "complete balance."[240]

With *Sieg,* Behrendt attempted to portray "the birth of the form of our time," which he called a "building style" and, in the end, christened "the technical style." But he also called this "form" a language and went so far as to acknowledge that the teaching of historical styles may be "necessary, even indispensable"[241] for training spatial thinking and cultivating the sense of form, "just as in higher education instruction in dead languages is continued to train one to think logically and to develop a sense for language." But, he insisted, "in the end it is imperative that we learn the syntax of our own *living* language, so that we can correctly construct the sentences in which we express our needs and say what disturbs or moves us."[242] Considered as language, the new building style was, in effect, a living system of mediated production, impossible to isolate as a thing independent of its activity. In the 1880s, Fiedler had already suggested that art, like language, was no mere imitation of reality, but constitutive of it. "The relation between thinking and speaking," he wrote in an aphorism, "is to be understood such that the kind of thinking that presents itself in language comes into being only in and through language, not only indissolubly tied to speech, but identical with it."[243] Ernst Cassirer's influential philosophy of symbolic forms, first published in 1923, also centered on a theory of language and culture as constitutive forms of mediation.[244]

What could here appear as a contradiction between the desire for immediacy and acceptance of mediation is resolved in the ideal of building style as a *natural* language, a transparent and frictionless form of communication, implied by Behrendt but never articulated as such. Moreover, it is precisely this resolution that distinguished Behrendt's building style from the style-architecture that Muthesius attacked so vehemently. Behrendt's admiration for the polemical writings of Gotthold Ephraim Lessing (1729–1781)—"my great friend and favorite author"[245]—is telling. For Lessing's distinctions between poetry and painting applied notions of natural signs and sensate intuition, which had been developed in German aesthetics of the late eighteenth century, to the evaluation of the arts as media, each capable of communicating and engendering imaginative freedom in its own way and to a different degree. For Lessing, poetry owed its superiority over the plastic arts to its more refined form of signification. As David Wellbery has observed, the sign was profoundly ambiguous for Enlightenment culture, allowing humanity to raise itself beyond immediate experience, to develop and perfect its knowledge, while simultaneously marking humanity's essential limitations, its inclination to error and delusion, and the finiteness of the human soul. Deeply suspicious of "its own conditions of possibility," the Enlightenment resolved this "conflict with itself by projecting an ideal future state free of the deceptive opacity of sign use."[246] In perfecting the specific logic of their medium, works of art were thought capable of producing something of that future proleptically, thereby hastening its coming. Similarly, Behrendt suggested seeing the rationalized and purified "aesthetic elements" common to his chosen examples, if not already in themselves the elements of a new style, "then as the yeasts or starting points for the formation of such" — able to minimize interference, distortion, and friction for the process of *Gestaltung*.

The model of culture that Behrendt presented in 1927 was distinct in its organicism from Häring's Neues Bauen and Schultze-Naumburg's "style," both of which assimilated the principle of physiognomic expression to a universalizing essentialism. Despite his predilection for the vernacular, Behrendt's "form of our time" was not a rigid uniform but an open architectonic system fluidly mediating the free self-generation of buildings within a constantly evolving historical environment, at once constructed and constructing. Notwithstanding his antagonism toward Schultze-Naumburg's mechanical historicism, Behrendt remained indebted to his comprehensive approach to modeling "the culture of the visible" as the basis for intervening in the process of historical change. The distinctness of Behrendt's position is revealed, perhaps most clearly, in a three-way dispute over "true tradition" played out in an exchange of letters published in *Die Form* in 1926. For the idea of tradition served as yet another figure for organic cultural unity, which Behrendt used interchangeably with style throughout his career.

The exchange began with a letter by Häring[247] responding to an attack on Neues Bauen by Schultze-Naumburg that had been published in the April edition of the popular magazine *Uhu*.[248] Schultze-Naumburg had by this time become one of the most prominent architects of his generation and one of the most effective proponents of *Heimatstil*. In his article in *Uhu*, Schultze-Naumburg characterized Neues Bauen as the invention of people who possessed neither culture nor tradition, let alone love of *Heimat*. Häring recounted Schultze-Naumburg's concern that "Mongoloid, Negroid, and many other bloods"[249] had come to play a significant role within the body politic of the German people, and that, without knowing it, they were seeking to free themselves from the Nordic form and cultural circle. Insisting that the moderns had no desire to speak in such terms, he felt obligated to intervene. While "not prepared to seek blood tests of the various proponents of style,"[250] he contended that surely the advocates of the new were the ones who belonged to this Nordic cultural circle, and that it was Schultze-Naumburg who carried alien traditions and forms derived from the East or the Mediterranean.

Häring argued that the new architecture had emerged on the ground of form invention which was truly the ground of the homeland in Germany — dedicated to the problems of life rather than problems of harmony and rhythm. He declared that "we will purify ourselves of the last traces of the invasion that installed a thousand-year hegemony of the form-transducing power of the Mediterranean." "Surely," he concluded, "Schultze-Naumburg will not let himself be taken over by this invading culture."[251] Be fundamental, he insisted.

The exchange continued in the July issue of *Die Form* with a reply from Schultze-Naumburg and a final rebuttal from Behrendt. Schultze-Naumburg sought to correct what he took to be Häring's misrepresentations and to expose his nationalist claims on Modernism's behalf as nothing more than a word game. Most people recognized what was meant by tradition, he said, and would consider the architecture promoted by Häring to be foreign, just as "one can admit that one is drawn to the physiognomy of a person or house, or is repelled."[252] He reiterated his commitment to the tradition of which Häring sought to purge the country. And he defended his own work as partaking in a sensible and rational tradition of good construction, economical and fundamental, without ornament. Throughout his life, he explained, he had fought against the cold formalism of a classicism that took Italian palaces as precedents.

Behrendt's intervention focused on clarifying the characteristics of tradition, which allowed him to then claim that, with the new architecture, we are experiencing the "emergence of a new tradition," which would be both internationalist and regionalist. Schultze-Naumburg would surely agree, he wrote, that tradition does not consist in passing down completed art forms. His own effort to reanimate the Biedermeier tradition had, in this sense, not been a strong formalism. However, it could not be taken as a land-based tradition either, but rather the last stage of classical eclecticism. Behrendt saw the failure of this effort, with which he too had been associated, as the definitive demonstration that it was not possible to give new life to old forms. He asked:

> Does the author of *Kulturarbeiten* not sense that the new impulse to form is unmistakably related to the one that created the bridges, silos, factories, and blast furnaces and defined the appearance of the new cultural landscape that he showed us so clearly in the seventh volume of his series? Does this relationship not point to a new feeling for form here, which can only mean the emergence of a new tradition?[253]

Following the eternal law of death and birth, Behrendt explained, old traditions that have become senseless go to their grave as new ones generate themselves in their place. While unfamiliar, the new forms are vital expressions of our changed forms of economy, life, and society. Whether the bourgeoisie would still be the carriers of the new forms, he preferred to leave cautiously to the future, along with any judgment of whether this new tradition was good or bad.

Where Häring argued against Schultze-Naumburg on his own terms, accepting the physiognomic theory as criteria for authentic and rooted national culture,[254] Behrendt did not refer to nationalism or race, and he circumscribed his use of physiognomic expression within an open conception of cultural work and architectural form. Not only was participation in the new building style to be freely chosen (he sought to persuade, not impose), but its aim was self-generation and differentiation through a system of means that was understood to maximize freedom—that sought to guarantee organicity through expressive process rather than formal attributes or physical features.

Behrendt's *Sieg* provokes a reconsideration of German functionalism as neither a monolithic nor a determinist ideology but rather a multifaceted quest for self-determination approached from a number of competing theoretical perspectives—long misunderstood in English-speaking architectural culture. In assembling his portrait of a new "building style," Behrendt drew implicitly on the theory of self-generation first proffered in biology around 1800 in opposition to the then prevalent theory of preformation, which held that the germs of all living beings had been preformed since the Creation.[255] Not only was the principle of self-generation absorbed during the nineteenth century into the reform of social institutions such as marriage as well as the arts, but by 1900 it had been subsumed in more advanced biology, in theories of evolution (Darwin) and ecology (Uexküll), which in turn inspired an array of developmental histories and theories of social and technological mediation in the social sciences. At the turn of the century, scientists such as the zoologist Ernst Haeckel and later the botanist Raoul France argued that knowledge from the life sciences should be used to guide human works and ways of life.[256] Even art critics such as Scheffler contended that "[w]hat the science associated with the name Darwin teaches us of the life of plants, animals, and people may very well be transposed to the laws of development in the building-art."[257] Informed by polemics like these to reground architecture on scientific principles, German functionalism extended and updated the organicism of the nineteenth century, which had itself, as Caroline van Eck has shown, transformed and transumed the use of nature as a model within Vitruvian classicism.[258] Considered in this context, Behrendt's model of material culture sought to win from the modern industrial world the possibility of a renewed state of organic unity. Having traced in *Kampf um den Stil* the process whereby modernization disintegrated the precapitalist matrix of economy, technology, and society, as well as its cultural forms, Behrendt constructed in *Sieg* a composite image of a new architectonic paradigm that he took to be immanent to modernization. Like Mies's urban plan for the Weissenhofsiedlung, Behrendt's paradigm—which he called interchangeably "building style," "language," and "form"—was to be a form of mediation, both technological and social, within which spatial organisms would unfold as if from themselves, producing an endlessly rich world of forms bound together in free relations.

Notes

1. Walter Curt Behrendt, *Der Sieg des neuen Baustils* (Stuttgart: Akademischer Verlag Dr. Fritz Wedekind & Co., 1927). Hereafter cited as *Sieg*, with the English translation from the present edition cited as *Victory*. Unless otherwise indicated, all other translations are my own.

2. Gottfried Semper, "Prolegomenon" to *Style in the Technical and Tectonic Arts; or, Practical Aesthetics*, in *The Four Elements of Architecture and Other Writings*, trans. Harry Francis Mallgrave and Wolfgang Herrmann (Cambridge: Cambridge Univ. Press, 1989), 182; Gottfried Semper, "Prolegomena" to *Der Stil in den technischen und tektonischen Künsten; oder, Praktische Aesthetik* (Frankfurt am Main: Verlag für Kunst und Wissenschaft, 1860–63): v: "*neben den glanzvollen Wundern der Gestirne mattschimmernde Nebelstellen... zwischen Zerstörung und Neugestaltung.*"

3. Gottfried Semper, "Prospectus: Style in the Technical and Tectonic Arts; or, Practical Aesthetics (1859)," in Semper 1989 (see note 2), 179; prospectus to *Der Stil in den technischen und tektonischen Künsten; oder, Praktische Äesthetik*. Semper Archiv, Institut für Geschichte und Theorie der Architektur, Eidgenössische Technische Hochschule Zürich. Manuscript 205, page 6 (exemplar of printed prospectus): "*die socialen Zustände der Gesellschaft und die Verhältnisse der Zeiten hinzu, deren künstlerisch monumentaler Ausdruck stets die höchste Aufgabe der Architektur war.*"

4. Gottfried Semper, "On Architectural Styles (1869)," in Semper 1989 (see note 2), 284; idem, "Ueber Baustile," in *Kleine Schriften,* ed. Hans and Manfred Semper (Berlin: W. Spemann, 1884; reprint, Mittenwald: Mäander Kunstverlag, 1979), 426: "*eine neue welthistorische... Idee.*" Semper (ibid.) was "*überzeugt, dass sich schon dieser oder jener unter unseren jüngeren Kollegen befähigt zeigen würde, einer solchen Idee, wo sie sich wirklich Bahn bräche, das geeignete architektonische Kleid zu verleihen*" (convinced that wherever such an idea would really take the lead, one or the other of our young colleagues will prove himself capable of endowing it with a suitable architectural dress).

5. See Timothy O. Benson, ed., *Expressionist Utopias: Paradise, Metropolis, Architectural Fantasy* (Los Angeles: Los Angeles County Museum of Art, 1993); Joan Weinstein, *The End of Expressionism: Art and the November Revolution in Germany, 1918–1919* (Chicago: Univ. of Chicago Press, 1990); Dorothea Dietrich, *The Collages of Kurt Schwitters: Tradition and Innovation* (Cambridge: Cambridge Univ. Press, 1993).

6. See Vittorio Magnago Lampugnani and Romana Schneider, eds., *Moderne Architektur in Deutschland, 1900 bis 1950*, vol. 1, *Reform und Tradition*, exh. cat. (Stuttgart: Gerd Hatje, 1992). On the relationship of the Stuttgart exhibition to the Darmstadt artists' colony, see Richard Pommer and Christian E. Otto, *Weissenhof 1927 and the Modern Movement in Architecture* (Chicago: Univ. of Chicago Press, 1991). On *Lebensreform* in the garden city of Hellerau, see Marco de Michelis, "Modernity and Reform: Heinrich Tessenow and the Institut Dalcroze at Hellerau," *Perspecta* 26 (1990), 143–70. On the garden city movement in Germany, see Kristiana Hartmann, *Deutsche Gartenstadtbewegung: Kulturpolitik und Gesellschaftsreform* (Munich: Heinz Moos, 1976). On reform in the applied arts, see Joan Campbell, *The German Werkbund: The Politics of Reform in the Applied Arts* (Princeton: Princeton

Univ. Press, 1978). On education reform, see Karl Kreuzer, *Jugendstil und Reform-pädagogik* (Munich: Profil, 1988).

7. On the Novembergruppe, see Helga Kliemann, *Die Novembergruppe* (Berlin: Gebr. Mann, 1969).

8. Walther Rathenau, *Der neue Staat* (Berlin: Fischer, 1919); *Die neue Wirtschaft* (Berlin: Fischer, 1918); *Die neue Gesellschaft* (Berlin: Fischer, 1919), translated by Arthur Windham as *The New Society* (New York: Harcourt, Brace & Company, 1921). Rathenau was born in 1867 and died in 1922. At the time of this trilogy, he had become one of Berlin's most influential figures. He was appointed foreign minister in early 1922 to negotiate reparations with the Allies and was murdered by anti-Semitic nationalists later that year. His many publications include *Zur Kritik der Zeit* (A critique of our time) of 1912, *Zur Mechanik des Geistes; oder, Vom Reich der Seele* (The mechanism of the mind; or, The realm of the soul) of 1913, and *Von kommenden Dingen* (translated as *In Days to Come*) of 1917.

9. Rathenau, *The New Society* (see note 8), 41. Rathenau, *Die neue Gesellschaft* (see note 8), 28: "*uns … anzupassen.*"

10. Rathenau, *The New Society* (see note 8), 103. Rathenau, *Die neue Gesellschaft* (see note 8), 72: "*so muss der Wille nach voller Bildung des Leibes, des Geistes und der Seele im Volke so stark werden, dass alle Fragen der Bequemlichkeit, des Genusses, der Geltung, der materiellen Interessen tief in den Schatten treten.*"

11. Rathenau, *The New Society* (see note 8), 41. Rathenau, *Die neue Gesellschaft* (see note 8), 28: "*der ärmlichen Zivilisation und der tiefgefährdeten Kultur.*"

12. Rathenau, *The New Society* (see note 8), 42. Rathenau, *Die neue Gesellschaft* (see note 8), 29: "*Wir lassen uns den Stolz des Leidensweges durch trügerische Löh-nung nicht verkümmern.*"

13. For a sociogenesis of the opposition between *Kultur* and *Zivilisation* in German usage, see Norbert Elias, *Über den Prozess der Zivilisation*, vol. 1, *Wandlungen des Verhaltens in den weltlichen Oberschichten des Abendlandes* (1937); translated by Edmund Jephcott as *The History of Manners*, vol. 1, *The Civilizing Process* (New York: Urizen Books, 1978).

14. Rathenau, *The New Society* (see note 8), 104. Rathenau, *Die neue Gesellschaft* (see note 8), 72: "*Der Begriff von der Bildung als von unserer wahren und einzigen Lebensmacht muss so tief verstanden werden, dass sie im öffentlichen Leben und in der Gesetzgebung das erste und letzte Wort hat. Wenn wir so arm werden wie die Kirchenmäuse, so müssen wir unseren letzten Pfennig daransetzen, Erziehung und Unterricht, Vorbild und Anschauung, Ansporn und Anspruch, Leistung und Atmo-sphäre so hoch zu spannen, dass der Eintritt in Deutschland den Eintritt in ein neues Zeitalter bedeutet.*"

15. On Hartlaub's exhibition at the Mannheim Kunsthalle, see Dennis Crockett, *German Post-Expressionism: The Art of the Great Disorder, 1918–1924* (University Park: Pennsylvania State Univ. Press, 1999). See also Franz Roh, *Nach-Expressionis-mus: Magischer Realismus, Probleme der neuesten europäischen Malerei* (Leipzig: Klinkhardt & Biermann, 1925). Hartlaub's show and Roh's book were followed by Rudolf Kurtz's critical manifesto for Constructivism, *Expressionismus und Film* (Berlin: Verlag der Lichtbildbühne, 1926) and Emil Utitz, *Die Überwindung des*

Expressionismus: Charakterologische Studien zur Kultur der Gegenwart (Stuttgart: Ferdinand Enke, 1927).

16. Wilhelm Worringer, "Das Porträt des Nach-Expressionismus," *Frankfurter Zeitung* (7 February 1926): *"Dieses Stück Magie ist ein Bodensatz vom kaltgewordenen Expressionismus."* On the "return to order," see Kenneth E. Silver, *Esprit de Corps: The Art of the Parisian Avant-Garde and the First World War, 1914–1925* (Princeton: Princeton Univ. Press, 1989); Elizabeth Cowling and Jennifer Mundy, *On Classic Ground: Picasso, Léger, de Chirico and the New Classicism, 1910–1930*, exh. cat. (London: Tate Gallery, 1990); Wieland Schmied, *Neue Sachlichkeit and German Realism of the Twenties,* exh. cat. (London: Arts Council of Great Britain, 1978).

17. As part of the Bauhaus exhibition of 1923, Gropius curated an exhibition of exemplary modern architecture that he called *Internationale Architektur.*

18. Walter Gropius, ed., *Internationale Architektur* (Munich: Albert Langen, 1925; reprint, Mainz: Florian Kupferberg, 1981). The series sought to corral the sprawling discourse of the avant-garde in order to make it accessible to a larger audience as a unified movement. It included books by Theo van Doesburg, Piet Mondrian, J. J. P. Oud, Oskar Schlemmer, Albert Gleizes, and Kazimir Malevich, as well as Gropius and Moholy-Nagy, many of which were translations of books and essays not previously available in German.

19. Adolf Behne, *Der moderne Zweckbau* (Munich: Drei Masken Verlag, 1926); translated by Michael Robinson as *The Modern Functional Building* (Santa Monica: Getty Research Institute for the History of Art and the Humanities, 1996).

20. Heinrich de Fries, *Junge Baukunst in Deutschland: Ein Querschnitt durch die Entwicklung neuer Baugestaltung in der Gegenwart* (Berlin: Otto Stollberg Verlag für Politik und Wirtschaft, 1926; reprint, Munich: Kraus-Thomson, 1980).

21. Gustav Platz, *Die Baukunst der neuesten Zeit* (Berlin: Propyläen-Verlag, 1927).

22. Adolf Behne, *Neues Wohnen — Neues Bauen* (Leipzig: Hesse & Becker Verlag, 1927); Ludwig Hilberseimer, ed., *Internationale neue Baukunst* (Stuttgart: Julius Hoffmann, 1927); Julius Vischer and Ludwig Hilberseimer, *Beton als Gestalter* (Stuttgart: Julius Hoffmann, 1928); Sigfried Giedion, *Bauen in Frankreich, Bauen in Eisen, Bauen in Eisenbeton* (Leipzig: Klinkhardt & Biermann, 1928), translated by J. Duncan Berry as *Building in France, Building in Iron, Building in Ferroconcrete* (Santa Monica: The Getty Center for the History of Art and the Humanities, 1995); Walter Müller-Wulckow, *Deutsche Baukunst der Gegenwart* (Königstein im Taunus: Karl Robert Langewiesche, 1925–29); Arthur Korn, *Glas im Bau und als Gebrauchsgegenstand* (Berlin: Ernst Pollak, [1929?]).

23. Bruno Taut, *Modern Architecture* (New York: Boni, 1929); Henry-Russell Hitchcock, Jr., *Modern Architecture: Romanticism and Reintegration* (New York: Payson & Clarke, 1929; reprint, New York: Hacker Art Books, 1970).

24. Henry-Russell Hitchcock, Jr., and Philip Johnson, *The International Style: Architecture since 1922* (New York: W. W. Norton, 1932). *Modern Architecture,* exh. cat. (New York: Museum of Modern Art, 1932).

25. Oechslin has analyzed the role of architectural publications in constructing the image as well as discourse of modern architecture as a new mainstream. See Werner Oechslin, "A Cultural History of Modern Architecture," part 1, "The 'Modern':

Historical Event vs. Demand," *Architecture and Urbanism,* no. 235 (1990): 50–64; idem, "A Cultural History of Modern Architecture," part 2, "Modern Architecture and the Pitfalls of Codification: The Aesthetic View," *Architecture and Urbanism,* no. 237 (1990): 29–37; idem, "A Cultural History of Modern Architecture," part 3, "The 'Picture': The (Superficial) Consensus of Modern Architecture," *Architecture and Urbanism,* no. 245 (1991): 28–38.

26. Riezler was a contemporary of Behrendt's who had been introduced to him by Muthesius in 1909; see letter from Hermann Muthesius to Walter Curt Behrendt, 7 September 1909, Hermann Muthesius Papers, Werkbund-Archiv, Berlin.

27. In its first incarnation, *Die Form* was the organ of the Deutsche Gewerbeschau, the German Werkbund, the Reichskunstwart, the Verband Deutscher Kunstgewerbevereine, the Wirtschaftsbund Deutscher Kunsthandwerker, and other associations.

28. *Die Form ohne Ornament,* introduction by Wolfgang Pfleiderer and foreword by Walter Riezler (Stuttgart: Deutsche Verlags-Anstalt, 1924).

29. The Werkbund exhibition *Die Wohnung* was open from July to September 1927 (extended to October).

30. Theo van Doesburg, "Stuttgart-Weissenhof 1927: *Die Wohnung,"* in *On European Architecture: Complete Essays from "Het Bouwbedrijf," 1924–1931,* trans. Charlotte I. Loeb and Arthur L. Loeb (Basel: Birkhäuser, 1990), 164. Idem, "Stuttgart 1927: Permanente Architectuurtentoonstelling Die Wohnung," in *De Stijl en de europese architectuur: De architectuuropstellen in "Het Bouwbedrijf," 1924–1931* (Nijmegen: SUN, 1986), 144: *"In plaats van tegenover, wilde men de bezoeker in het nieuwe plaatsen en van de 'beschouer,' een 'belever' maken."*

31. Doesburg 1990 (see note 30), 164. Doesburg 1986 (see note 30), 144: *"de eenheid van een collectief stijlstreven."*

32. Doesburg 1990 (see note 30), 164. Doesburg 1986 (see note 30), 144: *"verreweg de sterkste persoonlijkheid der Duitse constructivistengroep."*

33. Behrendt published a segment-precis of *Sieg* in *Die Form.* See Walter Curt Behrendt, "Zur Formproblem der Zeit," *Die Form* 1, no. 9 (June 1926): 187–94.

34. Several reviewers of Behrendt's *Sieg* associated the book with the Werkbund show. See E. Völter, *Die Baugilde* 9 (12 December 1927): 23; Franz Hallbaum, "Rückblick auf Stuttgart," *Die Gartenkunst* 40 (1927): 195–96.

35. Hilberseimer (see note 22). Originally published in *Moderne Bauformen: Monatshefte für Architektur und Raumkunst* 26 (1927): 325–64.

36. See Walter Curt Behrendt, "Skyscrapers in Germany," *Journal of the American Institute of Architects* 11, no. 9 (September 1923): 365–70.

37. Pommer and Otto (see note 6), 21.

38. Pommer and Otto (see note 6), 83, 227 n. 1: Fondation Le Corbusier, Weissenhof Box, Mies to Behrendt, 4 October 1926.

39. On the formation of Der Ring and Der Block, see Karin Kirsch, *The Weissenhofsiedlung: Experimental Housing Built for the Deutscher Werkbund, Stuttgart, 1927,* trans. David Britt (New York: Rizzoli, 1989), 16, and Pommer and Otto (note 6). The announcement of the founding of Der Ring in *Die Form* listed Behrendt as a member; see *Die Form* 1, no. 10 (July 1926): 225.

40. For details of Mies's disputes with the Stuttgart advocates of mass housing, and those with Döcker and Häring, see Pommer and Otto (note 6).

41. *Victory*, 97. *Sieg*, 11: *"einen neuen Formalismus."* Here Behrendt referred to the title of the Werkbund's own exhibition of 1923, *Die Form ohne Ornament,* as a catchphrase whose adherents in 1927 he considered formalists and opponents. Later, in *Sieg*, Behrendt characterized "Machine Romanticism" as a kind of formalism emerging within Modernism.

42. See Ludwig Mies van der Rohe, "Vorwort," *Bau und Wohnung* (Stuttgart: Deutscher Werkbund, 1927), 7; translated by Mark Jarzombek in Fritz Neumeyer, *The Artless Word: Mies van der Rohe and the Building Art* (Cambridge: MIT Press, 1991), 259. In a concurrent article, Mies was even more concrete (Ludwig Mies van der Rohe, "Introductory Remarks to the Special Issue 'Werkbundausstellung: Die Wohnung,'" in Neumeyer, *The Artless Word,* 261): "I have therefore not given out guidelines but have limited myself to solicit the cooperation of those whose work leads me to expect interesting contributions to the housing question. The exhibition was conceived from the beginning as experimental and thus has its value quite independent of the results achieved. Each participating architect has investigated the new materials available in the marketplace for their applicability, and each one has made the choice as to his construction according to his responsibility." ("Einleitung," *Die Form* 2, no. 9 [September 1927]: 257: *"Ich habe darum darauf verzichtet, irgendwelche Richtlinien aufzustellen, sondern mich darauf beschränkt, solche Persönlichkeiten für die Mitarbeit auszusuchen, deren Arbeit interessante Beiträge zu der Frage der neuen Wohnung erwarten liess. Die Austellung war von vornherein als Experiment gedacht und hat als solches ganz unabhängig von den erreichten Resultaten ihren Wert. Von jedem beteiligten Architekten sind die auf dem Markt befindlichen neuen Materialien auf ihre Verwendbarkeit untersucht worden und jeder hat nach dem Grad seiner Verantwortlichkeit die Wahl für seinen Bau getroffen."*)

43. The idea that new housing estates should be crowned by a communal building, a *Stadtkrone,* as the cathedrals had crowned the medieval city, was proffered most famously by Bruno Taut in his utopian resettlement projects in 1919–1921.

44. Richard Pommer and Christian Otto have characterized Behrendt's gesture as propaganda that "for more than fifty years afterward has obscured the strong resistance and opposition that it engendered, particularly in Germany." See Pommer and Otto (note 6), 145. Pommer and Otto echoed Henry-Russell Hitchcock who had already in 1929 called Behrendt's book, together with Behne's *Neues Wohnen — Neues Bauen,* "primarily criticism or at least propaganda." See Hitchcock (note 23), 241. In contrast, Reyner Banham called Behrendt's book "explanatory rather than propagandist in aim, though even he fell victim to an old-established exasperation of the propagandists," namely, attempting to coax clients away from their Louis XVI interiors and toward the architectural equivalent of their Rolls-Royce cars. See Reyner Banham, *Theory and Design in the First Machine Age* (London: Architectural Press, 1960), 305. Similarly, Manfredo Tafuri held that Behrendt's publication, like Gustav Platz's *Die Baukunst der neuesten Zeit* (1927), attempted a systematic historiography of Modernism, which he distinguished from the operative criticism of Adolf Behne, Persico, Pagano, and Morton Shand and the self-publicity of Le Corbusier, Ernst May, Bruno

Taut, and magazines such as *Frühlicht, L'esprit nouveau, Casabella, Das neue Frank-furt,* and *Wasmuths Monatshefte für Baukunst.* See Manfredo Tafuri, *Theories and History of Architecture,* trans. Giorgio Verrecchia (New York: Harper & Row, 1980), 153–54.

45. Walter Curt Behrendt, *Der Kampf um den Stil im Kunstgewerbe und in der Architektur* (Stuttgart: Deutsche Verlags-Anstalt, 1920), 20.

46. *Victory,* 126. *Sieg,* 42: *"neue ästhetische Elemente"*; ibid., *"[diese] inneren Kräftespannungen"*; ibid., *"in ein reines und ebenmässiges Verhältnis."*

47. Behrendt's review of *Frank Lloyd Wright, Chicago* (Berlin: Ernst Wasmuth, 1911) appeared in *Kunst und Künstler* 11, no. 9 (September 1913): 487.

48. See J. J. P. Oud, "Der Einfluss von Frank Lloyd Wright auf die Architektur Europas," in *Holländische Architektur* (Munich: Albert Langen, 1926; reprint, Mainz: Florian Kupferberg, 1976), 77–83. Behrendt reiterated much of Oud's assessment in Walter Curt Behrendt, *Modern Building: Its Nature, Problems and Forms* (New York: Harcourt, Brace & Co., 1937), 150–54.

49. For a fuller treatment of the unresolved tension between the desire for freedom and the quest for a new system in the history of avant-garde theory, see Matei Cali-nescu, *Five Faces of Modernity: Modernism, Avant-Garde, Decadence, Kitsch, Post-modernism* (Durham: Duke Univ. Press, 1987), 95–111. For a consideration of the way in which this aporia played itself out in the architectural avant-garde of the twentieth century, see Detlef Mertins, "System and Freedom: Sigfried Giedion, Emil Kaufmann, and the Constitution of Architectural Modernity," *Autonomy and Ideology: Position-ing an Avant-Garde in America,* ed. R. E. Somol (New York: Monacelli Press, 1997), 214–31.

50. This account of Behrendt's life and career is compiled largely from Lewis Mumford, "Walter Curt Behrendt (1884–1945)," *The Roots of Contemporary Archi-tecture* (New York: Reinhold, 1952), 421–22; Janos Frecot, "Biographische Daten von Werkbundmitgliedern, die dem Werkbund vor 1933 angehört haben," in *Zwischen Kunst und Industrie: Der Deutsche Werkbund,* exh. cat. (Munich: Die neue Sammlung, Staatliches Museum für angewandte Kunst, 1975; reprint, Stuttgart: Deutsche Verlags-Anstalt, 1987), 594; Reginald R. Isaacs, "Walter Curt Behrendt," *Macmillan Encyclo-pedia of Architects* (New York: Free Press, 1982) 1:164–65; Henry F. Withey and Elsie Rathburn Withey, "Walter Curt Behrendt (12/26/1884–4/26/1945)," *Biographical Dic-tionary of American Architects (Deceased)* (Los Angeles: Hennessey & Ingalls, 1970), 48; "Walter Curt Behrendt," *Who Was Who in America,* vol. 2, 1943–1950 (Chicago: A. N. Marquis, 1950), 55; and obituary, "Dr. W. C. Behrendt, City Plans Expert," *New York Times,* 27 April 1945, 19. The most extensive treatments of Behrendt's role in the reception of German Modernism in the United States are M. David Samson, "'Unserer Newyorker Mitarbeiter': Lewis Mumford, Walter Curt Behrendt, and the Modern Movement in Germany," *Journal of the Society of Architectural Historians* 55, no. 2 (June 1996), 126–39; Stanislaus von Moos, "The Visualized Machine Age; or, Mum-ford and the European Avant-Garde," in Thomas P. Hughes and Agatha C. Hughes, eds., *Lewis Mumford: Public Intellectual* (New York: Oxford Univ. Press, 1990), 181–232; and Robert Wojtowicz, *Lewis Mumford and American Modernism: Eutopian Theories for Architecture and Urban Planning* (Cambridge: Cambridge Univ. Press, 1996),

84–85, 107, 119. Some details of Behrendt's life are provided in Donald L. Miller, *Lewis Mumford: A Life* (New York: Weidenfeld & Nicolson, 1989), 176, 322, 413, 428–29, 440. There is also a wealth of personal detail in Correspondence between Walter Curt Behrendt and Lewis Mumford, 1925–1945, Lewis Mumford Papers, folders 362–366, Special Collections, Van Pelt–Dietrich Library Center, University of Pennsylvania (hereafter cited as LMP–UPenn).

51. Karl Scheffler, *Moderne Baukunst* (Leipzig: Julius Zeitler, 1908), 157–68. Behrendt cited Scheffler's dualism in his review of Henry van de Velde's *Vom neuen Stil,* published in *Neudeutsche Bauzeitung* 4, no. 3 (1908): 17–20.

52. Scheffler (see note 51), 103: "*es* [kann] *sich letzten Endes nie um einen Kampf für oder wider eine dieser beiden 'Richtungen' handeln.*"

53. Scheffler (see note 51), 166: "*die reifste und schönste der Kulturfrüchte*"; ibid., "*alle zusammenwirkenden Kräfte* [müssen] *gesättigt sein von Gesundheit und Zukunftswillen.*"

54. Scheffler (see note 51), 168: "*Etwas Abschliessendes lässt sich über die grosse und weitreichende Bewegung…noch nicht sagen*"; ibid., "*die stärkste architektonische Kraft der Gegenwart*"; ibid., "*sich diesem jäh erwachten und heftig ringenden Wollen rein und vertrauend hinzugeben.*"

55. Mumford (see note 50), 421–22.

56. For the religious affiliations of Behrendt and his wife, see Miller (note 50), 428.

57. See Barbara Miller Lane, *Architecture and Politics in Germany* (Cambridge: Harvard Univ. Press, 1968), 173, 260 n. 15.

58. Günter Feist with Ursula Feist, eds., *Kunst und Künstler: Aus 32 Jahrgängen einer deutschen Kunstzeitschrift* (Mainz: Florian Kupferberg, 1971), 398–99.

59. Fritz Neumeyer, "Alfred Messel: Der grosse Unbekannte," in Walter Curt Behrendt, *Alfred Messel* (reprint, Berlin: Gebr. Mann, 1998), 139–51. Karl Scheffler was a prominent art critic, editor of *Kunst und Künstler,* and author of numerous books on German Impressionists, including monographs on Max Lieberman and Adolf Menzel. In architecture and urbanism, his principal works include *Der Architekt* (1907), *Moderne Baukunst* (1908), *Berlin: Ein Stadtschicksal* (1910), *Henry van de Velde* (1913), *Die Architektur der Großstadt* (1913), *Geist der Gotik* (1919), and *Holland* (1930).

60. See Feist, ed. (note 58), 398–99.

61. In Walter Curt Behrendt to Lewis Mumford, 11 April 1926, LMP–UPenn, Behrendt recounted that he was writing this book, which "presents the artistic aims of the new international architectural movement." He asked Mumford to assist him with an American translation.

62. While Taut and even Gropius contributed to *Die Volkswohnung,* Behrendt did not contribute to *Frühlicht.*

63. Erwin Gutkind, *Neues Bauen: Grundlagen zur praktischen Siedlungstätigkeit* (Berlin: Verlag der Bauwelt, 1919). Several members of the editorial board of *Die Volkswohnung,* in addition to Behrendt, also contributed to this anthology: Otto Glas, Otto Bartning, and Gerhard Jobst. Behrendt's article was on art and technology.

64. There is of course a danger of overstating the distinction between reformers and avant-gardists, which was for many more of a continuum than a conflict. For

instance, Bruno Taut, like Behrendt, sought to straddle the two, and his essay, "Die Erde, eine gute Wohnung," published in *Die Volkswohnung* 1, no. 4 (24 February 1919): 45–48, hit close to the heart of the journal's ethos.

65. On the Bodenreform movement, see Adolf Damaschke, *Die Bodenreform: Grundsätzliches und Geschichtliches zur Erkenntnis und Überwindung der sozialen Not* (Jena: Gustav Fischer, 1913), and Heinrich Freese, *Die Bodenreform: Ihre Vergangenheit und Ihre Zukunft* (Berlin: Weichert, 1918).

66. Walter Curt Behrendt, "Die Normenbewegung im Bauwesen," *Die Volkswohnung* 1, no. 5 (10 March 1919): 57–59.

67. Otto Bartning, "Unser Ziel," *Die Volkswohnung* 2, no. 1 (1920): 4–7.

68. Walter Curt Behrendt, "Weg und Ziel," *Die Volkswohnung* 4, no. 1 (10 January 1922): 1: "*Herd der Unzufriedenheit und des Unfriedens*"; ibid., "*die menschliche Seele, die in diesem Kampf um ihre Rettung ringt*"; ibid., "*auf dem Wege, [eine neue Arbeitsordnung] zu gestalten.*"

69. Behrendt cited Wilhelm Heinrich Riehl's *Die deutsche Arbeit* (Stuttgart: J. G. Cotta, 1861), 3: "*Die Seele des Volkes springt aus seiner Idee der Arbeit hervor, wie aus seiner Praxis der Arbeit.*" (The soul of the people springs from its idea of work, as much as its praxis of work.) Later, in *Kampf um den Stil* (see note 45), he also referred to Riehl's classic social history, *Die Naturgeschichte des Volkes als Grundlage einer deutschen Social-Politik*, 4 vols. (Stuttgart: J. G. Cotta, 1854–55). Abridged translation by David J. Diephouse as *The Natural History of the German People* (Lewiston: Edwin Mellen Press, 1990).

70. Walter Curt Behrendt, "Unsere Aufgabe," *Der Neubau: Halbmonatsschrift für Baukunst* 1, no. 1 (10 January 1924): 1: "*das Verständnis für die ursprünglichsten Aufgaben baulicher Gestaltung wieder zu wecken*"; ibid., "*das Werk des Genies, des Geistes und der schöpferischen Kraft*"; ibid., "*den Boden vorzubereiten für das Werden und Wachsen der neuen Form.*"

71. See page 10 and note 47.

72. Behrendt (see note 36). The responses were George C. Nimmons, "Skyscrapers in America," and William Stanley Parker, "Skyscrapers Anywhere," 370–72, in the same issue.

73. Clarence Stein et al., "Die Entwicklung des Städtebaues in Amerika," *Der Neubau* 6, no. 12 (24 June 1924): 141–45.

74. See Adolf Rading, "Reise nach den Vereinigten Staaten," *Der Neubau* 7, no. 2 (February 1925): 29–33; and 7, no. 5 (March 1925): 57–60. In his letter to Behrendt of 3 March 1925, Rading gave him many suggestions for his trip, including hotels and names and addresses of people to meet. See Adolf Rading Correspondence, Rading-Archiv, Akademie der Künste, Berlin.

75. Walter Curt Behrendt, *Städtebau und Wohnungswesen in den Vereinigten Staaten: Bericht über eine Studienreise* (Berlin: Hackebeil, 1926).

76. *Victory*, 142. *Sieg*, 60: "[des] technischen *Stils*" (Behrendt's emphasis).

77. Rudolf von Delius, "Kunstform und Naturform," *Die Form* 1, no. 6 (March 1926): 109–10. Kurt Ewald, "Die Schönheit der Maschine," *Die Form* 1, no. 6 (March 1926): 111–16. Walter Gropius, "Wo berühren sich die Schaffensgebiete des Technikers und Künstlers," *Die Form* 1, no. 6 (March 1926): 117–22. Werner Gräff, "Zur

Form des Automobils," *Die Form* 1, no. 9 (June 1926): 195–202. Gräff's articles appeared in the same issue as an early draft of *Sieg* (see note 33) and an essay by Riezler on Ford.

78. Lewis Mumford, *Sticks and Stones: A Study of American Architecture and Civilization* (New York: Boni and Liveright, 1924).

79. Lewis Mumford, "Die Form in der amerikanischen Zivilisation," *Die Form* 1, no. 2 (November 1925): 26–29. Lewis Mumford, "Amerikanische Baukunst," *Die Form* 1, no. 5 (February 1926): 102–4. Lewis Mumford, "Die Stadt der Zukunft," *Die Form* 1, no. 8 (May 1926): 176–79. All of these articles were translated by Margarete Mauthner.

80. While Erich Mendelsohn had already offered to have a translation done in 1924, it was Behrendt's proposal that Mumford accepted. See Lewis Mumford, *Vom Blockhaus zum Wolkenkratzer: Eine Studie über amerikanische Architektur und Zivilisation* (From log cabin to skyscraper: A study of American architecture and civilization), trans. Margarete Mauthner (Berlin: Cassirer, 1925). In his preface, Mumford thanked Behrendt for his interest in promoting the translation. Behrendt reviewed the translation in *Die Form* 1, no. 2 (November 1925): 34. By insisting that photographs accompany Mumford's articles in *Die Form* and guiding Mumford to photographers in New York, Behrendt also appears to have encouraged his incorporation of illustrations into the German edition of Mumford's book (Walter Curt Behrendt to Lewis Mumford, 22 May 1925 and 25 August 1925, LMP–UPenn). For the original American edition, Mumford had eschewed the use of images, preferring to tease readers into making their own first hand "regional surveys" of the American metropolis. Mumford's later books on the history of cities developed a strategic use of images to present a concise graphic version of his story. It was the publisher Bruno Cassirer who proposed the "more journalistic" title for the translation in order to appeal to the German audience. (Walter Curt Behrendt to Lewis Mumford, 13 May 1925 and 11 April 1926, LMP–UPenn).

81. See Wojtowicz (note 50), 85–86. For further details on Behrendt's relationship with Mumford, see Samson (note 50), Miller (note 50), and the Behrendt–Mumford Correspondence, LMP–UPenn. It was through Mendelsohn that Mumford published an essay on Wright in the Dutch journal *Wendigen*. See Lewis Mumford, "The Social Back Ground [*sic*] of Frank Lloyd Wright," *Wendigen* 7 (1925): 65–79.

82. Mumford (see note 78), 209.

83. Mumford (see note 78), 199.

84. Mumford (see note 78), 196.

85. While Behrendt himself did not use the term *modern vernacular* or even *vernacular* (*volkstümliche Baukunst* or *Volkskunst,* although the latter refers more to folk art), David Samson has used it to designate the populist orientation and love of folk ways that Behrendt and Mumford shared. See M. David Samson (note 50). Similarly, Francesco Passanti has recently mined Le Corbusier's reading of Karl Scheffler's conception of a metropolitan or modern *Volkskunst,* with which Behrendt would also have been familiar. See Francesco Passanti, "The Vernacular, Modernism, and Le Corbusier," *Journal of the Society of Architectural Historians* 56, no. 4 (December 1997): 438–51. Passanti uses the term *vernacular* in "its most generic sense, embracing ethnic, folk, regionalist, primitive, etc." (438), oriented toward the ideal of original purity.

86. Walter Curt Behrendt, "Zum Formproblem der Zeit," *Die Form* 1, no. 9 (June 1926): 187–94.

87. Walter Curt Behrendt et al., *Gegenwartsprobleme der Technik,* Schriften des Frankfurter Massamts 11 (Frankfurt am Main: Selbstverlag des Messamts, 1927) and Walter Curt Behrendt, *Die holländische Stadt* (Berlin: Cassirer, 1928).

88. Walter Curt Behrendt to Lewis Mumford, 31 July 1933, LMP–UPenn.

89. Walter Curt Behrendt to Lewis Mumford, 3 January 1934, LMP–UPenn.

90. The correspondence between Behrendt and Mumford reveals that Behrendt and his wife, Lydia, visited the United States for several months in early 1934 to explore opportunities for immigration and employment. They returned to Berlin for the summer, having arranged a one-year teaching contract at Dartmouth College. Throughout this process, the Behrendts were assisted especially by their friends Clarence Stein and Lewis Mumford. See LMP–UPenn.

91. Behrendt described hiring a young graduate recommended by Eero Saarinen as his assistant in preparing the master plan in Walter Curt Behrendt to Lewis Mumford, 8 November 1938, LMP–UPenn.

92. Isaacs (see note 50), 164–65.

93. Behrendt (see note 48). Mumford promoted the book to the publisher, read drafts of the manuscript, helped find illustrations, and attended to its production. See various letters from Mumford to Behrendt during 1936 and 1937.

94. Obituary, "Dr. W. C. Behrendt, City Plans Expert" (see note 50), 19.

95. Mumford, "Behrendt," *Roots* (see note 50), 421–22.

96. See Philip Johnson, *Writings* (New York: Oxford Univ. Press, 1979).

97. See Kathryn Bloom Hiesinger, "Introduction," *Art Nouveau in Munich: Masters of Jugendstil,* exh. cat. (Philadelphia: Philadelphia Museum of Art in association with Prestel-Verlag, 1988), 11–23.

98. Carl Bötticher, "Das Prinzip der hellenischen und germanischen Bauweise hinsichtlich der Übertragung in die Bauweise unserer Tage," *Allgemeine Bauzeitung* 11 (1846): 111–25; translated by Wolfgang Herrmann as "The Principles of the Hellenic and Germanic Ways of Building with Regard to Their Application to Our Present Way of Building," in *In What Style Should We Build? The German Debate on Architectural Style* (Santa Monica: The Getty Center for the History of Art and the Humanities, 1992), 147–67. See also Mitchell Schwarzer, "Ontology and Representation in Karl Bötticher's Theory of Tectonics," *Journal of the Society of Architectural Historians* 52, no. 3 (September 1993), 267–80.

99. Alfred Gotthold Meyer, *Eisenbauten: Ihre Geschichte und Aesthetik* (Esslingen: Paul Neff, 1907).

100. Friedrich Naumann, "Kunst und Industrie: 'Das Deutsche Kunstgewerbe 1906,'" reprinted in *Zwischen Kunst und Industrie* (see note 50), 38: "*die Sprache der Maschine.*"

101. For a more extended account and analysis of the Werkbund's promotion of quality in the context of the early history of commodity culture and its critics, see Frederic J. Schwartz, *The Werkbund: Design Theory and Mass Culture before the First World War* (New Haven: Yale Univ. Press, 1996).

102. See, for instance, Peter Behrens, "Art and Technology, 1910," in Tilmann

Buddensieg, in collaboration with Henning Rogge, *Industriekultur: Peter Behrens and the AEG,* trans. Iain Boyd White (Cambridge: MIT Press, 1984), 212–19. See also Tilmann Buddensieg, *"Industriekultur:* Peter Behrens and the AEG, 1907–1914," 8–95.

103. Riegl presented his theory of the *Kunstwollen* most fully in *Die spätrömische Kunstindustrie nach den Funden in Österreich-Ungarn,* part 1 (1901; reprint of 2d edition of 1927, Darmstadt: Wissenschaftliche Buchgesellschaft, 1964); translated by Rolf Winkes as *Late Roman Art Industry* (Rome: G. Bretschneider, 1985). See also Otto Pächt, "Art Historians and Critics, IV: Alois Riegl," *Burlington Magazine* 105 (May 1963): 188–93; Margaret Iversen, *Alois Riegl: Art History and Theory* (Cambridge: MIT Press, 1993), 2–18; and Margaret Olin, *Forms of Representation in Alois Riegl's Theory of Art* (University Park: Pennsylvania State Univ. Press, 1992), 148–54.

104. Hermann Muthesius, *Stilarchitektur und Baukunst: Wandlung der Architektur im XIX. Jahrhundert und ihr heutiger Standpunkt* (Mülheim an der Ruhr: K. Schimmelpfeng, 1902; 2d ed., 1903); translated by Stanford Anderson as *Style-Architecture and Building-Art* (Santa Monica: The Getty Center for the History of Art and the Humanities, 1994).

105. See Wladyslaw Tatarkiewiz, "Form: History of One Term and Five Concepts," in *A History of Six Ideas: An Essay on Aesthetics* (The Hague: Martinus Nijhoff, 1980), 220–43.

106. Muthesius 1994 (see note 104), 78. Muthesius 1903 (see note 104), 49: *"Die Welt liegt im Banne des Wahngebildes einer 'Stilarchitektur.' Dass die eigentlichen Werte in der Baukunst von der Stilfrage gänzlich unabhängig sind, ja dass eine echte Betrachtungsweise bei einem Architekturwerk gar nicht von Stil reden wird, dies zu begreifen ist dem heutigen Menschen nicht möglich."*

107. Muthesius 1994 (see note 104), 81. Muthesius 1903 (see note 104), 54–55: *"Wenn es gelänge, den Begriff Stil zunächst einmal ganz zu verbannen, wenn sich der Baukünstler mit Absehnung von allem Stil zunächst immer klar und in erster Linie an das hielte, was die besondere Art der Aufgabe von ihm verlangt, so wären wir von dem richtigen Wege zu … dem wirklichen neuen Stil nicht mehr weit entfernt."*

108. Muthesius 1994 (see note 104), 100. Muthesius 1903 (see note 104), 81: *"Fesseln …, in denen sie während eine Jahrhunderts festgebannt lag"*; ibid., *"die Strahlen eines neuen künstlerischen Lebens."*

109. Hermann Muthesius, "Die Bedeutung des Kunstgewerbes: Vortrag, Handelshochschule Berlin, 1907," in *Zwischen Kunst und Industrie* (see note 50), 41: *"auf der Grundlage einer absolut selbständigen Gestaltung Werke von überzeugender, künstlerischer Wirkung zu schaffen."*

110. Muthesius 1994 (see note 104), 87: "fashion seized the whiplash line as the characteristic of the new style that it had so long awaited." Muthesius 1903 (see note 104), 60: *"die Mode hat die geschwungene Linie als das Charakteristische desjenigen neuen Stils aufgefasst, auf den sie schon so lange gewartet zu haben schien."*

111. Muthesius 1994 (see note 104), 83. Muthesius 1903 (see note 104), 57: *"im Grunde also wieder die alte Stil- und Ornamentmisère."*

112. Muthesius 1994 (see note 104), 83. Muthesius 1903 (see note 104), 57: *"eine Kinderkrankheit ist, durch die sich eine heraufkommende wirkliche neue Kunstauffassung durchzuwinden im Begriff steht."*

113. Muthesius 1994 (see note 104), 83–84. Muthesius 1903 (see note 104), 58: "*eine freie, durch keine Fesseln beengte Gestaltung, die den jedesmaligen Sonderumständen Rechnung trägt, die sich flüssig jedem Bedürfnis anpasst, dem inneren Wesen der Aufgabe nachspürt und dieses äusserlich auszudrücken sucht.*" In the first edition of 1902, Muthesius used the word *Formgebung* rather than *Gestaltung*.

114. Muthesius 1994 (see note 104), 84. Muthesius 1903 (see note 104), 58: "[hierin liegt] *ein Sieg des Gegenwartsgeistes ausgedrückt, dem die Bewegung entsprungen ist.*"

115. Muthesius 1994 (see note 104), 98. Muthesius 1903 (see note 104), 78: "*die beginnende neue Stellung zur Stilfrage.*"

116. Muthesius 1994 (see note 104), 99. Muthesius 1903 (see note 104), 80.

117. Muthesius 1994 (see note 104), 79. Muthesius 1903 (see note 104), 51: "*eine strenge, man möchte sagen, wissenschaftliche Sachlichkeit, eine Enthaltung von allen äussern Schmuckformen, eine Gestaltung, die genau nach dem Zweck, dem das Werk dienen soll, getroffen ist.*"

118. Muthesius 1994 (see note 104), 91. Muthesius 1903 (see note 104), 68.

119. Muthesius 1994 (see note 104), 98. Muthesius 1903 (see note 104), 78: "*während sich die Mutter Architektur auf Abwegen befand, selbst Formen für das, was es an Neuem hervorbrachte, die anspruchslosen Formen der reinen Sachlichkeit, es schuf unsere Maschinen, Wagen, Geräte, eisernen Brücken, Glashallen. Indem es dabei ganz nüchtern vorging, indem es praktisch, man möchte sagen rein wissenschaftlich verfuhr.*"

120. Muthesius 1994 (see note 104), 98. Muthesius 1903 (see note 104), 78.

121. Muthesius 1994 (see note 104), 96. Muthesius 1903 (see note 104), 75.

122. Muthesius was concerned that "*Es ist, als ob die Menge unfähig sei, die Kernfragen menschlicher Probleme zu begreifen*" (Muthesius 1994 [see note 104], 87; Muthesius 1903 [see note 104], 60: "It is as if the masses are incapable of grasping the fundamental nature of human problems"). See Schwartz (note 101) on the problematic of fashion in the pre–World War I Werkbund discourse. For a broader treatment of the issue within architectural Modernism, see Mark Wigley, *White Out: Fashioning the Modern* (Cambridge: MIT Press, 1996) and Deborah Fausch et al., eds., *Architecture, in Fashion* (New York: Princeton Architectural Press, 1994).

123. Muthesius 1994 (see note 104), 97. Muthesius 1903 (see note 104), 77: "*echte Kunst*"; ibid., "*echte Menschen.*"

124. At the turn of the century, Schultze-Naumburg had been active in conservative reform movements and was closely associated with Ferdinand Avenarius. Portions of *Kulturarbeiten* were first published in Avenarius's *Der Kunstwart*, which was one of the most influential reform journals prior to World War I, catalyst for the formation of the Deutscher Bund Heimatschutz and the Dürerbund. Schultze-Naumburg was himself a founding member of the Heimatschutz in 1904, as well as the German Werkbund in 1907. The wide-ranging influence of *Kulturarbeiten* extended into the Werkbund, and its technique of comparisons between good and bad was emulated even among the avant-garde. But Schultze-Naumburg is remembered in history primarily as a theorist of cultural racism and a supporter of Hitler. In 1928 he published the tract *Kunst und Rasse*. In 1929 he became a member of the Kampfbund für Deutsche Kultur, and in

1931 leader of its division devoted to architecture and engineering. See Norbert Borrmann, *Paul Schultze-Naumburg, 1869–1949: Maler, Publizist, Architekt: Vom Kulturreformer der Jahrhundertwende zum Kulturpolitiker im Dritten Reich* (Essen: Richard Bacht, 1989).

125. Paul Schultze-Naumburg, *Kulturarbeiten* 1 (Munich: Kunstwart, 1901), unpaginated foreword: *"entsetzliche Entstellung der Physiognomie unseres Landes"*; ibid., *"der entsetzlichen Verheerung unseres Landes … entgegenzuarbeiten."*

126. Schultze-Naumburg (see note 125), 2: *"der Idee die Realität verleihen."*

127. Schultze-Naumburg (see note 125), unpaginated foreword: *"Die Kultur des Sichtbaren umfasst nicht allein Häuser und Denkmale, Brücken und Strassen, sondern auch Kleider und gesellige Formen, Forste und Viehzucht, Maschinen und Landesverteidigung."*

128. Schultze-Naumburg (see note 125), 3: *"die Veränderung der ganzen Erdoberfläche durch Menschenhand"*; ibid., *"der Bauer und der Ingenieur, der Kaufmann wie der Gärtner, der Seemann wie der Soldat, der Förster wie der Baumeister"*; ibid., *"tatsächlich gehört alles Gestalten derselben Familie."*

129. Schultze-Naumburg (see note 125), 3: *"nur wenn es Gestaltung der 'Idee' ist, hat es Kulturwert. Nur, heisst das, wenn es in vollkommenster Weise seinem Zwecke dient und sich diese Vollkommenheit auch in seiner äusseren Form ausdrückt."*

130. Schultze-Naumburg (see note 125), 3: *"das Einzelne [wird] die Harmonie eines ethischen Weltbildes zur Anschauung bringen."*

131. Schultze-Naumburg (see note 125), 4: *"Im tiefsten Grunde berührt sich Schönheit mit Ethik, indem sie uns das im weitesten Sinne für den Menschen 'Gute' als 'Schön' sichtbar macht und ihn es lieben lehrt."*

132. Schultze-Naumburg (see note 125), 5: *"Gibt es einen stärkeren Ausdruck der durch die Menschheit gebändigten Naturkräfte, als einen Eisenbahnzug? Wenn das Ungeheuer mit seinen glühenden Augen daherkommt, wie es in der grossen Kurve dort auf dem Boden dahinschiesst, dann auf dem Bahnhof laut keuchend und pustend kaum zu Atem kommt und nun mit tiefem Aufstöhnen von neuem die Last aufnimmt?"*

133. On Conrad Fiedler and his context, see Harry Francis Mallgrave and Eleftherios Ikonomou, "Introduction" and "Conrad Fiedler," in *Empathy, Form, and Space: Problems in German Aesthetics, 1873–1893* (Santa Monica: The Getty Center for the History of Art and the Humanities, 1994), 1–85, 319. See also Philippe Junod, *Transparence et opacité: Essai sur les fondements théoriques de l'art moderne: Pour une nouvelle lecture Konrad Fiedler* (Lausanne: Éditions L'âge d'homme, 1976). In introducing Behrendt to Riezler in 1909, Muthesius associated Riezler with a circle of "Hildebrand critics" formed in Munich around Adolf Hildebrand's book of 1893, *The Problem of Form*, including Theodor Fischer, Richard Riemerschmid, Fritz Schumacher, and Dr. [Wolf?] Dohrn. See letter from Hermann Muthesius to Walter Curt Behrendt, 7 September 1909, and letter from Behrendt to Muthesius, 9 September 1909. In his reply, Behrendt expressed his sympathy for the Hildebrand circle. Hermann Muthesius Correspondence, Werkbund-Archiv, Berlin.

134. Conrad Fiedler, *On Judging Works of Visual Art*, trans. Henry Schaefer-Simmern and Fulmer Mood (Berkeley: Univ. of California Press, 1949), 46. Conrad Fiedler, *Über die Beurteilung von Werken der bildenden Kunst*, in *Schriften zur Kunst,*

ed. Hermann Konnerth (Munich: R. Piper, 1913–14; reprint, Munich: Wilhelm Fink, 1971), 1:50: "*Die künstlerische Tätigkeit ist weder sklavische Nachahmung, noch willkürliche Erfindung, sondern freie Gestaltung.*"

135. Fiedler 1949 (see note 134), 48. Fiedler 1913–14 (see note 134), 1:52: "*die Welt durch und für das künstlerische Bewusstsein.*"

136. Fiedler 1949 (see note 134), 48. Fiedler 1913–14 (see note 134), 1:52: "*einem unendlich Rätselhaften*"; ibid., "*wo er, von einer inneren Notwendigkeit getrieben, die verworrene Masse des Sichtbaren, die auf ihn einstürmt, mit der Macht seines Geistes ergreift und zum gestalteten Dasein entwickelt.*"

137. Fiedler 1949 (see note 134), 53–54. Fiedler 1913–14 (see note 134), 1:57: "*die Welt der Erscheinungen im eigenen Bewusstsein zu immer reicherer Entfaltung, zu immer vollendeterer Gestaltung zu bringen.*"

138. Fiedler 1949 (see note 134), 48–49 (translation modified). Fiedler 1913–14 (see note 134), 1:53: "*das vom menschlichen Geiste noch Unberührte ist es, was ihre Tätigkeit erregt.... Sie* [die Kunst] *geht nicht vom Gedanken, vom geistigen Produkte aus, um zur Form, zur Gestalt hinabzusteigen, vielmehr steigt sie vom Form- und Gestaltlosen zur Form und Gestalt empor, und auf diesem Wege liegt ihre ganze geistige Bedeutung.*"

139. Fiedler 1949 (see note 134), 54. Fiedler 1913–14 (see note 134), 1:58: "*Das Reich der Erscheinungen wird ihm grenzenlos, weil es unter seiner grenzenlosen Tätigkeit entsteht.*"

140. For instance, Wölfflin's conception of the history of art as a history of vision was indebted to Fiedler.

141. *Victory*, 109. *Sieg*, 22: "konstruieren, *vom lateinischen* construere, *in der Bedeutung von erfinden, herleiten, bilden, formen,* gestalten" (Behrendt's emphases).

142. *Victory*, 109. *Sieg*, 21: "[von] *ästhetischen Elementen: in der knappen Prägnanz ihrer Linienführung, in der vollendeten Reinheit ihrer Proportionen, in der straffen Gespanntheit ihrer ebenen und geschwungen Flächen, in der leuchtenden Farbigkeit ihrer Anstriche und Lacke, in dem spiegelnden Glanz ihrer Polituren.*"

143. *Victory*, 109. *Sieg*, 22: "*dürfen, wenn nicht selbst etwa schon als Elemente eines neuen Stils, so doch als Fermente und Anknüpfungspunkte für die Bildung eines solchen angesehen werden.*"

144. *Victory*, 107. *Sieg*, 20: "*nicht alle Zeiten das Beste, was sie zu sagen haben, gerade in der Kunst ausdrücken.*"

145. Behrendt (see note 45), 219.

146. Adolf Hildebrand, *Das Problem der Form in der bildenden Kunst* (Strasbourg: Heitz & Mündel, 1893). English translation as "The Problem of Form in the Fine Arts," in Mallgrave and Ikonomou, eds. (see note 133), 227–79.

147. *Victory*, 126. *Sieg*, 42: "*Ein und dieselbe Triebkraft bringt Formen und Proportionen untrennbar vereinigt hervor: eine Eigentümlichkeit, die Jakob Burckhardt als das entscheidende Merkmal aller ursprünglichen, aller organischen Stile bezeichnet hat.*"

148. Hermann Muthesius, "Das Formproblem im Ingenieurbau," in *Die Kunst in Industrie und Handel*, Jahrbuch des Deutschen Werkbundes 1913 (Jena: Eugen Diederichs, 1913).

149. Muthesius (see note 148), 28: "*Bei allen sichtbaren Gestalten* [ist] [u]*nser Auge … der ständige Kontrolleur dessen, was wir sichtbar tun, wobei wir die Form nach einem unserem Gehirne eingepflanzten Gesetze bilden, beurteilen und handhaben.*"

150. Muthesius (see note 148), 28: "*Bei der Schönheit handelt es sich um ein Problem der Form und um nichts anderes, bei der Nützlichkeit um die nackte Erfüllung irgend eines Dienstes. … Das Schöne mit dem Nützlichen zu verschmelzen, und zwar bis zu einer möglichst restlosen Erfüllung beider Forderungen ist, wie bekannt, die eigentliche Aufgabe der Architektur.*"

151. Muthesius (see note 148), 30: "*Genau dieselben Gestaltungstendenzen kehren wieder beim Kunsthandwerker, beim Architekten, beim Ingenieur, beim Werkzeugverfertiger, beim Schneider, bei der Putzermacherin, beim simplen Handwerker, bei der Mutter, die ihrer Kleinen ein Kleid zurechtschneidert. Es handelt sich immer um die gleichen Dinge: gute Proportionierung, Abstimmung der Farben, wirkungsvollen Aufbau, Rhythmus, ausdrucksvolle Form.*"

152. The publication of Hermann Konnerth's book of 1909 on Fiedler and his 1913–1914 edition of Fiedler's writings refueled interest among artists, architects, and theorists. See Hermann Konnerth, *Die Kunsttheorie Conrad Fiedlers: Eine Darlegung der Gesetzlichkeit der bildenden Kunst* (Munich: R. Piper, 1909) and Fiedler 1913–14 (see note 134).

153. Muthesius (see note 148), 30: "*allgemeiner, sozusagen kosmischer Art*"; ibid., "*unserer Gehirntätigkeit immanent.*"

154. Walter Gropius, "Der stilbildende Wert industrieller Bauformen," in *Der Verkehr,* Jahrbuch des Deutschen Werkbundes 1914 (Jena: Eugen Diederichs, 1914), 29–32. Reprinted in Hartmut Probst and Christian Schädlich, eds., *Walter Gropius,* vol. 3, *Ausgewählte Schriften* (Berlin: Ernst & Sohn, 1988), 58–59.

155. Gropius (see note 154), 31: "*dieser Drang zum Gestalten in unseren Tagen* [beginnt sich] *gerade bei der Entwicklung industrieller Formen mit ursprünglicher Frische zu betätigen.*" Reprinted in Probst and Schädlich, eds. (see note 154), 58.

156. Gropius (see note 154), 29: "*Solange eben die geistigen Begriffe der Zeit noch unsicher schwanken, ohne ein einiges festes Ziel, solange fehlt auch der Kunst die Möglichkeit, Stil zu entwickeln, d.h. den Gestaltungswillen der vielen in* einem *Gedanken zu sammeln*" (Gropius's emphasis). Reprinted in Probst and Schädlich, eds. (see note 154), 59. For a consideration of Gropius's theoretical writings in relation to Riegl's historiography, see Karin Wilhelm, *Walter Gropius: Industrie Architekt* (Braunschweig: Friedr. Vieweg & Sohn, 1983), 30–33. Wilhelm interprets Gropius's writings and architectural projects in relation to then-current theories of technology, aesthetics, and history.

157. Karl Scheffler, "Die Volkskunst," *Dekorative Kunst* 4, no. 4 (1901): 140–44. Karl Scheffler, *Berlin: Ein Stadtschicksal* (reprint of the 1910 edition, Berlin: Fannei & Waltz, 1989). Karl Scheffler, *Die Architektur der Großstadt* (Berlin: Bruno Cassirer, 1913).

158. Georg Simmel, "The Metropolis and Mental Life, 1903," in *On Individuality and Social Forms,* ed. Donald N. Levine, trans. Edward A. Shils (Chicago: Univ. of Chicago Press, 1971), 324–39. Originally published as "Die Großstadt und das

Geistesleben," in *Die Großstadt: Vorträge und Aufsätze zur Städteausstellung,* ed. Theodor Petermann, Jahrbuch der Gehe-Stiftung zu Dresden, vol. 9 (Dresden: von Zahn & Jaensch, 1903), 185–206. See Ferdinand Tönnies, *Gemeinschaft und Gesellschaft: Grundbegriffe der reinen Soziologie* (Berlin: Fues, 1887); translated by Charles P. Loomis as *Community and Society* (East Lansing: Michigan State Univ. Press, 1957; reprint, New York: Harper & Row, 1963).

159. Endell drew on an Impressionist mode of seeing to portray the distinctive beauty of the metropolis. At the same time, he depicted the city as a form creation (*Gestaltung*), a working entity (*Arbeitswesen*), nature, noises, and landscape. See August Endell, *Die Schönheit der grossen Stadt* (Stuttgart: Strecker & Schröder, 1908). See also his earlier pamphlet outlining his conception of a new nonrepresentational, empathetic, and abstract art of forms: August Endell, *Um die Schönheit* (Munich: Emil Franke, 1896). See also Lothar Müller, "The Beauty of the Metropolis: Towards an Aesthetic Urbanism in Turn-of-the-Century Berlin," in Charles W. Haxthausen and Heidrun Suhr, eds., *Berlin: Culture and Metropolis* (Minneapolis: Univ. of Minnesota Press, 1990), 37–57.

160. Karl Scheffler, *Henry van de Velde: Vier Essays* (Leipzig: Insel, 1913), 95: "*ein grosser Organisator lebendiger Kräfte.*"

161. Scheffler (see note 160), 92: "*eine von neuer Klassizität regierte Zukunft.*"

162. Scheffler (see note 160), 96.

163. Behrendt (see note 45), 20. In so doing, he drew on Nietzsche's vitriolic critique of academic historicism and his alternative of a critical history, summarized in the following passage from his essay on history of 1874: "When the past speaks it always speaks as an oracle: only if you are an architect of the future and know the present will you understand it … only he who constructs the future has a right to judge the past. If you look ahead and set yourself a great goal, you at the same time restrain that rank analytical impulse which makes the present into a desert and all tranquillity, all peaceful growth and maturing almost impossible. Draw about yourself the fence of a great and comprehensive hope, of a hope-filled striving. Form within yourself an image to which the future shall correspond." See Friedrich Nietzsche, "On the Uses and Disadvantages of History for Life (1874)," *Untimely Meditations,* trans. R. J. Hollingdale (Cambridge: Cambridge Univ. Press, 1985), 94.

164. Behrendt (see note 45), 77. On the reception of Nietzsche in the arts in Germany at this time, see Seth Taylor, *Left-Wing Nietzscheans: The Politics of German Expressionism, 1910–1920* (Berlin: Walter de Gruyter, 1990) and Steven E. Aschheim, *The Nietzsche Legacy in Germany, 1890–1990* (Berkeley: Univ. of California Press, 1992). In reiterating Nietzsche's call for images of the future, Behrendt participated in the utopian discourse promoted by the AfK with which he was initially affiliated. Adolf Behne, most notably, had made a similar reference to Nietzsche in *Zur neuen Kunst* (Berlin: Der Sturm, 1915; reprinted in the series Sturm-Bücher, Kraus: Nendeln/Liechtenstein, 1974), 32.

165. For a more extensive treatment of this, see Detlef Mertins, "Anything but Literal: Sigfried Giedion and the Reception of Cubism in Germany," in *Architecture and Cubism,* eds. Eve Blau and Nancy J. Troy (Cambridge: MIT Press; Montreal: Canadian Centre for Architecture, 1997), 219–51.

166. Behrendt (see note 45), 20.

167. Schwartz (see note 101) provides an insightful treatment of the issue of commodification in the prewar discourse of the Werkbund, mapping the exchanges between political economy, sociology, and the applied arts.

168. Behrendt (see note 45), 52: *"ein neues 'realistisches' Gestaltungsprinzip entgegen, nach welchem die Form organisch aus ihrer Funktion abgeleitet werden sollte, als ein künstlerisches Symbol ihres tektonischen Zweckes."*

169. Behrendt (see note 45), 52.

170. Behrendt (see note 45), 20.

171. Behrendt (see note 45), 72.

172. Behrendt (see note 45), 132. Here Behrendt cited Goethe's principle of self-fashioning in the context of engineering.

173. Behrendt (see note 45), 90.

174. In Behrendt (see note 45), Behrendt used the term *Gestaltung* to designate expression in form (p. 14), the form creation of life (p. 20), the organic (p. 52), creative forces (p. 72), the process of spiritualization (p. 90), and self-fashioning (p. 132).

175. Behrendt (see note 45), 132–33.

176. Behrendt (see note 45), 134–35.

177. Behrendt (see note 45), 131: *"Der Geist der Zeit ist ein Geist dauernder Bewegung und rastloser Aktivität. Für ihn gibt es kein Fertiges und Endgültiges, sondern nur ein unablässiges Streben nach einer besseren und vollkommeneren Lösung. So kennt auch die Zeit keine Reife und Harmonie, sondern nur einen ständigen Wechsel und alle Dissonanzen neuen Werdens."*

178. Behrendt (see note 45), 136: *"Erst wenn die Architekten den Mut und die Kraft finden werden, dem akademisch überlieferten Dekorationsschema zu entsagen und sich selbst wieder zu Ingenieuren, zu Technikern, zu Handwerkern..., wird sich die Hoffnung auf einen neuen, selbständigen Stil in der Baukunst vielleicht erfüllen."*

179. Speaking of the implications of iron and concrete structures developed for buildings serving global transportation and commerce, Behrendt identified *"die Entwicklung eines konstruktiven Gerüststils im gotischen Sinne, eines Bausystems, in dem die architektonische Form unmittelbar aus ihrer Funktion abgeleitet, die Konstruktion also bewusst wieder zum Träger des künstlerischen Ausdrucks erhoben wird"* (the development of a constructional *Gerüststil* in the Gothic sense, a building system in which architectonic form is derived directly from its function — construction elevated once again to be the carrier of artistic expression). Behrendt (see note 45), 214–15.

180. Walter Curt Behrendt, "Einleitung," in Paul Mebes, *Um 1800: Architektur und Handwerk im letzten Jahrhundert ihrer traditionellen Entwicklung* (3d ed., Munich: F. Bruckmann, 1920), 7–12.

181. *Victory*, 89. *Sieg*, 22: *"gewaltige[s] Schauspiel eines umfassenden Gestaltwandels...vollzieht sich vor unseren Augen."*

182. For a full treatment of these interrelated themes, see Harry Lieberman, *Fate and Utopia in German Sociology, 1870–1923* (Cambridge: MIT Press, 1988).

183. Adolf Behne, *Die Wiederkehr der Kunst* (Leipzig: Kurt Wolff, 1919), especially 59, 73.

184. See Walter Gropius, "Was ist Baukunst?" in *Flugblatt zur Ausstellung für*

unbekannte Architekten (Berlin: Arbeitsrat für Kunst, Graphisches Kabinett von J.B. Neumann, 1919). Reprinted in Probst and Schädlich, eds. (see note 154), 3:63–64.

185. Theo van Doesburg et al., "Manifest I von 'Der Stil,' 1918" *De Stijl* 2, no. 1 (November 1918): 5: "*ans Licht gebracht*"; ibid., "*im äuszerlichen Leben zu realisieren.*" Reprinted in *De Stijl,* vol. 1, 1917–1920 (Amsterdam: Athenaeum, 1968), 239.

186. Theo van Doesburg, "'Der Wille zum Stil' (Neugestaltung von Leben, Kunst und Technik)," part 1, *De Stijl* 5, no. 2 (February 1922): 23–32. Reprinted in *De Stijl,* vol. 2, 1921–1932 (Amsterdam: Athenaeum, 1968), 174–82.

187. Piet Mondrian, "Die neue Gestaltung in der Musik und die Futuristischen Italienischen Bruitisten," part 1, *De Stijl* 6, no. 1 (March 1923): 1–9, and part 2, *De Stijl* 6, no. 2 (April 1923): 19–25. Reprinted in *De Stijl,* vol. 2, 1921–1932 (see note 186), 329–33 and 342–45. This essay originally appeared in Dutch as "De 'Bruiteurs futuristes italiens' en 'het' nieuwe in de muziek." The German version was translated by Max Burchartz from Mondrian's own French translation, published under the modified title "La manifestation du néo-Plasticisme dans la musique et les bruiteurs italiens futuristes."

188. Doesburg (see note 186), 25: "*Gesamtausdruck eines Volkes*"; ibid., "*Physiognomie jeder Kunstperiode.*" Reprinted in *De Stijl,* vol. 2, 1921–1932 (see note 186), 179.

189. Doesburg (see note 186), 23: "*Problem der wirtschaftlichen und ökonomischen Neugestaltung Europas.*" Reprinted in *De Stijl,* vol. 2, 1921–1932 (see note 186), 174.

190. Theo van Doesburg, "'Der Wille zum Stil' (Neugestaltung von Leben, Kunst und Technik)," part 2, *De Stijl* 5, no. 3 (March 1922): 33: "*Die Maschine ist das Phänomen geistiger Disziplin par exellençe.*" Reprinted in *De Stijl,* vol. 2, 1921–1932 (see note 186), 187.

191. Doesburg (see note 190): 34: "*Die neue geistige Kunstauffassung hat nicht nur die Maschine als Schönheit empfunden, sondern sie hat ihre unendlichen Ausdrucksmöglichkeiten für die Kunst sofort anerkannt.*" Reprinted in *De Stijl,* vol. 2, 1921–1932 (see note 186), 187.

192. Werner Lindner with Georg Steinmetz, eds., *Die Ingenieurbauten in ihrer guten Gestaltung* (Berlin: Ernst Wasmuth, 1923). An earlier version of this was published in the journal *Die Form* 1, no. 2 (1922): 5–8. The same issue of the journal included an editorial by Riezler on nature and machines. A follow-up publication appeared in 1927: Werner Lindner, *Bauten der Technik: Ihre Form und Wirkung* (Berlin: Ernst Wasmuth, 1927).

193. Walter Gropius, "Monumentale Kunst und Industriebau," in Probst and Schädlich, eds. (see note 154), 3:28–51. This was an illustrated lecture given at the Folkwang-Museum in Hagen on 10 April 1911.

194. Lindner and Steinmetz, eds. (see note 192), 7: "*Die Bauten der modernen Ingenieurkunst sind neben ihren sonstigen Leistungen bewunderungswert wie kaum sonst Menschenwerk.*"

195. G 1 (July 1923): 1: "*Die allgemeine Situation der Kunst und des Lebens zu klären.*" Reprinted in Marion von Hofacker, ed., *G: Material zur elementaren Gestaltung, Herausgeber Hans Richter, 1923–1926* (Munich: Der Kern, 1986), insert.

196. Doesburg (see note 190): 35: "*In mannigfaltigen Erscheinungen offenbart sich das neue Stilwollen. Nicht nur in der Malerei, Plastik und Architektur, in Literatur, Jazz-Band und Kino, sondern vor allem in rein utilistischer Produktion.*" Reprinted in *De Stijl*, vol. 2, 1921–1932 (see note 186), 188.

197. See Werner Gräff, "Über die sogenannte G-Gruppe," *Werk und Zeit* 11 (1962): 3–5; idem, "Concerning the So-called G Group," with introduction by Howard Dearstyne, *Art Journal* 23, no. 3 (Spring 1964): 280–82; and Raoul Hausmann, "More on Group 'G,'" *Art Journal* 24, no. 4 (Summer 1965): 350–51.

198. Theo van Doesburg, "Zur Elementaren Gestaltung," *G* 1 (July 1923): 2: "*Aus den elementaren Mitteln wächst die neue Gestaltung. In ihr werden die verschiedenen Künste sich so zu einander verhalten, dass sie imstande sind, ein Maximum von (elementarer) Ausdruckskraft zu entfalten.*" Reprinted in Hofacker, ed. (see note 195), insert.

199. Mies van der Rohe, "Bürohaus," *G* 1 (July 1923): 3; translated by Mark Jarzombek as "Office Building," in Neumeyer (see note 42), 241 (translation modified).

200. El Lissitzky, "Suprematism in World Reconstruction," in Sophie Lissitzky-Küppers, *El Lissitzky: Life, Letters, Texts* (New York: Thames and Hudson, 1980), 331.

201. El Lissitzky, "PROUN: Not World Visions, BUT — World Reality," in Lissitzky-Küppers (see note 200), 348. Originally published as "PROUN: Nicht Weltvision, SONDERN — Weltrealität," *De Stijl* 5, no. 6 (June 1922): 81–85: "*der Proun* [geht] *über das Gemälde und dessen Künstler einerseits, die Maschine und den Ingenieur andererseits hinaus und schreitet zum Aufbau des Raumes…und baut eine neue vielseitige, aber einheitliche Gestalt unserer Natur.*"

202. See Giedion (note 22). László Moholy-Nagy, *Von Material zu Architektur* (Munich: Albert Langen, 1929); later translated and expanded as László Moholy-Nagy, *The New Vision* (New York: George Wittenborn, 1947).

203. Hans Richter, "G," *G* 3 (June 1924): 1: "[in] *dem heillosen Chaos unserer Tage*"; ibid., "*in der gründlichen Auflösung*"; ibid, 2: "*das Spiel der Lebenskräfte*"; ibid., 2: "*das allgemeine Existenzproblem*"; ibid., 1: "*Dokumente eines einheitlichen Lebenstriebes.*" Reprinted in Hofacker, ed. (see note 195), 11–13.

204. Raoul Haussmann, "Ausblick," *G* 3 (June 1924): 6: "[zeigen] *die Tiefe unseres Erinnerungsvermögens*"; ibid., 7: "*Wir können und müssen die Biozönose umformen, wenn wir das organische Denken und die daraus entspringende Tat und Tatsächlichkeit ernstlich in das Milieu, in das Gesamtmiterlebensgebiet hineintragen oder besser aus ihm herausarbeiten.*" Reprinted in Hofacker, ed. (see note 195), 14–17.

205. Walter Curt Behrendt, "Geleitwort," *Die Form* 1, no. 1 (October 1925): 1–2: "*Die Zeitschrift wird die Aufgaben der Formgestaltung für alle Gebiete des gewerblichen und künstlerischen Schaffens behandeln. Alle gestaltende Arbeit findet ihr Ende und ihren sichtbaren Ausdruck in der Form. Form ist Ordnung. Die neue Welt der Arbeit aber, die um uns erstanden ist, hat für sich bisher noch keine Ordnung gefunden. Die Grundlagen der gestaltenden Arbeit haben eine vollständige Umwandlung erfahren.… Wir sind uns bewusst, dass die Formprobleme der gestaltenden Arbeit, mit denen wir uns in dieser Zeitschrift zu beschäftigen haben, nur im Zusammenhang mit jenen übergeordneten Problemen behandelt werden können, die in der Gestaltung*

einer neuen Arbeitsordnung und der Bildung neuer Lebensformen bestehen.... [D]ie Form für uns [ist] nicht ein ästhetisches, sondern vorwiegend ein konstruktives Problem. Uns geht hier weniger die fertige Form an und ihre kritische Bewertung nach überlieferten Schönheitsbegriffen. Wir werden uns vielmehr mit dem Gestaltungsprozess, mit dem Weg zur Form, mit der Formwerdung beschäftigen. Wir werden die Gestaltungsmethoden aufzeigen, die auf allen Gebieten des gewerblichen und künstlerischen Schaffens unserer Zeit zu neuen und oft ungewohnten Formen geführt haben."

206. Gropius, "Vorwort," in Gropius, ed. (see note 18), 5: *"eines allgemeinen Gestaltungswillens von grundlegend neuer Art."*

207. Gropius (see note 206), 6–7: *"Eine neue wesenhafte Baugesinnung entfaltet sich gleichzeitig in allen Kulturländern. Die Erkenntnis wächst, dass ein lebendiger Gestaltungswille, in der Gesamtheit der Gesellschaft un ihres Lebens wurzelnd, alle Gebiete menschlicher Gestaltung zu einheitlichem Ziel umschliesst — im Bau beginnt und endet.... [D]er neue Gestaltungsgeist, der sich langsam zu entwicklen beginnt, geht wieder auf den Grund der Dinge: um ein Ding so zu gestalten, dass es richtig funktioniert, ein Möbel, ein Haus, wird sein Wesen zuerst erforscht.... [D]er Wille zur Entwicklung eines einheitlichen Weltbildes, der unsere Zeit kennzeichnet, setzt die Sehnsuch voraus, die geistigen Werte aus ihrer individuellen Beschränkung zu befreien und sie zu objektiver Geltung emporzuheben. Dann folgt die Einheit der äusseren Gestaltungen, die zur Kultur führen von selbst nach"* (Gropius's emphases).

208. For a fuller treatment of the role of aesthetic theory in the pedagogy of the Bauhaus, see Detlef Mertins, "Bauhaus," *Encyclopedia of Aesthetics* (Oxford: Oxford Univ. Press, 1998): 1:219–27.

209. Hugo Häring, "Wege zur Form," *Die Form* 1, no. 1 (October 1925): 3–5.

210. Hugo Häring (see note 209), 4: *"das Ergebnis einer Ordnung vieler einzelner Dinge im Raum, in Hinsicht auf eine Lebensentfaltung und Leistungserfüllung sowohl des Einzelnen wie des Ganzen."*

211. Hugo Häring (see note 209), 5: *"Dieses Ganze ist die Gestalt unseres Lebens."*

212. Hugo Häring (see note 209), 5: *"Wir wollen aber nicht die Dinge, sondern nur ihre Herstellung mechanisieren.... Die Herstellung mechanisieren indessen heisst Leben gewinnen."*

213. Häring, like Behne, makes a claim to autonomy, albeit through the notion of the organic rather than the geometric-classical.

214. Behne 1996 (see note 19), 146. Behne 1926 (see note 19), 72: *"die starken dynamischen Spannungen, die eine lebendige Baukunst...immer in sich aufnehmen muss,...zu stabilisieren."*

215. Behne 1996 (see note 19), 142. Behne 1926 (see note 19), 68: *"macht den Bau zur lebendigen, konkreten 'Gestalt.'"* Paul Tillich, *Das System der Wissenschaften nach Gegenständen und Methoden* (Göttingen: Vandenhoeck & Ruprecht, 1923). English translation by Paul Wiebe as *The System of the Sciences according to Objects and Methods* (London: Associated Univ. Presses, 1981).

216. Behne 1996 (see note 19), 143. Behne 1926 (see note 19), 69: *"der Mensch [ist] zwei Welten verhaftet: der Welt der biologischen Notwendigkeiten, einem dunklen Naturgrund voller Härten, und einer geistigen Welt mit spezifischem Inhalt und*

Gehalt." Behrendt cites a paraphrase of Alfred Vierkandt, *Der Dualismus im modernen Weltbild*, (Berlin: Pan-Verlag, 1923), from a review by Christian Hermann, "Dualismus," *Sozialistische Monatshefte* (1923), 287.

217. Behne 1996 (see note 19), 143–44. Behne 1926 (see note 19), 69: *"Seine konkrete Gestalt ist das Kompromiss zwischen Individuum (Funktion) und Gesellschaft (Form).... Seine reine Gestalt ist lebendiges Gleichgewicht, Verwirklichung eines nach vielen Seiten spielenden Verhaltens, offen und doch bestimmt."*

218. Behrendt wrote a positive review of the German translation of Le Corbusier's *Vers une architecture* in *Die Form* 1, no. 10 (1926): 228. Later, however, he suggested that Le Corbusier's formula, "the house is a machine for living," had led to misconceptions and to an abstract and systematic approach, despite the fact that he was clearly an artist. Behrendt commended him for providing the most concise statement of the structural transformations (economic, social, technological, and emotional) affecting the design of building organisms. He ended this article by setting *Bauen* and Frank Lloyd Wright against architecture and Le Corbusier as unnaive and overwhelmingly intellectual. Walter Curt Behrendt, "Le Corbusier," *Kunst und Künstler* 30, no. 2 (November 1931): 53–58. In the preface to *Modern Building* (see note 48), Behrendt continued to cite Häring as a significant influence.

219. In *Modern Building*, Behrendt reiterated almost verbatim J. J. P. Oud's conception of a "classical Cubism," first offered in the early 1920s in response to van Doesburg's conception of a formless Cubist architecture. The work of Frank Lloyd Wright was taken by Oud and Behrendt to be exemplary of Cubism. See Behrendt (note 48), 147–55. Also see J. J. P. Oud, "Über die zukünftige Baukunst und ihre architektonischen Möglichkeiten," 1921, and "Der Einfluss von Frank Lloyd Wright auf die Architektur Europas," 1925, in Oud (see note 48), 63–76, 77–83.

220. Behne continued, "It is a complete joy to know that someone of such modern sensibility and openmindedness occupies an influential post in the Prussian Ministry of Finance. This careful and well-grounded book is most highly recommended." (*Eine ebenso temperamentvolle wie kenntnisreiche Deutung des neuen Bauwillens, die durch eine besonders reiche Illustrierung unterstüzt wird. Es ist überaus erfreulich, einen Mann so moderner Empfindung und so vorurteilsloser Gesinnung an einflussreicher Stelle im Preussischen Finanzministerium wirkend zu wissen. Die sorgfältig gedruckte Schrift sei bestens empfohlen.*) Adolf Behne, review of *Der Sieg des neuen Baustils,* by Walter Curt Behrendt, *Reclams Universum* 44.2, no. 32 (3 May 1928): 732. I am indebted to Kai Gutschow for finding this.

221. Behrendt had already mobilized the term *Baustil* to designate the new historical formation in architecture in a lecture given in the spring of 1926 to the Schlesischer Landesverband des Deutschen Werkbundes. Titled "Der neue Baustil," it was reported briefly in the "Mitteilungen des Deutschen Werkbundes," *Die Form* 1, no. 8 (May 1926): unpaginated insert.

222. *Victory,* 107. *Sieg,* 17: "[w]*as die neue Bewegung treibt und trägt."*

223. *Victory,* 137. *Sieg,* 55: *"die Legitimität der neuen Gestaltungsweise."*

224. *Victory,* 142. *Sieg,* 60: *"den Weg..., dem alles ursprüngliche Gestalten folgt";* ibid., *"die Grundsätze alles ursprünglichen, alles organischen Gestaltens."*

225. See, for instance, J. J. P. Oud, who concludes his essay "Über die zukünftige

Baukunst und ihre architektonischen Möglichkeiten, 1921" (note 219) with the ideal of classical purity. In his *Klassik-Barok-Modern,* Theo van Doesburg had called the modern a self-conscious classicism.

226. *Victory,* 107. *Sieg,* 17: *"der Wille zurückzukehren zu den Grundlagen und Elementarregeln alles Bauens und es wieder genau so zu machen wie die Alten"*; ibid., *"das Begehren, sich auseinanderzusetzen mit den neuen Gegebenheiten der Zeit und ihren neuen Lebensinhalten."*

227. Much of the German avant-garde discourse preferred the passive form, which gave to things the capacity to self-generate, and thereby avoided anthropomorphic projection. While Behrendt did not use this way of referring to origins, Behne did in *Wiederkehr der Kunst* (see note 183).

228. *Victory,* 107. *Sieg,* 18: *"das Gesicht unserer Zeit."*

229. See also Fritz Neumeyer, "Der neue Mensch: Körperbau und Baukörper in der Moderne," in *Moderne Architektur in Deutschland, 1900 bis 1950,* vol. 2, *Expressionismus und Neue Sachlichkeit,* eds. Vittorio Magnago Lampugnani and Romana Schneider, exh. cat. (Stuttgart: Gerd Hatje, 1994), 15–32.

230. *Victory,* 129. *Sieg,* 45.

231. *Victory,* 126. *Sieg,* 42: *"einzelne Teile sich gegenseitig bedingen und in Spannung halten."*

232. Raoul Heinrich Francé, *Die technischen Leistungen der Pflanzen* (Leipzig: Veit, 1919). In this book as well as others, the celebrated botanist and monist promoted examples of nature's forms and constructional modalities as exemplary for human artifacts and engineering works. Speaking of the "principle of construction," he compared the limited range of human culture to the remarkable system of construction of diatom (*Kieselalge*), a kind of algae capable of producing over four thousand kinds of configurations. He suggested that the inventions of plants pointed to a hundred possible applications in the design of great halls, furniture, cases, and articles of everyday use. See *Die technischen Leistungen,* 35.

233. *Victory,* 134. *Sieg,* 51: "[wo] *sich um eine geschwungene Treppe als Rückgerät die Räume des Hauses so angliedern, dass sie sich den ganz individuellen Bedürfnissen des häuslichen Betriebes aufs genaueste anschmiegen."*

234. *Victory,* 134. *Sieg,* 51: "[in] *freierer Weise"*; ibid., *"unter nahezu völliger Auflösung ihrer Begrenzungen untereinander in Fluss gebracht"*; ibid., *"auch wieder aneinander gebunden durch die Wechselbeziehungen ihrer inneren Spannungen."*

235. Helmut Müller-Sievers, *Self-Generation: Biology, Philosophy, and Literature around 1800* (Stanford: Stanford Univ. Press, 1997).

236. Behrendt's characterization of organisms was consistent with cell theory as understood in biology. While cells had already been posited in the seventeenth century as the basic building blocks of living organisms, by the late nineteenth century the actions of cellular material were thought to be responsible for organic development and differentiation. Evolutionary theory, promoted in Germany most notably by Ernst Haeckel, also assigned cells a key role in the development of species. For an introduction to the history of cell theory, see Jane Maienschein, "Cell Theory and Development," in R. C. Olby et al., eds., *Companion to the History of Modern Science* (London: Routledge, 1990), 357–73.

237. *Victory*, 137. *Sieg*, 53: "*in ständiger Wechselwirkung.*"

238. *Victory*, 134 (translation modified). *Sieg*, 53: "[wird] *jetzt als das aufgefasst..., was sie in Wirklichkeit ist: nämlich* ein lebendiger Organismus, *der in seinem Gerüst und in seinem Aufbau so zu gestalten ist, dass er die mannigfachen* Lebensfunktionen, *die er zu erfüllen hat, so vollkommen, so reibungslos als möglich zu höchster Leistungsfähigkeit entfalten kann*" (Behrendt's emphases).

239. *Victory*, 137. *Sieg*, 53: "*nach den inneren Wechselwirkungen, nach dem Spannungsdruck, in dem sie zueinander stehen.*"

240. *Victory*, 137. *Sieg*, 53: "*im Gleichgewicht.*"

241. *Victory*, 141. *Sieg*, 58: "*notwendig, ja unentbehrlich.*"

242. *Victory*, 141. *Sieg*, 59: "*so wie in den höheren Schulen der Unterricht in den toten Sprachen gepflegt wird, um das logische Denken zu schulen und das Sprachgefühl zu entwickeln. Aber schliesslich und vor allem müssen wir doch auch die Syntax unserer eigenen, unserer* lebendigen *Sprache erlernen, damit wir die Sätze richtig konstruieren können, in denen wir unsere Nöte ausdrücken, mit denen wir sagen, was uns bedrängt und bewegt*" (Behrendt's emphases).

243. Conrad Fiedler, "Aphorismen, #106," in Fiedler 1913–14 (see note 134), 2:77: "*Das Verhältnis von Denken und Sprechen ist so zu verstehen, dass dasjenige Denken, welches sich in der Sprache darstellt, auch nur in und mit der Sprache entsteht, nicht nur mit der Sprache unauflöslich verbunden, sondern mit ihr identische ist....*"

244. Ernst Cassirer, *Philosophie der symbolischen Formen*, vol. 1, *Die Sprache* (Berlin: Bruno Cassirer, 1923); translated by Ralph Manheim as *The Philosophy of Symbolic Forms*, vol. 1, *Language* (New Haven: Yale Univ. Press, 1955).

245. Behrendt referred to Lessing as "my great friend and favored author, Gotthold Ephrain Lessing, whose polemical writings I always read with high admiration," in a letter to Mumford dated 16 February 1939 (LMP–UPenn). He also referred to Lessing earlier in his review of Le Corbusier's *Vers une architecture*, *Die Form* 1, no. 10 (1926): 228.

246. David E. Wellbery, *Lessing's Laocoon: Semiotics and Aesthetics in the Age of Reason* (Cambridge: Cambridge Univ. Press, 1984), 5.

247. Hugo Häring, "Die Tradition, Schultze-Naumburg und wir," *Die Form* 1, no. 8 (May 1926): 180.

248. Paul Schultze-Naumburg, "Wer hat Recht?" *Uhu* (April 1928): 30.

249. Häring (see note 246), 180, citing Schultze-Naumburg: "*mongolides, negrides, und manches andere Blut.*"

250. Häring (see note 246), 180: "*Wir wollen uns nun nicht auf eine Untersuchung der Blutsubstanz der verschiedenen Stilbekenner... einlassen.*"

251. Häring (see note 246), 180: "[Boden des nordischen Kulturkreises], *den wir damit von den letzten Spuren des Einbruchs reinigen, den vor etwas mehr als 1000 Jahren die gestaltgeberischen Mächte der Mittelmeerkulturen in ihn unternahmen. Freilich meint Sch.-N. gerade diese Einbruchskultur..., als deutscher Mann sich nicht nehmen lassen zu dürfen.*"

252. Paul Schultze-Naumburg, "Tradition," *Die Form* 1, no. 10 (July 1926): 226: "*Man kann bekennen, dass man sich zu der Physiognomie eines Menschen oder Hauses hingezogen oder von ihm abgestossen fühlt.*"

253. Walter Curt Behrendt, "Schlusswort der Schriftleitung," *Die Form* 1, no. 10 (July 1926): 227: *"Spürt der verdiente Verfasser der 'Kulturarbeiten' nicht, dass dieser Formtrieb eine unverkennbare Verwandtschaft aufweist mit jenem Formtrieb, der die Brücken, Silos, Fabriken und Hochöfen geschafften und das Gesicht jener neuen Kulturlandschaft geprägt hat, die er uns im 7. Bande seines Werkes so anschaulich schildert? Deutet diese Verwandtschaft nicht darauf hin, dass hier ein neues Formgefühl, und das heisst doch nichts anderes als eine neue Tradition, im Entstehen begriffen ist?"*

254. In a later essay, Häring continued to use the principle of physiognomy with respect to the cultural expression of races. See "Probleme der Stilbildung," *Deutsche Bauzeitung* 43 (24 October 1934): 841–46, and 47 (21 November 1934): 919–25; reprinted in Heinrich Lauterbach and Jürgen Joedicke, *Hugo Häring: Schriften, Entwürfe, Bauten* (Stuttgart: Karl Krämer, 1965), 35–43, especially 41–43.

255. See Müller-Sievers (note 234).

256. Before Francé, Haeckel had suggested that the world of nature provided a bountiful reservoir of models for the applied arts. His field of study, however, was not botany but zoology, or more precisely microscopic organisms. See, for instance, Haeckel, *Kunstformen der Natur* (Leipzig: Verlag des Bibliographischen Instituts, 1904) and Francé, *Die technischen Leistungen der Pflanzen* (note 232). In other writings, Haeckel also suggested that nature be the model for society and politics in order to solve what he called the "world riddle," while Francé proffered healthy ways of living that were understood to conform to the norms and principles of nature. See Haeckel, *Die Welträtsel: Gemeinverständliche Studien über monistische Philosophie* (Stuttgart: E. Strauss, 1899); translated by Joseph McCabe as *The Riddle of the Universe at the Close of the Nineteenth Century* (New York: Harper & Bros., 1900; reprint, Buffalo: Prometheus Books, 1992). See Francé, *Bios: Die Gesetze der Welt*, 2 vols. (Munich: Franz Hanfstaengl, 1921) and *So musst du leben: Eine Anleitung zum richtigen Leben* (Dresden: Carl Reissner, 1930).

257. Scheffler, *Moderne Baukunst*, 3: *"Was die Wissenschaft, die mit dem Namen Darwin verknüpft ist, vom Leben der Pflanzen, Tiere und Menschen lehrt, kann man sehr wohl auf die Entwicklungsgesetze der Baukunst übertragen."* He characterized the architect as carrying life forces and art ideas into life-forms; see *Moderne Baukunst*, 158.

258. See Caroline van Eck, *Organicism in Nineteenth-Century Architecture: An Inquiry into Its Theoretical and Philosophical Background* (Amsterdam: Architectura & Natura, 1994). Despite van Eck's illuminating treatment of organicism in the nineteenth century as alternatively a strategy of invention and a strategy of interpretation and her persuasive account of its antecedents in Vitruvianism, her conclusion that twentieth-century functionalism marked the end of the organicist tradition appears premature and inadequate to the proliferation as well as persistence of organic metaphors throughout twentieth-century architecture.

The Victory of the New Building Style

The Victory of the
New Building Style

Introduction

Influenced by the powerful spiritual forces in which the creative work of our time is embodied, the mighty drama of a sweeping transformation is taking place before our eyes. It is the birth of the *form of our time*. In the course of this dramatic play—amid the conflict and convulsion of old, now meaningless traditions breaking down and new conventions of thinking and feeling arising—new, previously unknown forms are emerging. Given their congruous features, they can be discussed as the elements of a new style of building.

Though the public regards these new building forms with immediate and visible excitement, their unfamiliar appearance often leads to a feeling of unease and incomprehension. For the public, and at best for those members of the profession who have not been hardened by the dead certitude of a doctrine, only one path leads to a vital understanding of the new architecture. These new forms must be shown to be inevitable, so that they will be seen as a natural consequence and logical result of a changed formulation of the problem.

This is the approach taken in the following remarks. Their aim is to make a broader circle of people familiar with the crucial building problems of the time; to show that these problems concern not purely aesthetic issues or the vain conceits of a company of misfits but rather quite universal and concrete questions. These questions, moreover, are of interest not just to architects but to us all, and they can therefore be discussed in a very specific way.

The New Architectural Form

Let us begin by describing very superficially the exterior attributes of the buildings of the new style, which, owing to a number of unmistakable features, stand out against their surroundings so emphatically. As the accompanying illustrations show, they are usually works with a simple, austere form and a clear organization, with smooth, planar walls, and always with a flat roof and straight profiles. The building body is generally articulated by a more or less lively gradation of masses and by the distribution of windows and openings in the wall surfaces. It is also apparent that the openings, the windows, and occasionally also the balconies (quite contrary to tradition) are placed at the corners of the building, where formerly we were accustomed to seeing the load-bearing parts of the building or the solid masonry of corner piers. Further, we notice that these buildings altogether lack the familiar and

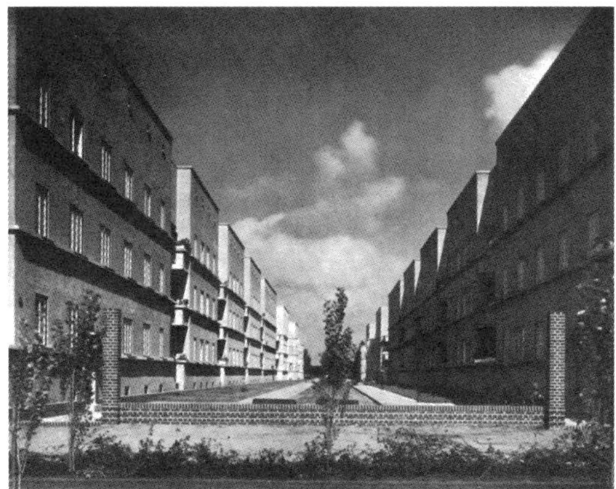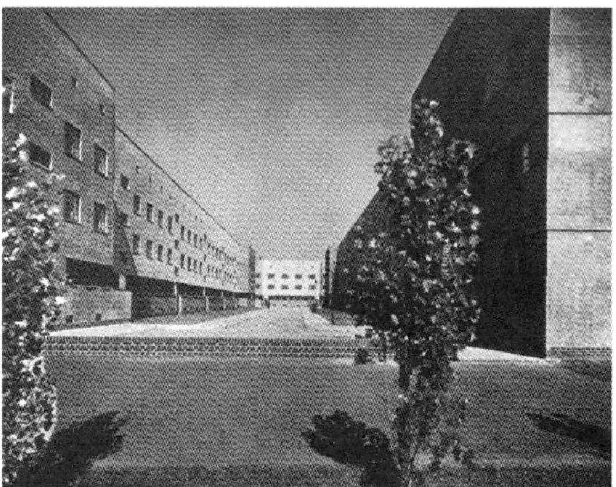

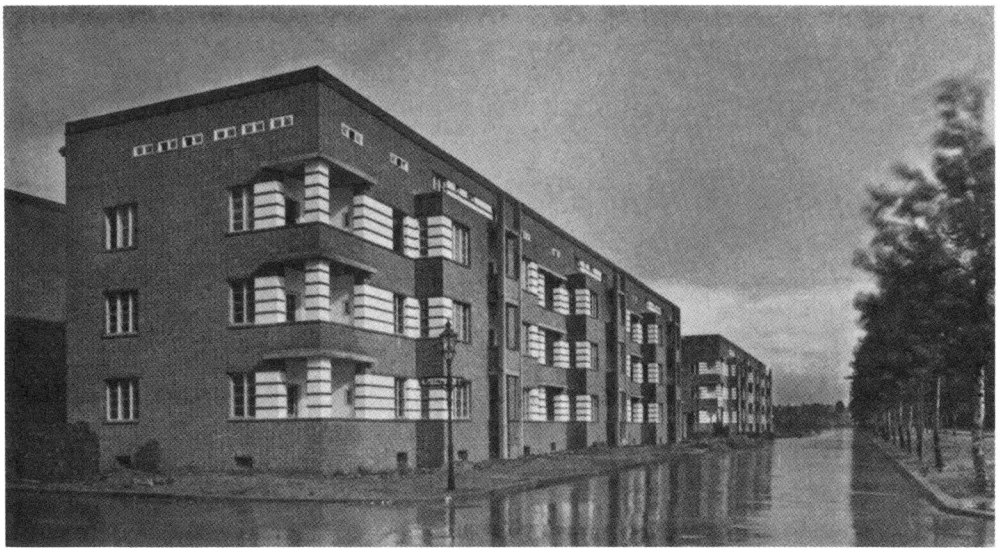

Figs. 1, 2. [Konrad] Rühl, Magdeburg
Residential street, Magdeburg

Fig. 3. Bruno Taut, Berlin
Apartment houses, Berlin

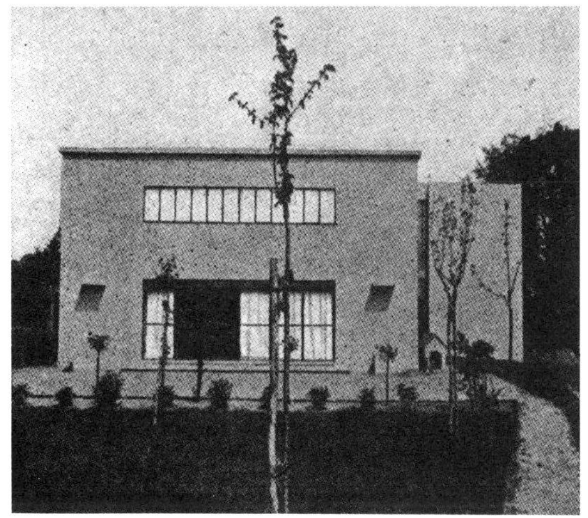

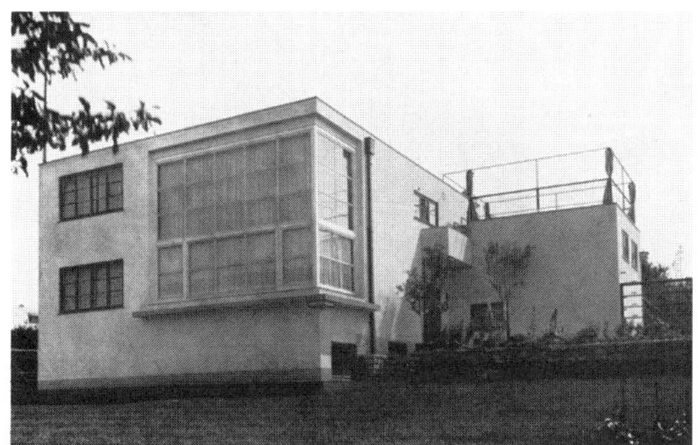

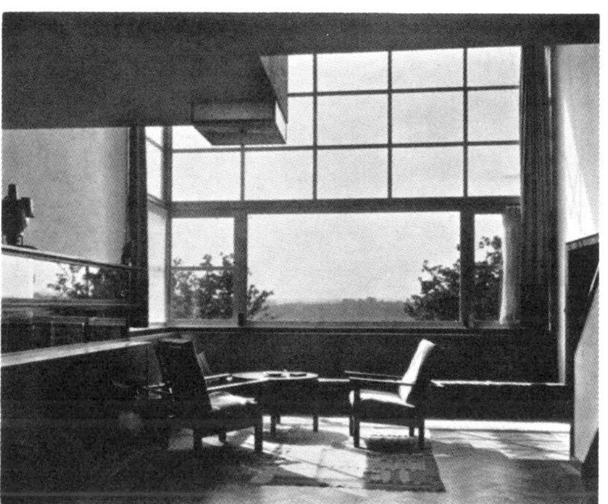

Fig. 4. Le Corbusier, Paris
House [in Vaucresson, near Paris]

Figs. 5, 6. E[rnst] May, Frankfurt am Main
May House, Frankfurt am Main

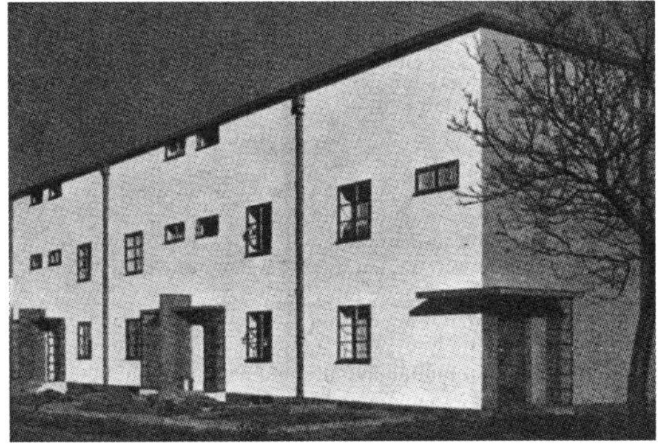

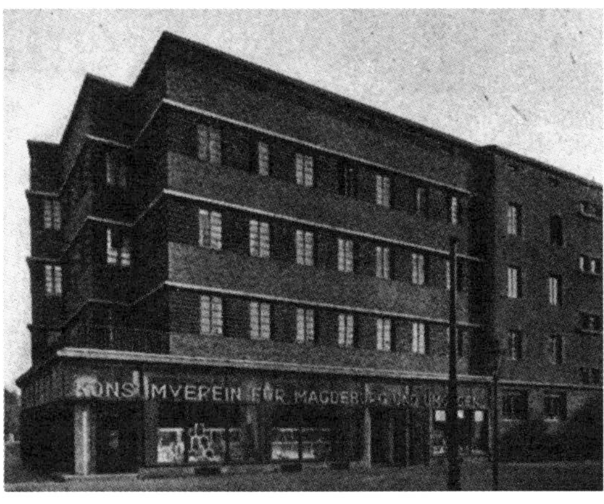

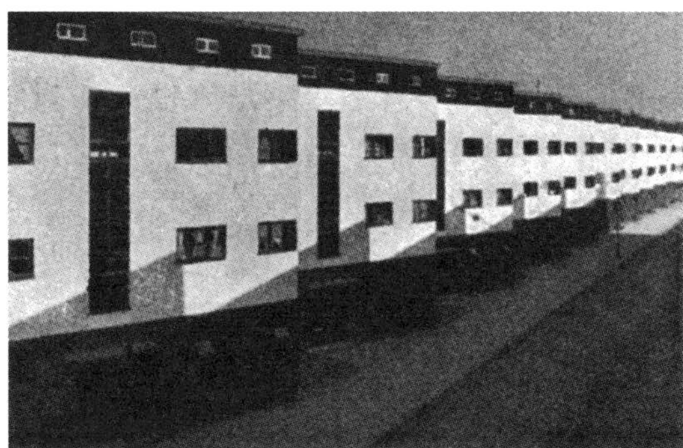

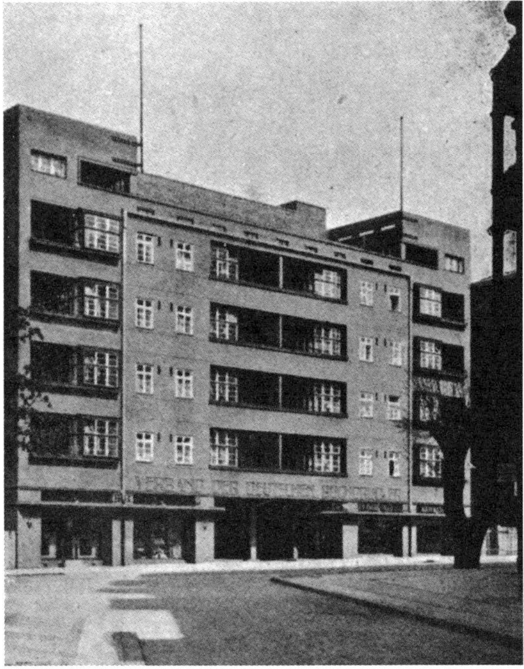

Fig. 7. E[rnst] May
Praunheim, near Frankfurt am Main

Fig. 8. E[rnst] May with [C. H.] Rudloff
Apartment houses, Frankfurt am Main

Fig. 9. [Konrad] Rühl, Magdeburg
Apartment and office building, Magdeburg

Fig. 10. Max Taut, Berlin
Printers' union house, [Berlin]

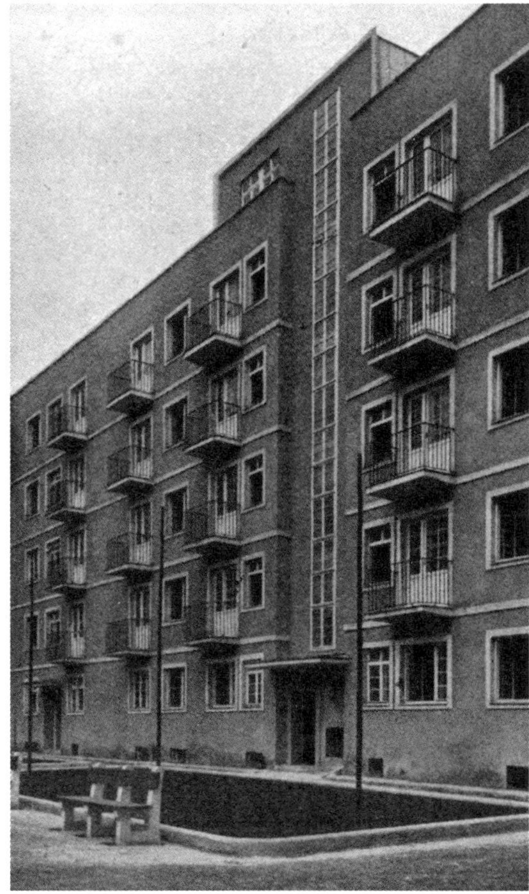

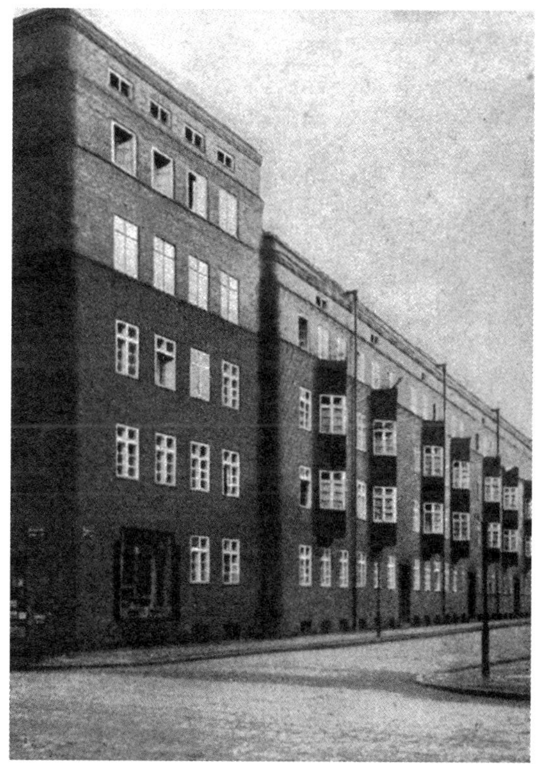

Fig. 11. Theo Effenberger, Breslau
Apartment house, Breslau

Fig. 12. Josef Frank, Vienna
Apartment house, Vienna

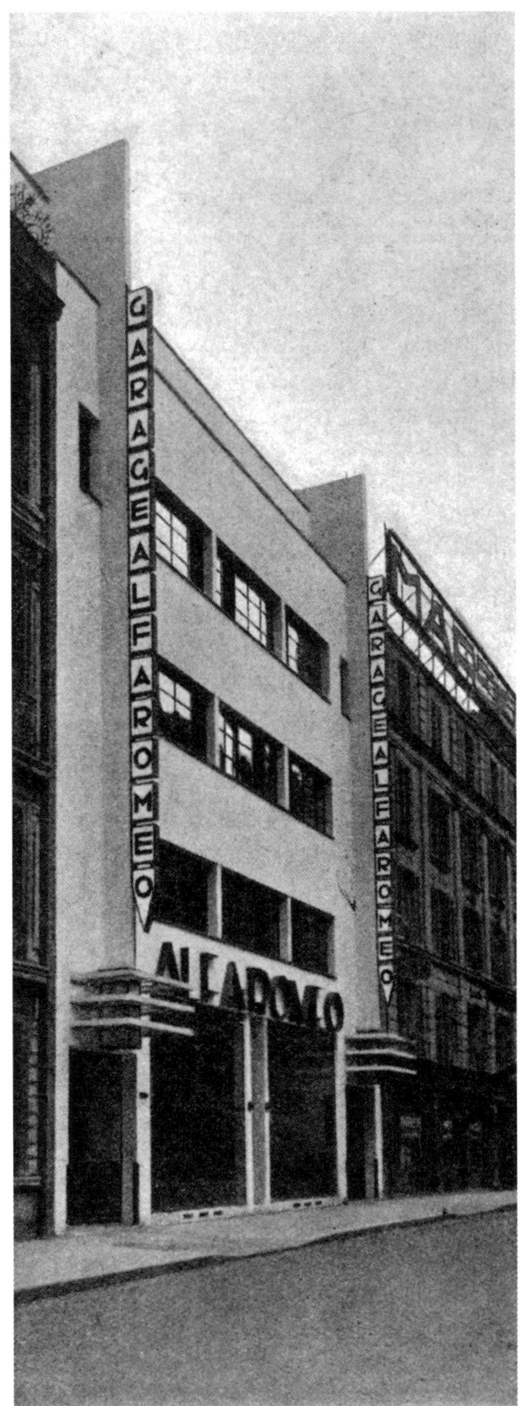

Fig. 13. Robert Mallet-Stevens, Paris
Office building, Paris

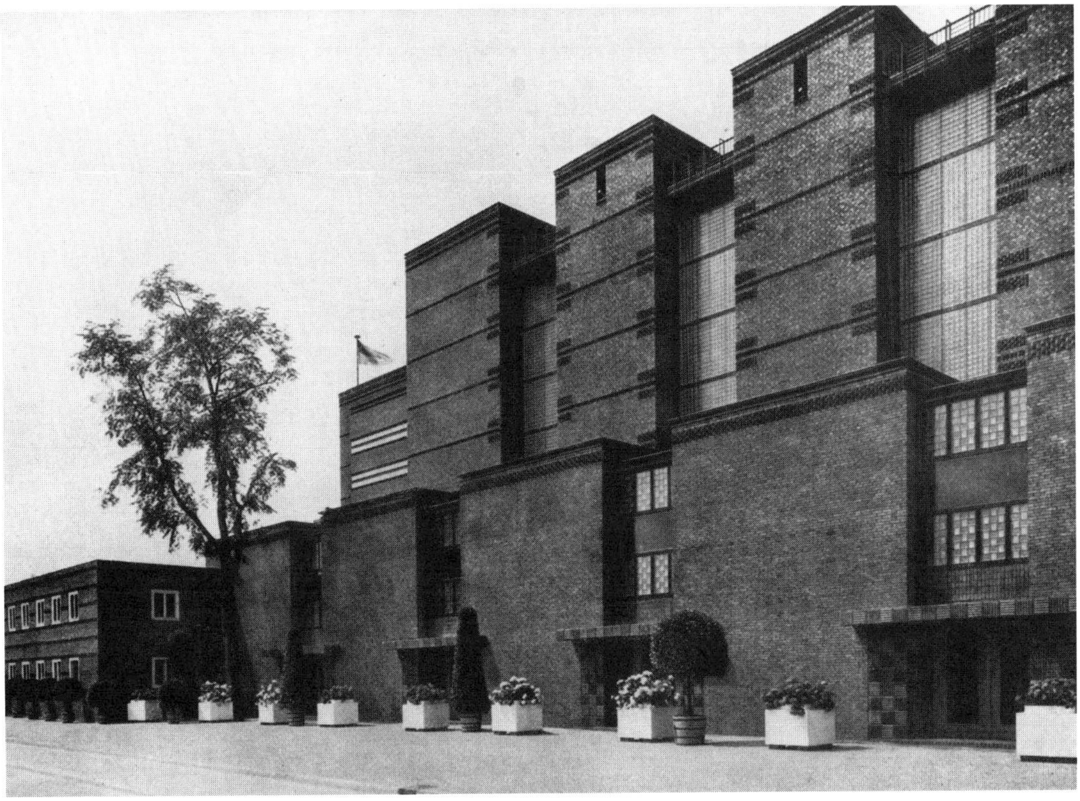

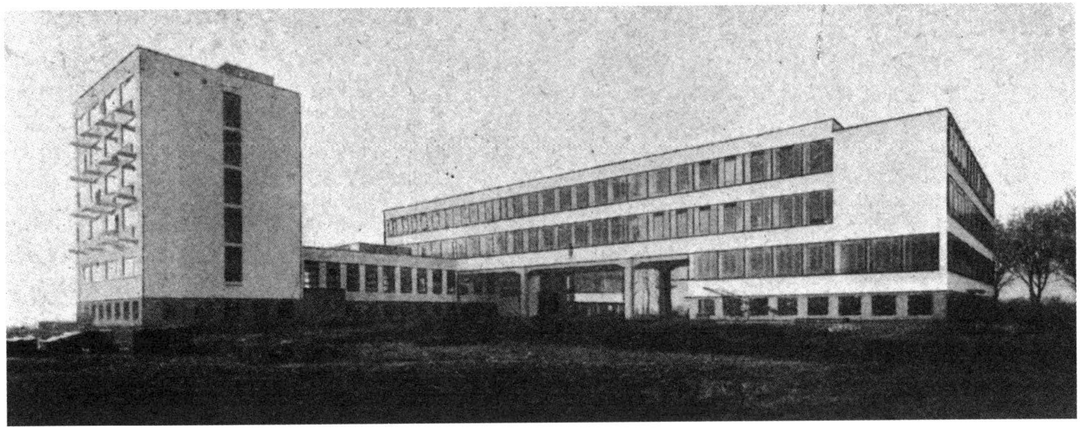

Fig. 14. Johannes Göderitz, Magdeburg
City hall, Magdeburg

Fig. 15. Walter Gropius, Dessau
Classroom building, Dessau Bauhaus

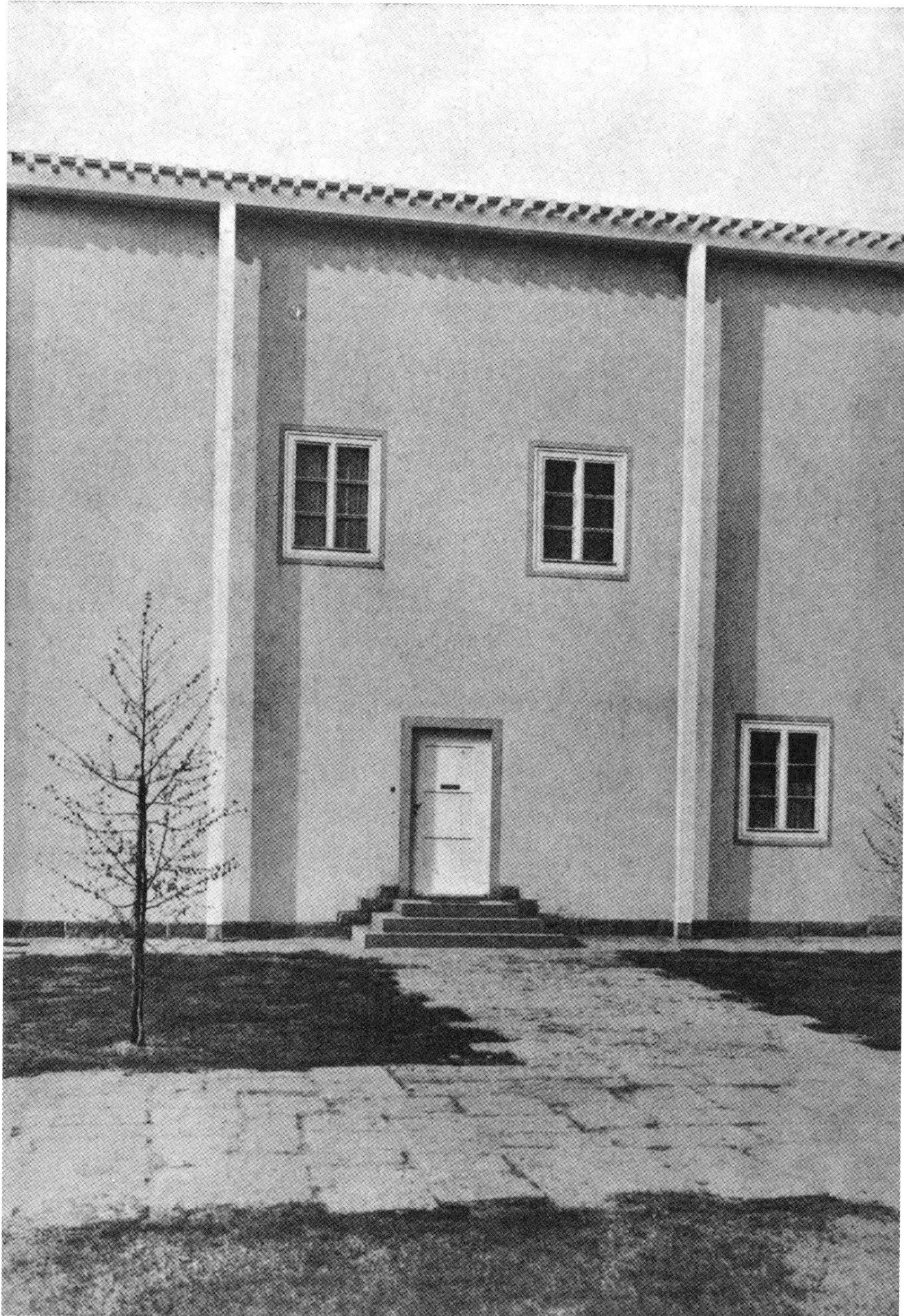

Fig. 16. Hans Tessenow, Berlin
State school, Dresden

customary means of decoration. The advocates of the new building attitude seem to have a particularly keen dislike for the column, that popular show-piece of academic architecture, and they are notably cool toward any kind of ornament or decorative detail. Ornament—the decorative accessory, the detail in the old sense—has completely disappeared. They prefer smooth walls and consciously exploit the wall's planar attributes as an architectural design tool. They compose simple building bodies, which are themselves plastically articulated, and create a powerfully punctuated rhythm of movement by linear accents or occasionally by overhanging slabs and deeply shaded projections, which emphasize and strengthen the impression of the corporal, the spatial, and the three-dimensional.

The most curious and striking feature of the new architecture is the absence of any kind of exterior ornament, which is then usually the first criticism leveled against it. This is completely understandable. In many areas of our life today we stand under the crippling weight of traditional views that cloud our judgment. Our artistic judgment is also greatly confused by the widespread superstition that art is synonymous with decoration. This deeply rooted belief makes it inevitable that not only the lay world but also professionals look upon the unadorned and therefore unfamiliar works of the new architecture as cold and dry, raw and unfinished, purely and simply as inartistic. They miss in these buildings the familiar charm of decorations. They are put off by linear, hard, and angular forms. And we must concede that such a limited judgment is to some extent justified, that the buildings of the new style do lack the effect of the pleasing, the artistic, the emotional that was evoked by the sensuous charm of detail in historical works.

The Opponents

Next, let us speak of the opponents of the new architecture. They can be divided into three groups, of which the most dangerous are the *opportunists*. With the skill of all profiteers, they make the outward characteristics of the new art their own, and with an adroitness unique to them, they know how to express themselves in that idiom *as well*. They discredit the new movement with their catchphrase "form without ornament," chosen purely for its assonance, thereby evoking with their spiteful slogan the specter of a new formalism, which, even with its algebraic sign changed, is no better than any other.

Of the other two groups, one consists of the opponents of principle, the opponents out of conviction, who regard themselves as the guardians or supporters of sanctified traditions and who use this sentiment to oppose the emerging new style. They see the traditional rules of their academic teachings and the laws of their professional judgment overturned by the works of the new building style, and therefore call for resisting the spread of such subversive radicalism. With these opponents, there can be no quarrel. Their case is hopeless; they misconstrue the idea of tradition. They fail to see that this idea, if it means preserving inherited possessions, also entails the mass of traditional and still-unresolved problems that must be addressed and, whenever

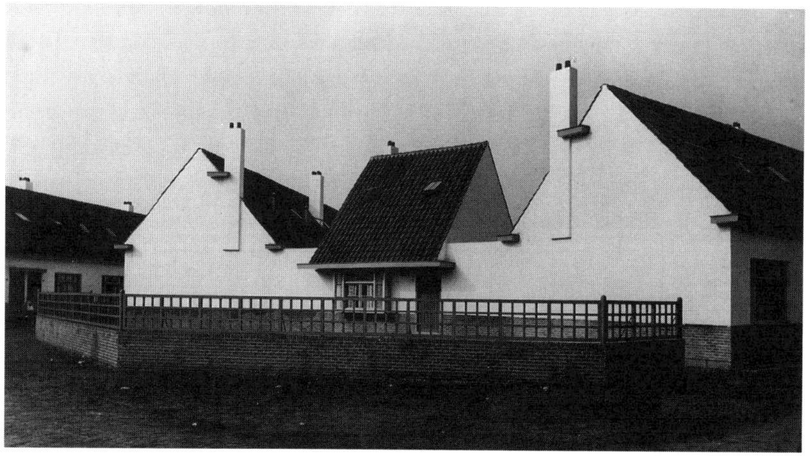

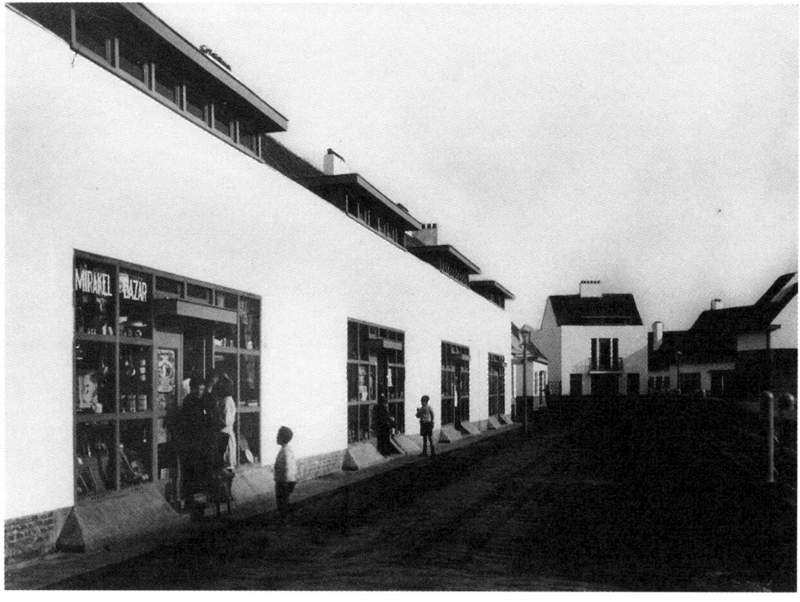

Figs. 17, 18. J. J. P. Oud, Rotterdam
Oud-Mathenesse housing estate, near Rotterdam

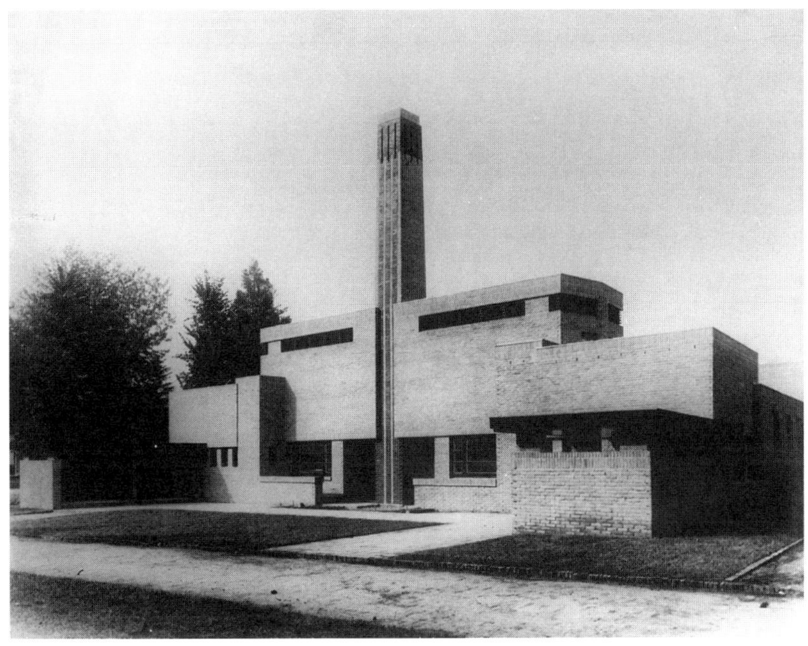

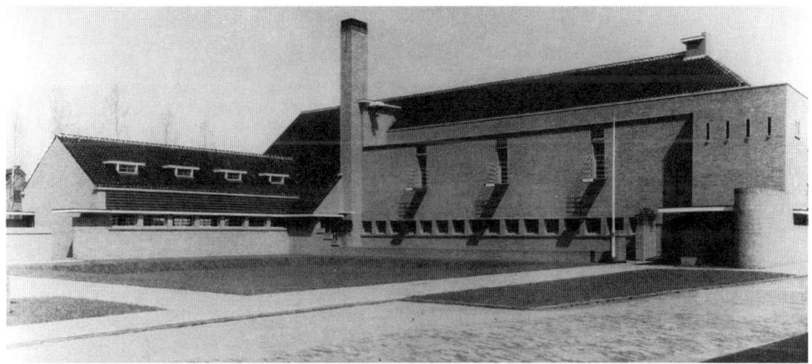

Fig. 19. W[illem Marinus] Dudok, Hilversum
Swimming pool, Hilversum

Fig. 20. W[illem Marinus] Dudok, Hilversum
School, Hilversum

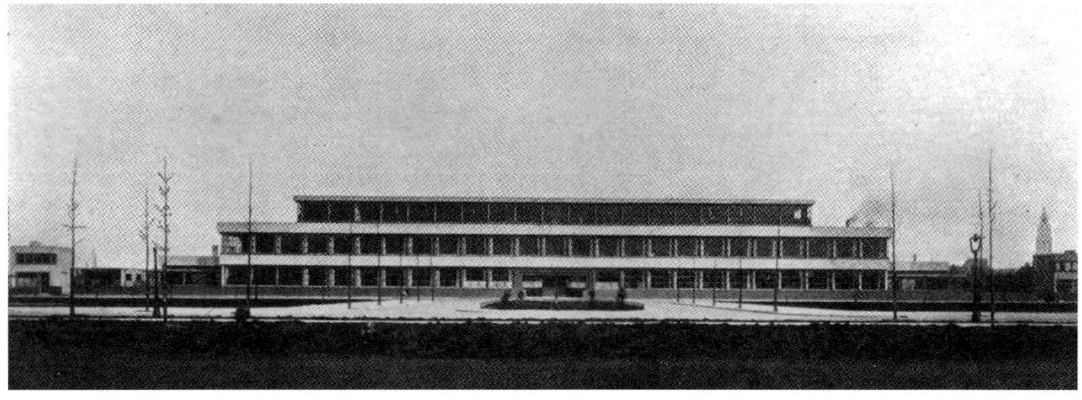

Fig. 21. [L. C.] van der Vlugt and [Jan] Wiebenga, Rotterdam
Arts and crafts school, Groningen

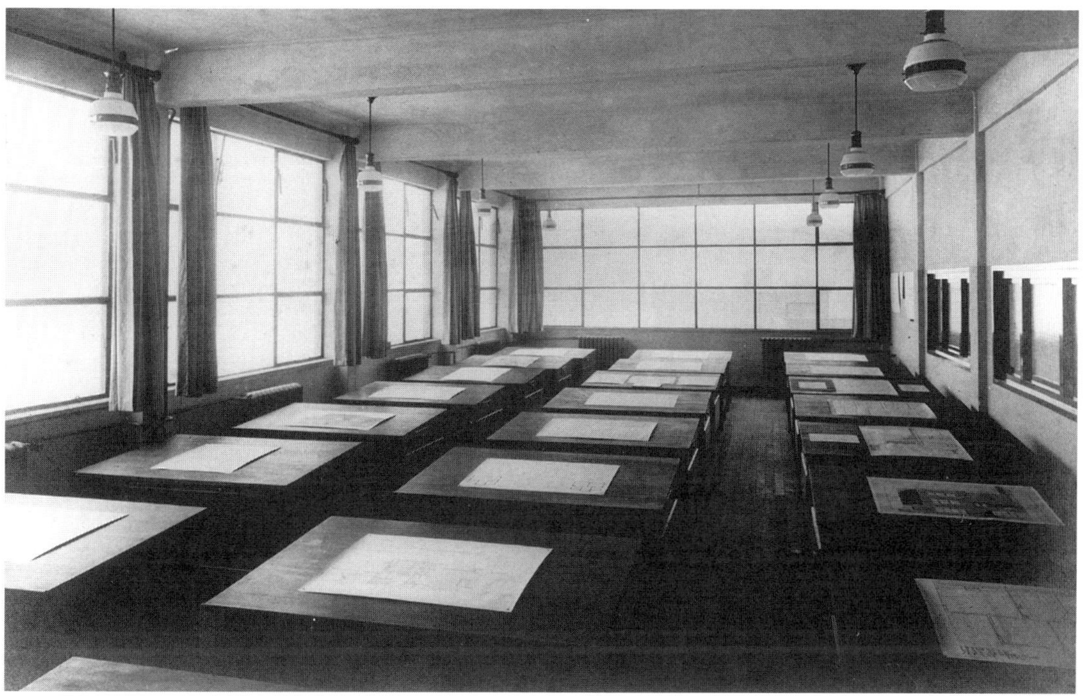

Fig. 22. [L. C.] van der Vlugt and [Jan] Wiebenga, Rotterdam
Drafting room, arts and crafts school, Groningen

possible, brought closer to a solution. These faithful followers of tradition sense nothing of the change of form; they know nothing of the profound meaning of "*Stirb und werde*" (Die and become); they fail to understand that every construction entails destruction, that "both the man who destroys and the man who builds are manifestations of will: one prepares the work; the other finishes it."

The other group is more benign and is not hardened by basic principles. They regard the works of the new architecture as the harmless folly of the artist and see it only as one of several new artistic fashions that have rapidly succeeded one another in the last few years.

This supposed artistic fashion is, by the way, not as altogether harmless as it appears to these more restrained opponents, as evinced by the concern it has meanwhile aroused in parliamentary circles. A short time ago a faction in the Prussian Diet, responding to the perfectly understandable interests of its constituents, addressed an interpellation to the state government, in which it pointed out "that because of the fashion of straight-line forms in house building as well as in interior furnishings, the carving and wood-turning trades suffer from severe unemployment." Because quality craftsmen in these noble artistic professions are in danger of becoming extinct, the state government has been asked whether it is prepared to promote the two affected trades by awarding contracts, and with that, as it literally goes on to say, "to change the trend of fashion." This heroic attempt in the name of art to appeal to the salvation of the middle class has something touching about it, but it misconstrues the situation if it considers a far-reaching artistic movement to be a frivolous artistic fashion hostile to the middle class, which can be most quickly and effectively rendered harmless by awarding state contracts.

The Style Movement

The efforts to renew architecture examined here concern a spiritual movement, not a fleeting artistic fashion or some new "ism." The originality of this movement and its intimate connection with the spiritual life of our time is well attested to by its international character—the fact that it has arisen in various countries simultaneously and with similar goals. Manifestations of this movement, with certain nuances conditioned by national characteristics, can be found in America as well as in almost every European country: in Germany and Holland, in Austria and Czechoslovakia, in Italy, France, and Russia.

There can be no better evidence for the living relevance of the ideas that support this movement. A movement so elemental and so widespread internationally, which has arisen spontaneously in various places with similar goals, may hardly be considered a transitory and thus frivolous artistic fashion. But neither will a purely aesthetic consideration of its achievements up to now allow us to appreciate its aims. We cannot properly evaluate the creations of this new building attitude using the more or less casual sympathies or antipathies of personal taste. To understand their nature, we must

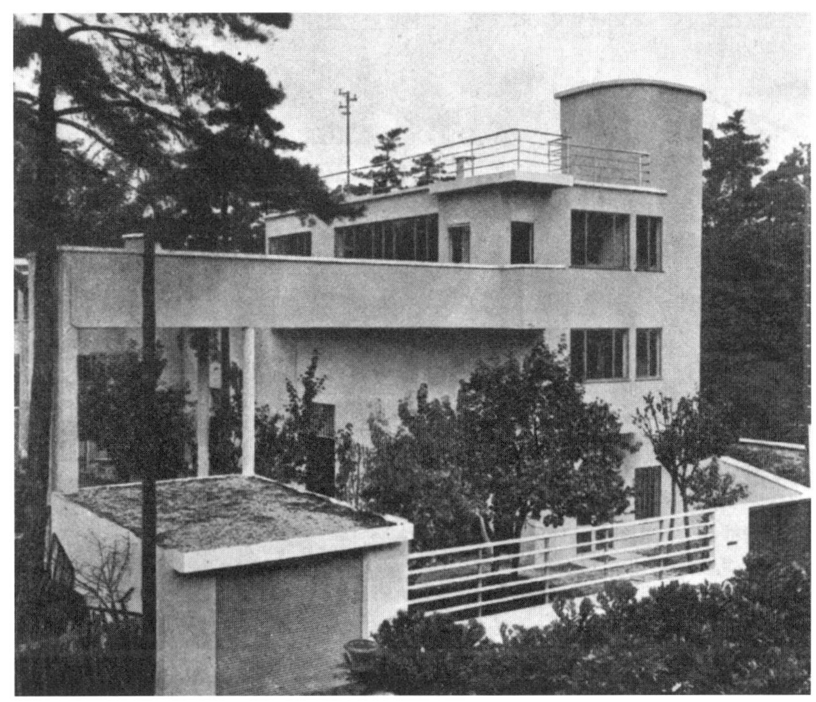

Fig. 23. Le Corbusier, Paris
House in Pessac

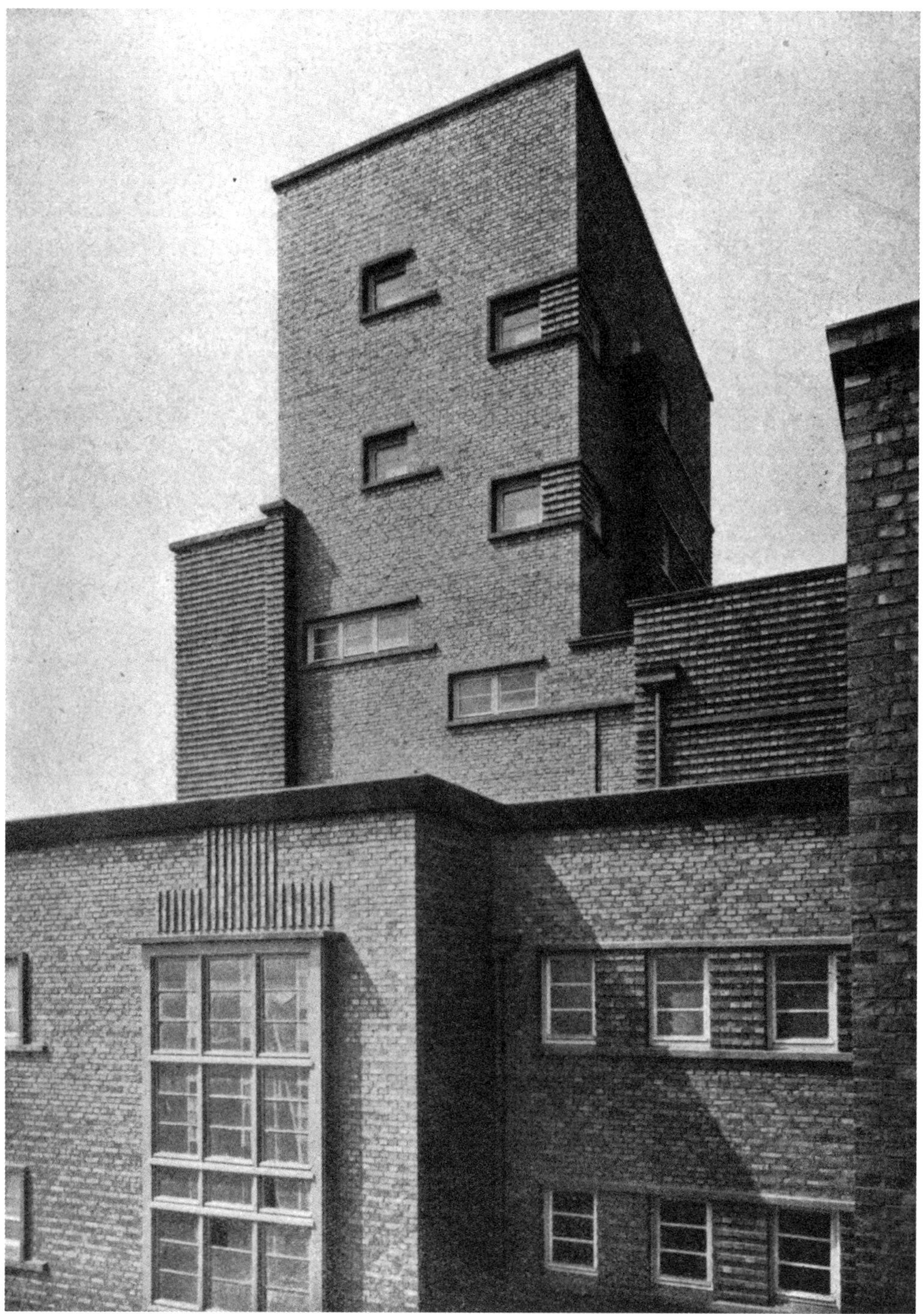

Fig. 24. Alfred Fischer[-Essen], Essen
Municipal offices, Hans-Sachs-Haus, Gelsenkirchen

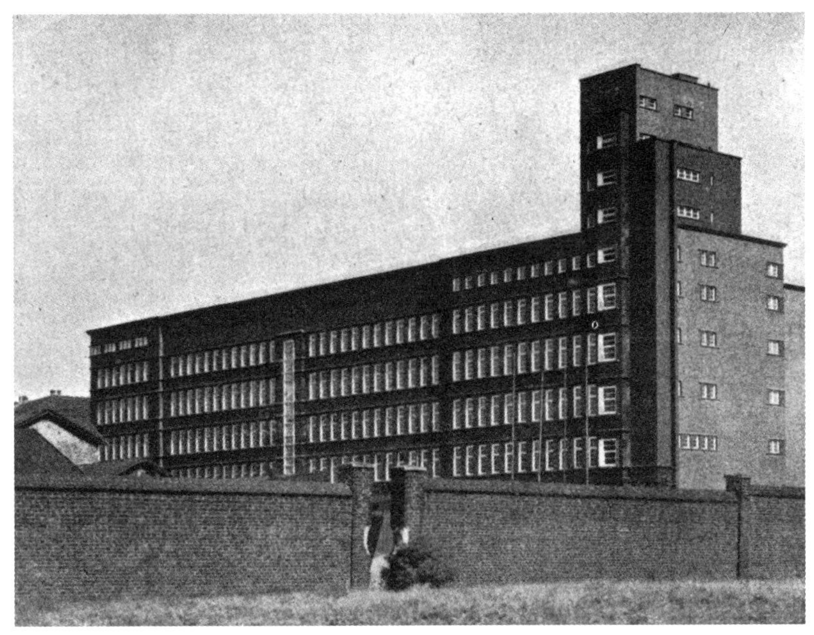

Fig. 25. Alfred Fischer[-Essen], Essen
Municipal offices, Hans-Sachs-Haus, Gelsenkirchen

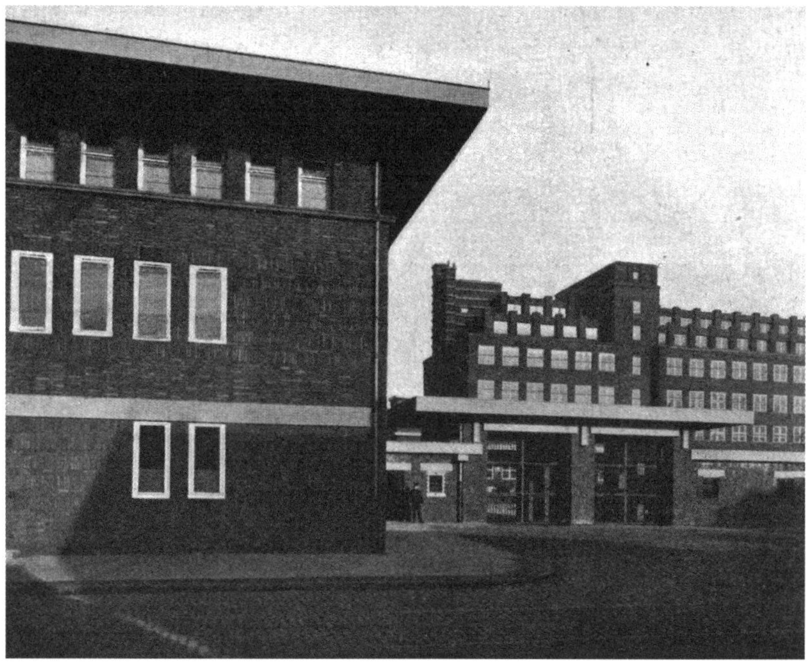

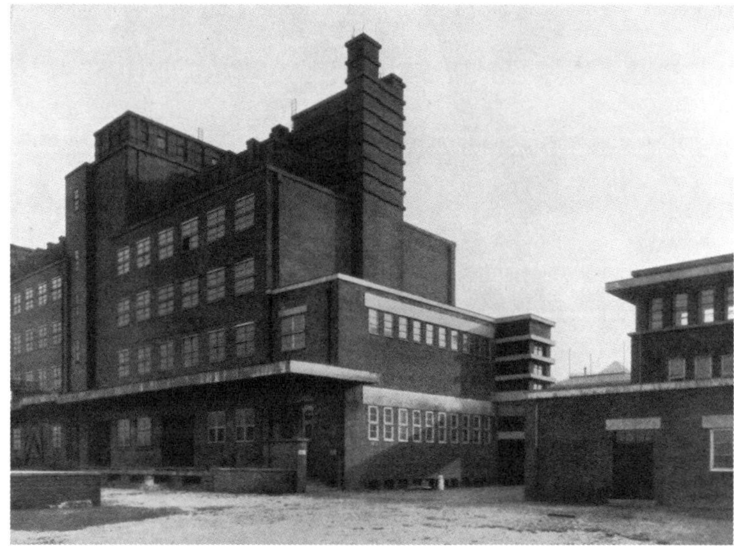

Figs. 26, 27. Peter Behrens, Berlin
Offices and warehouse of the Gute Hoffnungshütte, Oberhausen

probe deeper and seek out, above all, the spiritual ambience in which this movement has grown.

What supports and drives the new movement is neither a craze for innovation nor some cheap need for sensation, such as the desire to impress or do something different no matter what. Rather, it is the opposite. It is the will to return to basic principles and elementary rules of building and once again to build exactly as the ancients did. It is the desire to come to terms with the new realities of our time and the new life they entail. It is the endeavor to shape these new realities spiritually and to master them *creatively through design* [*gestaltend, durch Gestaltung*]. It is the striving to free ourselves from the stifling burden of now meaningless traditions and rigid ideas of form and thus to work unselfconsciously, free of prejudice, and with originality—just as is happening everywhere today in those creative fields where mass production defines the face of our time. It is the longing to enrich architecture with the same creative approach to design that rules in our technical and individually produced work, and thereby to make architecture once again a productive and vital part of our time.

It is therefore a very modern striving, a very natural and understandable desire, and a thoroughly unromantic longing! It is a striving that pursues a vital and most relevant task, one supported by the knowledge that everything shaped at a given time is born out of one and the same instinct, one and the same sense of form. It struggles to reclaim this lost unity today by attempting to place artistic creation at the same spiritual wellspring from which the new wealth of forms in technical design have arisen. It is a striving that, once it attains its goal, will ultimately bring about that unity of formal expression that has always been the unerring feature of any style.

Let us now examine it in somewhat greater detail.

Technical Design

In all creative fields having nothing to do with art, or rather in those areas untouched by the direct influence and intervention of art (which is to say in all fields of technical design), a formative power is at work today that has created an entire world of new, previously unknown forms. The wealth of these forms is immeasurable, and the richness and diversity of these new things belie the frequently heard complaint about our era's poverty of design and lack of formative power. At the same time, however, precisely the wealth of this new store of forms arising around us in every field of technical design clearly confirms the memorable words of Conrad Fiedler, who once said that not all times express the *best* of what they have to say in *art*. The formal energy of our time is certainly not lesser or weaker than in times past (no one can dispute that, given our many creations), but our design potential up to now has not manifested itself most strongly and purely in art, but rather in the fields of applied art or in technical and industrial production.

All these many forms of technical design—our machines and mechanical devices, our instruments and utensils, our modern vehicles, ships, airplanes,

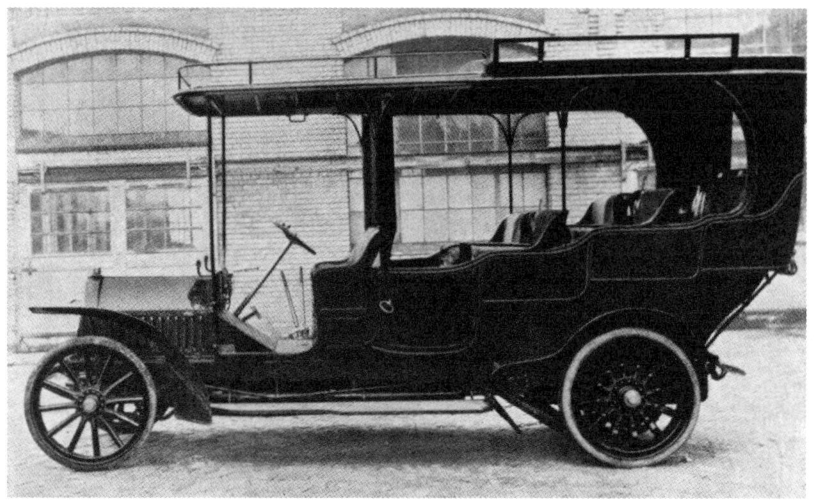

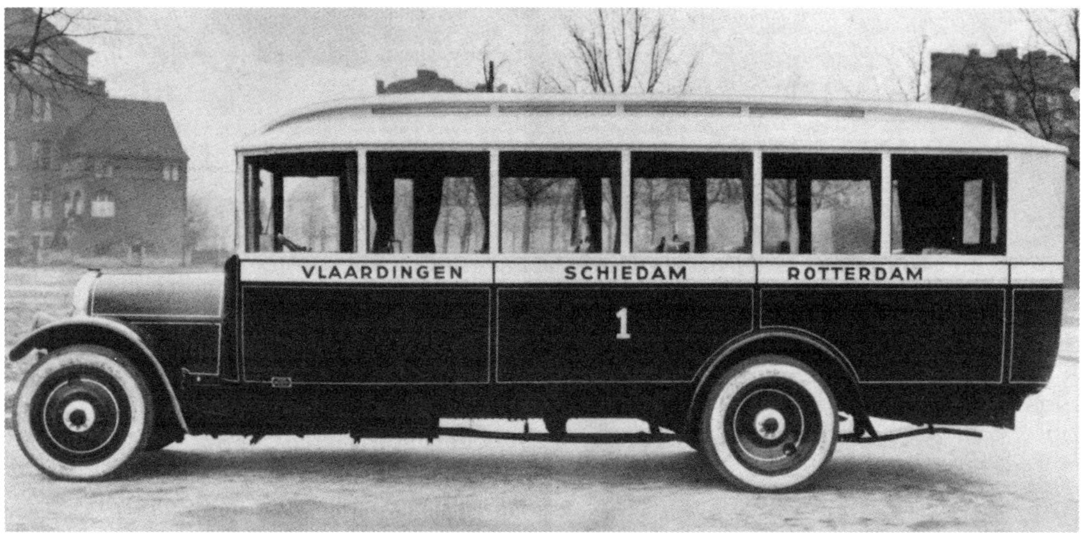

Fig. 28. Older-type motorcoach by NAG, Berlin-Oberschönweide

Fig. 29. Modern motorcoach
Body by Lange & Gutzeit, Berlin

automobiles, and so on—are functional forms. They were created with a specific performance standard in mind, and to fulfill a purpose most perfectly. This goal was not achieved overnight or at first try: every goal presumes a path. So too these forms, advancing progressively toward a given goal from trial to trial and result to result, were very gradually extracted, developed, and shaped from others, always more rigorously and more exactly accommodated to new production processes, machine methods, and the specific limits of the material and construction, yet always with a greater knowledge of and clearer insight into the performance standard.

In the individual stages of this form selection, we can also clearly follow how the sense of form became simultaneously refined and perfected with a greater awareness of the performance standard. The formal evolution of locomotives, airplanes, and automobiles that we are witnessing today firsthand (figs. 28, 29) vividly illustrates this process.

All these forms, as we said, are *functional creations* [*Zweckgebilde*]. Selecting their appropriate form is not an aesthetic problem but a constructional one. Nevertheless, these forms contain a whole series of aesthetic elements: clean and precise lines, the consummate purity of their proportions, the taut tension of their flat and curved surfaces, the colorfulness of their paints and varnishes, and the sparkling sheen of their finishes. The aesthetic elements of these creations are so numerous that it is typically said that the elegant styling of a modern luxury automobile can be considered a handicraft creation of our time, just as a royal carriage of Frederick the Great was for the age of the Rococo. Thus these aesthetic elements may be seen, if not already as elements of a new style in themselves, then as the yeasts or starting points for the formation of such.

If architecture, which is itself predominantly a field of technical design, today seeks again to orient itself to these methods of form selection, if in this effort at orientation it begins to emulate those aesthetic elements apparent in the creations of technical design, it does not do so in a superficial, formal sense by simply imitating these forms. This would only be a new kind of formalism, the visible manifestations of which have been, very appropriately, termed "Machine Romanticism"! It should, on the contrary, be a conscious renunciation of every formalism. Likewise, the new architectural attitude no longer regards form simply as an aesthetic problem, but at the same time and decidedly as a constructional one. I mean this not in a naturalistic sense or as some form of Constructivism, that is to say, neither the now-fashionable dogma of Russian descent nor the older teachings of a faded materialism from the time of Viollet-le-Duc and the Neogothic school, which saw form as a product of purpose, material, and construction. Rather, it should be taken quite literally: "to construct" [*konstruieren*] derives from the Latin verb *construere,* meaning "to invent, to deduce, to shape, to form, to *design*."

Modern Utility Buildings

It is no coincidence that, in architecture as well, new and previously unknown forms were created on precisely those occasions when a form was selected in the objective and impersonal way of a technical design, as a constructional problem — that is, with the tasks of the modern *utility building:* factories, workshops, warehouses, silos, water towers, and so on. Here the building was dealt with strictly under the constraints of a specific and clearly defined performance standard, which, moreover, appeared rigid and implacable in its economic demands. The nature and character of these building tasks entail the pressing demand to seek a solution irrespective of any representational, artistic, or decorative intentions, with a frank regard for the performance standard. They also make full use of the new manufacturing processes, the new material limits and methods of construction, and they stand in a conscious, logical, and systematic compliance with these new realities. And it has happened that completely new forms have been developed first with those tasks of industrial building that, with respect to the technical selection of form, were conceived and executed *constructionally* and *creatively.* They are fundamentally new forms that also unmistakably carry the new aesthetic elements. They are forms of a new architecture style that, as it cannot be otherwise, display in their nature an inner kinship with, in their effect an unmistakable similarity to, the aesthetic elements seen in the new creations of technical design (figs. 32–35).

New Realities

In order to approach the new style's formal problems — to discern them more clearly and grasp them more vividly — we must now inquire into the *new realities of our time* with which the *architect* today has to come to terms in his approach to design.

What are these realities?

The *first reality* is a series of new tools, new machines, and new methods of construction. To deny their existence would be self-delusion; to reject their use would be a waste of energy. Using mechanical means of production for the entire building industry (and not just for civil engineering, where it has long been adopted) is an economic necessity. The industrialization of the building industry will certainly find acceptance on an ever-larger scale and at an accelerating pace, at least within the field of housing, which provides for the needs of the masses. Although trained artisans and specialists are essential to many commissions in the building trades, and especially cultural and luxury buildings, and although future building will remain also in large part a highly skilled and seasoned trade, trained personnel in many fields are nevertheless being replaced more and more by machines and industrial technologies.

Further realities are a number of new building materials, such as iron, concrete, and glass. Previously these materials were either altogether unknown or not used to the same extent or in the same way as today. With their adoption

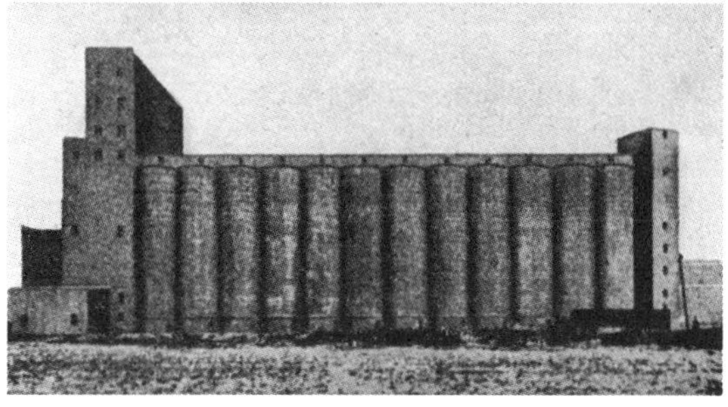

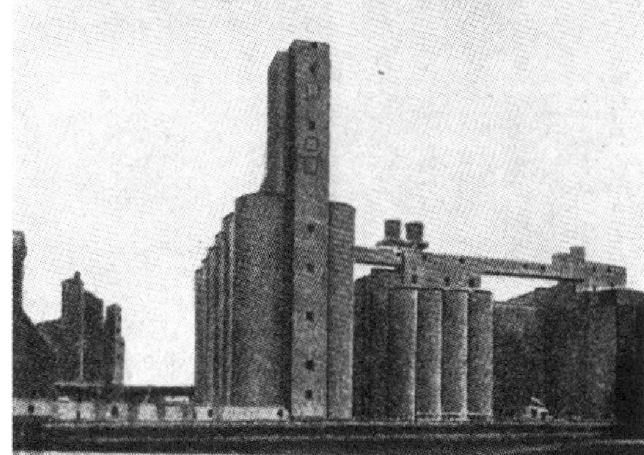

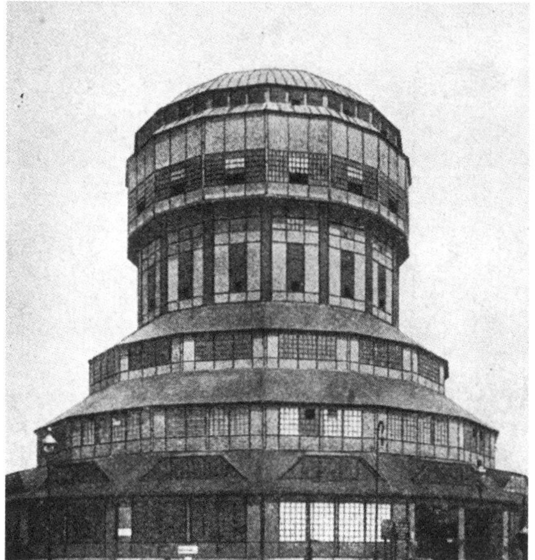

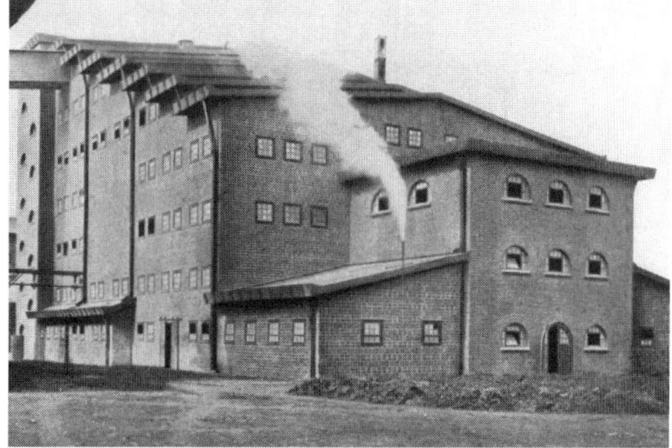

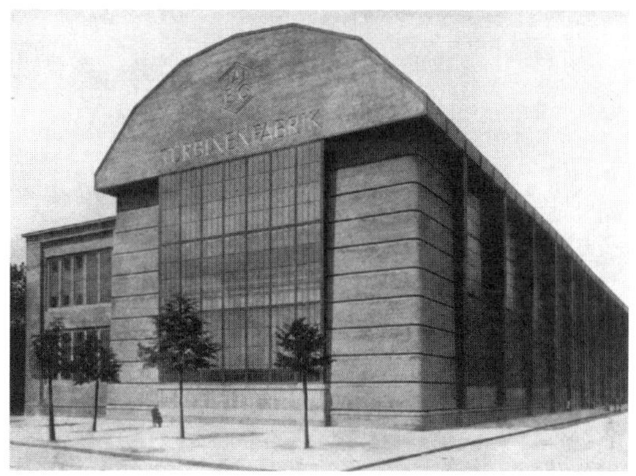

Fig. 30. [South] American grain silo

Fig. 31. Silo in Buffalo

Fig. 32. Hans Poelzig, Potsdam-Wildpark
Water tower, Posen

Fig. 33. Hans Poelzig, Potsdam-Wildpark
Sulfur phosphate factory, Luban, Silesia

Fig. 34. Peter Behrens, Berlin
AEG turbine hall, Huttenstrasse, Berlin

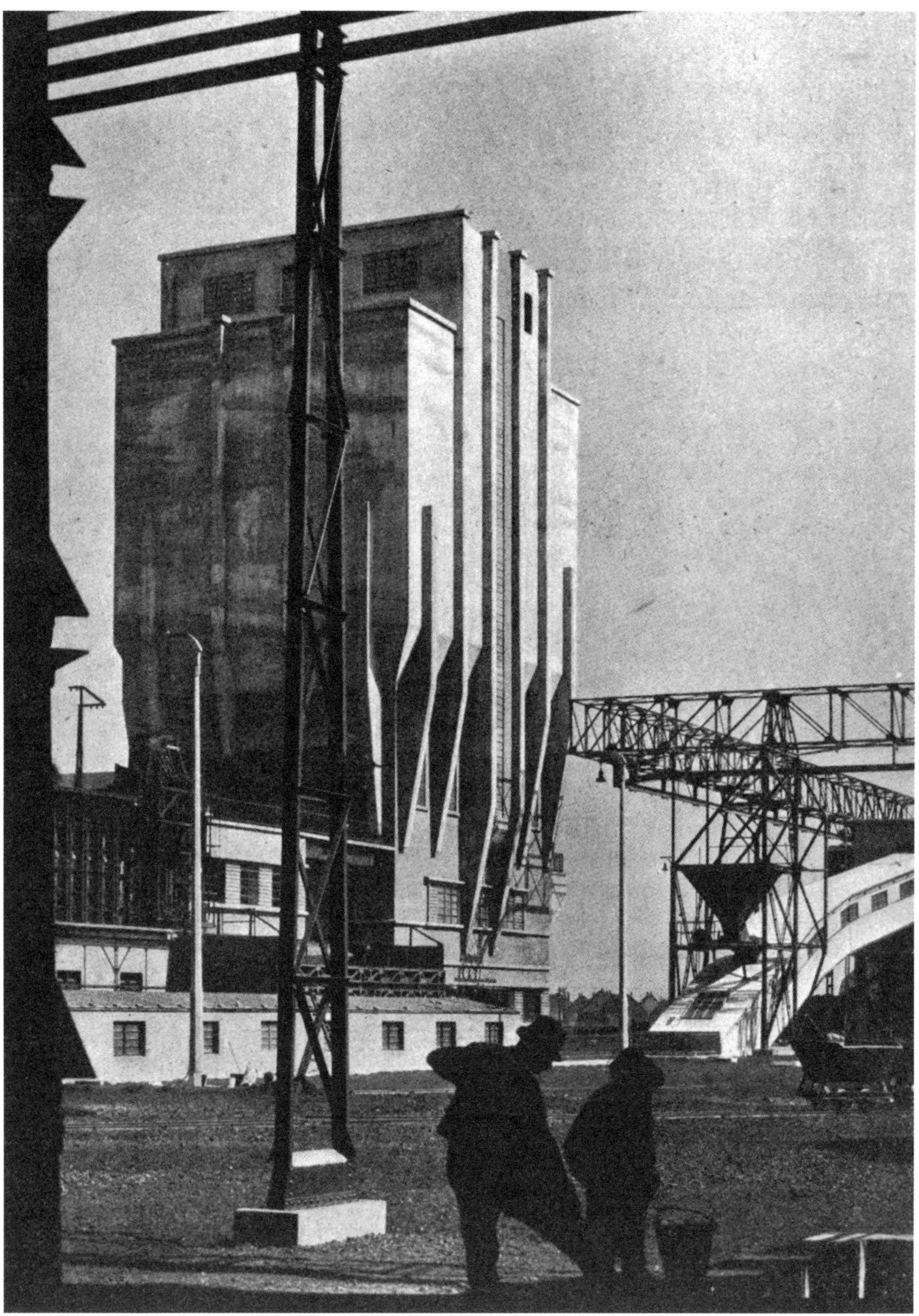

Fig. 35. Alfred Fischer[-Essen], Essen
Coal tower, Saxon mine, Hamm, Westphalia

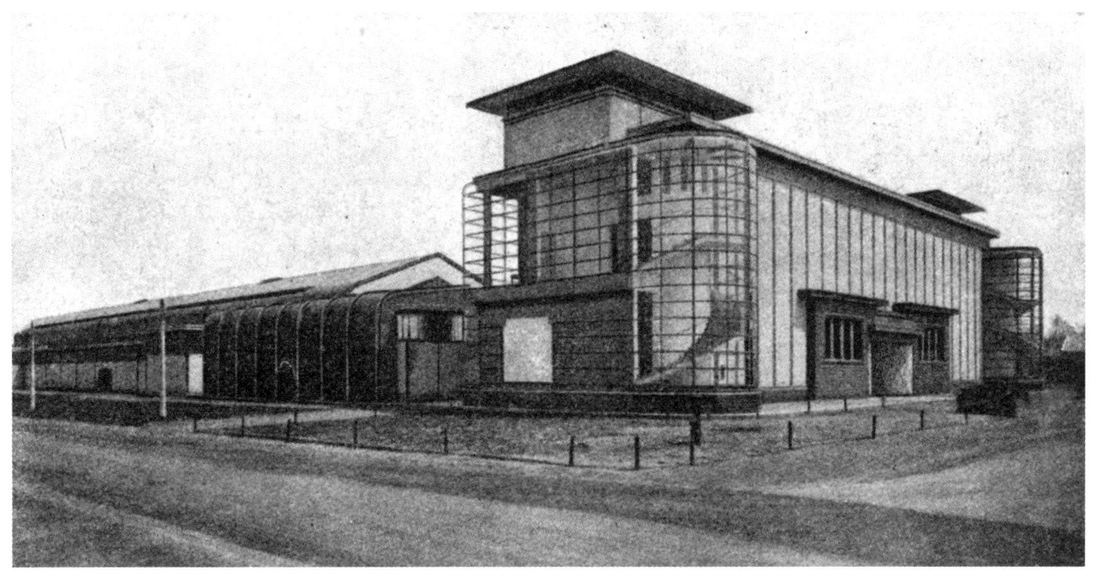

Fig. 36. Walter Gropius, Dessau
Factory building, German Werkbund exhibition 1914, Cologne

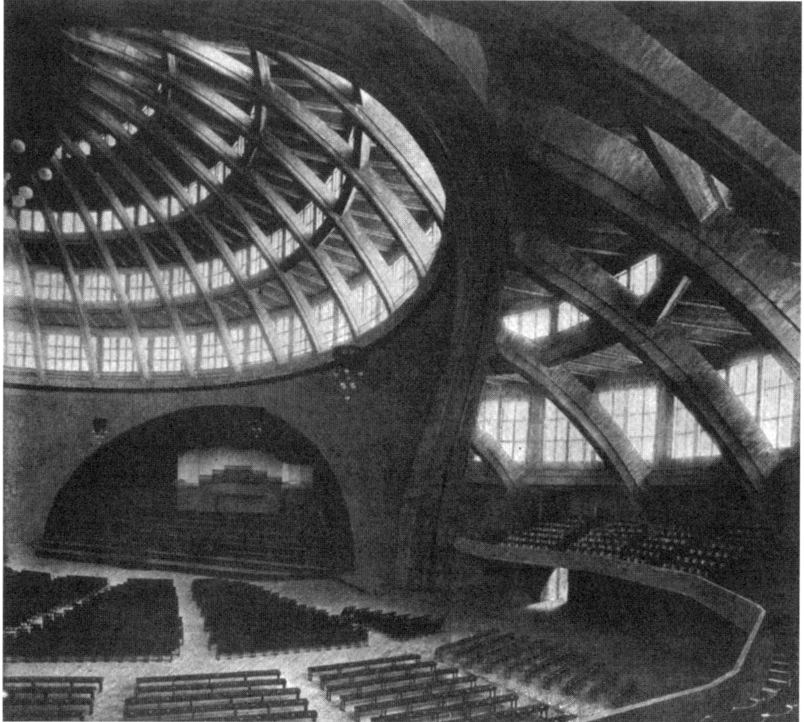

Fig. 37. Max Berg, Berlin
Interior of Century Hall, 1913, Breslau

and use, however, they have fundamentally altered traditional building and construction practices.

With these new realities, architecture has been enriched *first of all materially* with a number of new possibilities. To mention just one of these achievements (perhaps not the most important in its nature but the most obvious in its effect), the scale of building today, thanks to the inventiveness of the engineer, far exceeds the limits formerly imposed on it, because of the new methods of iron and reinforced-concrete construction. In fact, every shackle in this regard has been undone. These new construction methods, whose influence has recently also become evident in expanded possibilities for wood construction, make it possible to span the greatest openings and create almost unlimited spaces with no internal supports (fig. 37).

In addition to this material enrichment, however, the adoption of new building materials and construction processes has *also* induced a *spiritual upheaval*. The introduction of these materials and processes has changed completely the basic principles of building—spatial ideas as well as structural concepts. This upheaval is no less far-reaching in its effects than the change of perspectives that took place in medieval building with the invention of the Gothic vault. As with that invention, the upheaval has raised a whole series of formal problems.

Specialization of the Building Profession: The Engineers

It is rather remarkable that these new problems, several of which we will shortly consider in greater detail, were scarcely considered until now, and that they are still not recognized in most works of contemporary architecture. This is true even though the new means of expression have been eagerly accepted everywhere, and every material enrichment has been used extensively. To seek in passing an explanation for this remarkable fact, we might note that the development, refinement, and application of new construction processes have been almost exclusively the concern of *engineers*. Systematic investigation of the technical and structural properties of new building materials required extensive theoretical and mathematical knowledge, which could only be acquired through detailed and time-consuming specialization. Therefore, the engineer has developed alongside the architect as a specialist in the technical and constructional tasks of building. Thus the principle of the division of labor, which has had a decisive effect on the industrial production of our time, has also found acceptance in the building trades, much to the detriment of architecture.

Specialization in the building profession, incidentally, took place very early. First, in the field of military engineering the task of building fortifications became a specialized branch of architecture. Then, with the founding of the École des Ponts et Chaussées (School of bridges and roads) in Paris in 1747, the fields of hydraulic and road construction were excluded from the sphere of architects and assigned to specially trained experts, *architectes constructeurs*. In the course of the nineteenth century additional branches, especially those related to transportation, were also removed from the sphere of architects. Bridge building evolved into a private concern of engineers; train stations and factory buildings were handed over to them; and in recent decades all new and truly vital building tasks have devolved to them. By contrast, the architect for his part has now evolved into a specialist or virtuoso of decoration: seeking the solution to his task in amassing ready-made decorative forms and making new variations on the five column orders. In this preoccupation with employing decoration with the greatest virtuosity, the architect has completely forgotten construction, design, and building. This fatal one-sidedness has caused him to lose sight totally of the many formal problems that have since been raised by the new realities of our time.

New Formal Problems

From the wealth of these new formal problems let us single out a few of the most elementary cases to illustrate the nature of the new design tasks. One is the example of *load and supports,* the other is that of the *wall.*

The adoption of iron and reinforced-concrete construction has radically altered the traditional *relationship of load and supports*. The development of so-called *cantilevered construction* has combined the formerly discrete building elements of beams and columns: if not as one homogeneous element (as in concrete construction), then into a unit welded together with joints (as in iron construction). In their simplest structural form, as composite iron supports, these cantilevered girders are being used extensively in the new platforms of the German railway (fig. 38).

Figure 39 shows the same construction in *reinforced concrete,* again for a train platform. Figure 40 once more shows iron cantilevered girders in a large structure, a hall, where the one-directional cantilevered girders in the side wall can be distinctly recognized.

The new use of this cantilevered construction allows the upper parts of the structure to project far beyond the lower parts, without using supports.

The signal tower in Laon (fig. 41) shows this type of construction used in a superstructure raised above a railway platform. The switch tower itself rests on cantilevered girders supported on slender columns so as not to narrow the platform or obstruct traffic. Figure 42 shows another example of the same type of construction in concrete—a coal bunker, where the conveyer belt for the automatic transport of the coal to the bunker pocket is placed in the upper, cantilevered part.

The development of cantilevered construction has enriched architecture by a *new function*—that of being suspended—a function whose development, formation, and design constitutes one of the most interesting formal problems in the new style.

The office building in figure 43 shows an attempt in this direction; the projection of the upper story has the practical purpose of increasing the floor space and thereby compensating for limitations of the site—a narrow and shallow corner lot.

The new possibility has been developed more freely as architectural form and incorporated into the plan of a villa (fig. 44).

Let us now consider the second example—the wall.

As the industrialization of the building trades advances, *precast construction* will find increasing acceptance. In building construction, and especially in housing, the individual components will be produced in large plants (as has already long been the case in iron construction), cut to specified norms, and assembled or installed at the building site. *Walls* will then no longer be built of brick but formed as large uniform *plates* composed of weatherproof, thermally advantageous material—or better still, a seamless and jointless wall will be fabricated by pouring or layering materials (figs. 45, 46).

As such building methods develop, the wall will lose its traditional character and change its function from a *supporting* to a *supported* element. No longer needing to support itself, it will stretch across the inner supporting framework like an outer protective skin, a skin that whenever possible will be wall *and* roof at the same time.[1] As a skin without a bearing function, the wall

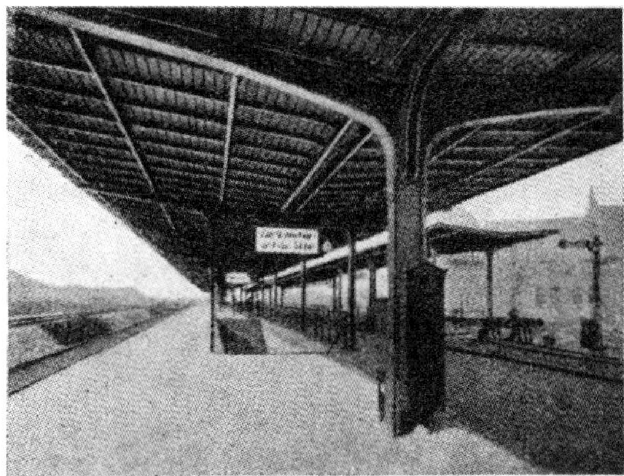

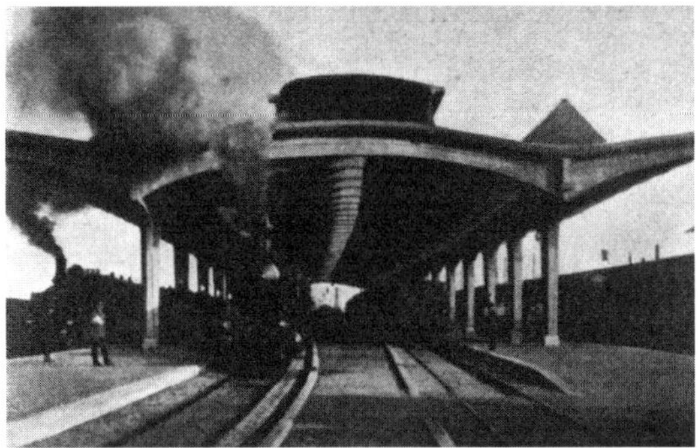

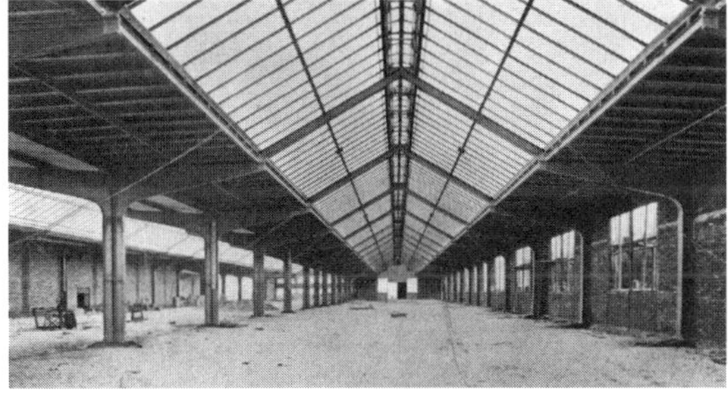

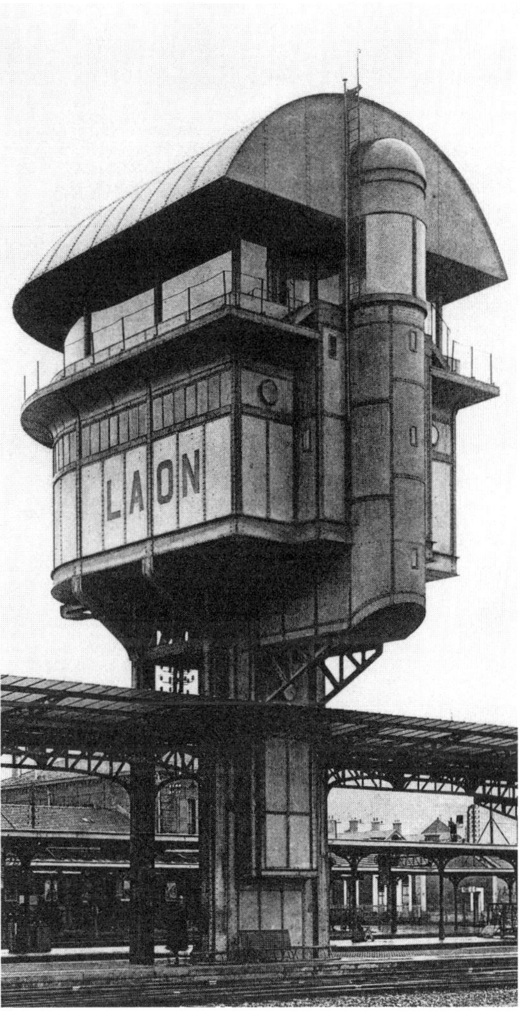

Fig. 38. Railway platform
Iron cantilevered girder

Fig. 39. Railway platform
Cantilevered girders in reinforced concrete

Fig. 40. Assembly hall
Iron cantilevered girders

Fig. 41. Signal tower, Laon

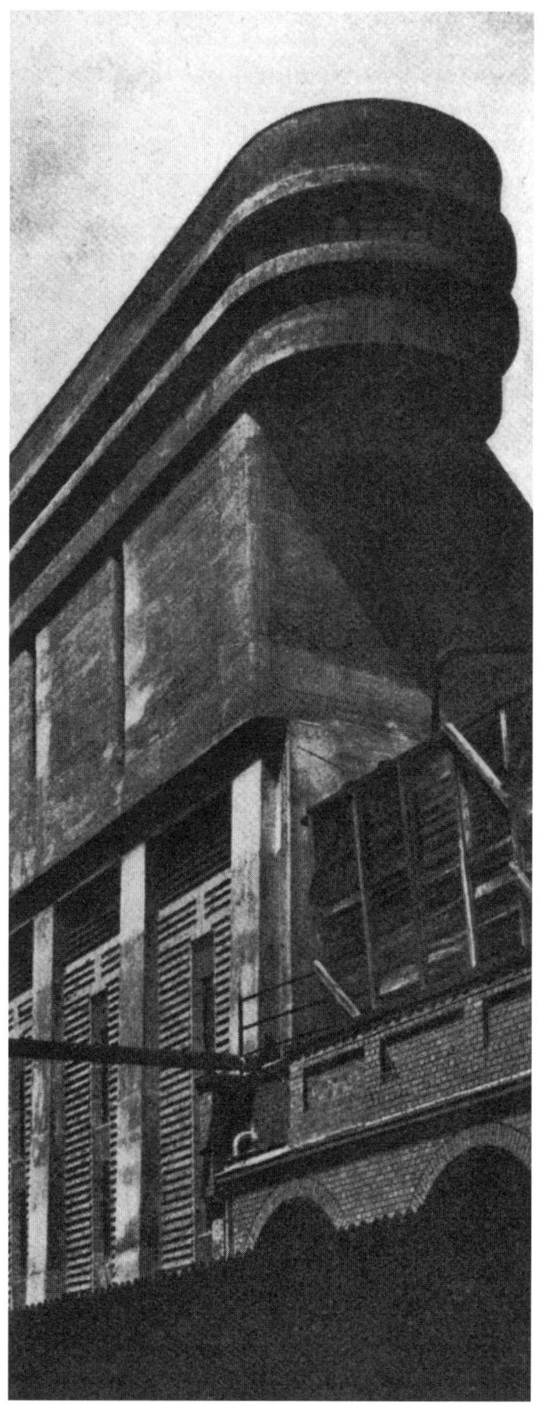

Fig. 42. Johannes Göderitz, Magdeburg
Coal bunker, municipal slaughterhouse, Magdeburg

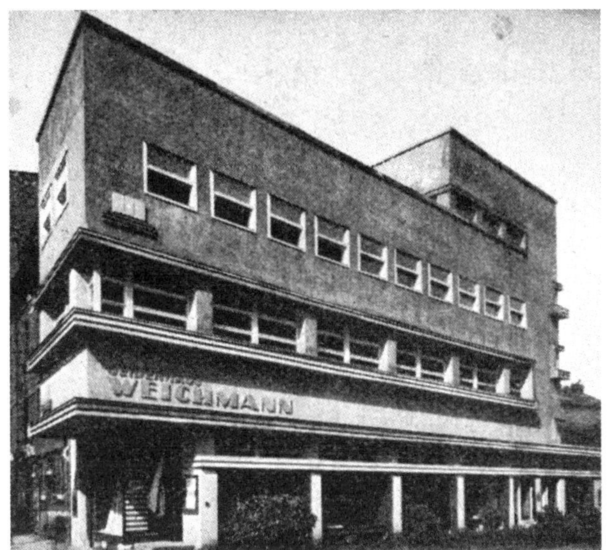

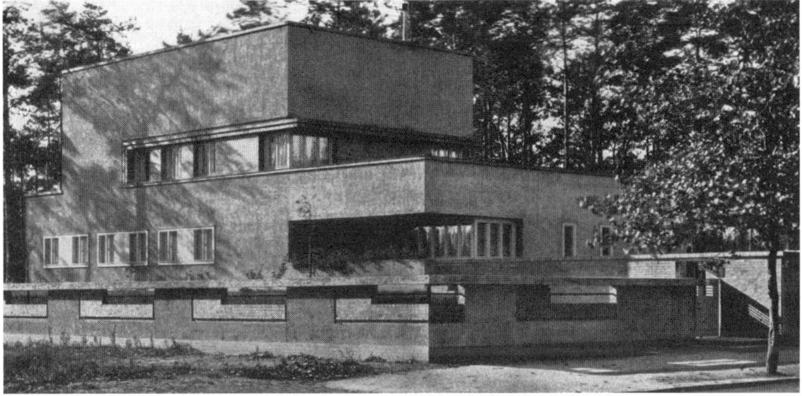

Fig. 43. Erich Mendelsohn, Berlin
Weichmann silk shop, Gleiwitz

Fig. 44. Erich Mendelsohn, Berlin
House in Berlin-Westend

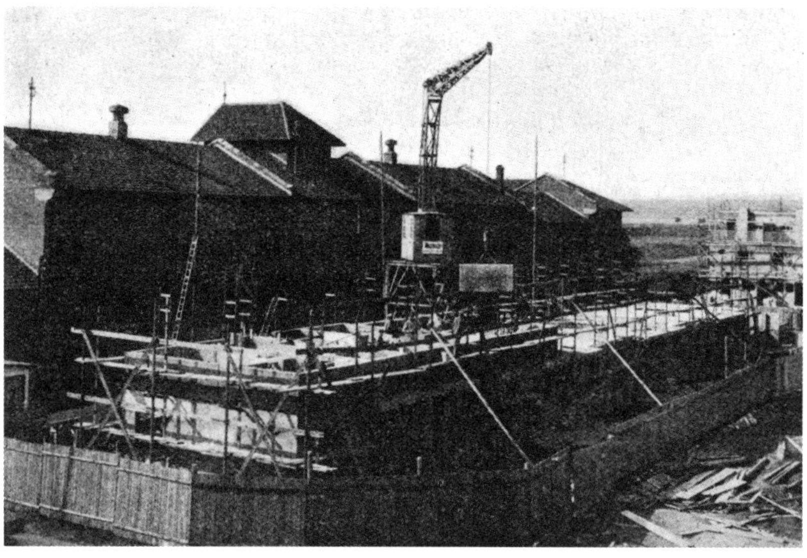

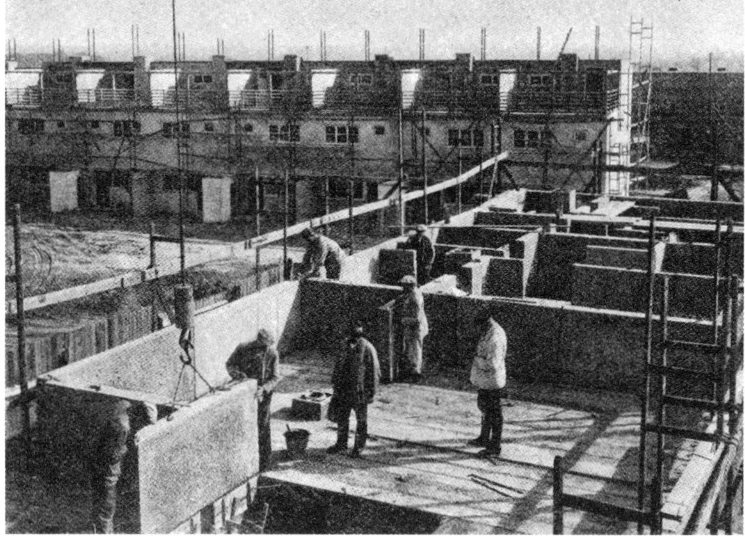

Figs. 45, 46. E[rnst] May, Frankfurt am Main
Praunheim *Siedlung* (panel construction), near Frankfurt am Main

will always tend to become lighter and above all thinner; theoretically, a material of membranelike strength would be sufficient for this purpose. With that, the wall will also change its architectural character. Whereas formerly the thickness of the bearing wall offered ample opportunities for plastic articulation and modeling, such modeling becomes impossible as soon as the wall is reduced to the slight dimension of a skin.

The use of *glass* is a stage in the wall's transformation from a supporting to a supported element. The relieved opening has now replaced the bearing wall: an event that vividly demonstrates the functional change.

The factory building shown in figure 47 is a logically designed example of this developmental stage. Because large windows are required for the lighting of the workshops, the exterior walls are predominantly glass. The "relieved opening" is especially noticeable in the left corner of the building. The nature of the relieved opening is seen still more clearly in the design of an office building (fig. 48). In this reinforced-concrete building the exterior walls (wall parapets in this case) are supported by interior cantilevered construction similar to that shown in figures 37 and 38. The intervening openings are enclosed with a glass skin.

The changed function of the wall—its transformation from a supporting to a supported element—is clearly seen in the buildings of the Bauhaus at Dessau, which contain several floors of superimposed teaching studios (fig. 49). An immense glass apron suspended from an upper concrete frame creates a completely translucent exterior wall. The next step would be to make the wall completely out of glass, as is done with the factory's stair tower (fig. 50; see also fig. 36).

The *wall's functional change* is also made abundantly clear in American *high-rise buildings*. In the early period of the skyscraper, the high-rise was treated architecturally as an ordinary building—as it could not be otherwise—and differed from the traditional multistory building only in having more floors and thus greater height. Figure 51 shows one such high-rise of the oldest type, which in its architectural development represents one of the most successful examples of this kind of treatment, although its styling today appears antiquated in the same way as, say, an older type of automobile. This conception normally resulted in those hulking stone colossi consisting of stacked rows of columns and temple motifs that dominate the city and streetscapes of large American cities (figs. 52, 53).

If, as the older examples show, the high-rise was really only an enlarged building whose walls rise up from the earth below, the masonry of the lower stories would have to be so thick in order to carry the load above that window openings would no longer be possible and no natural light could penetrate into the lower floors. But in fact these walls no longer rise up from the ground. The construction of the high-rises, or the so-called skyscrapers, first became practical only with the invention of the *steel frame* or "iron birdcage" construction. Figure 54 presents such a steel frame and thus the actual shell of a modern high-rise. Enclosing this frame allows the wall panels to be

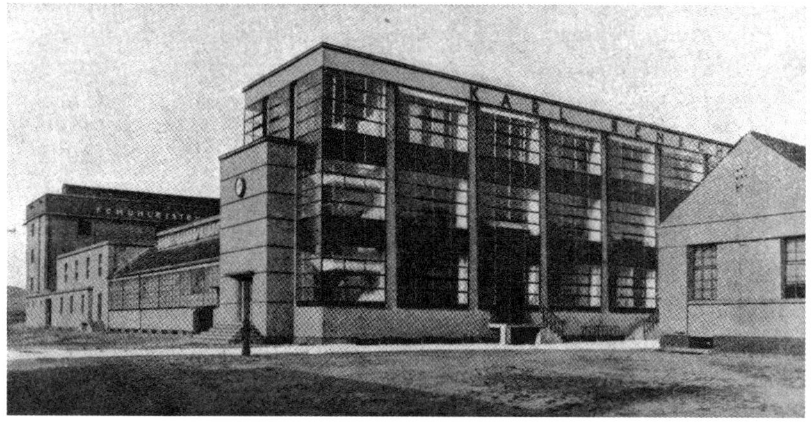

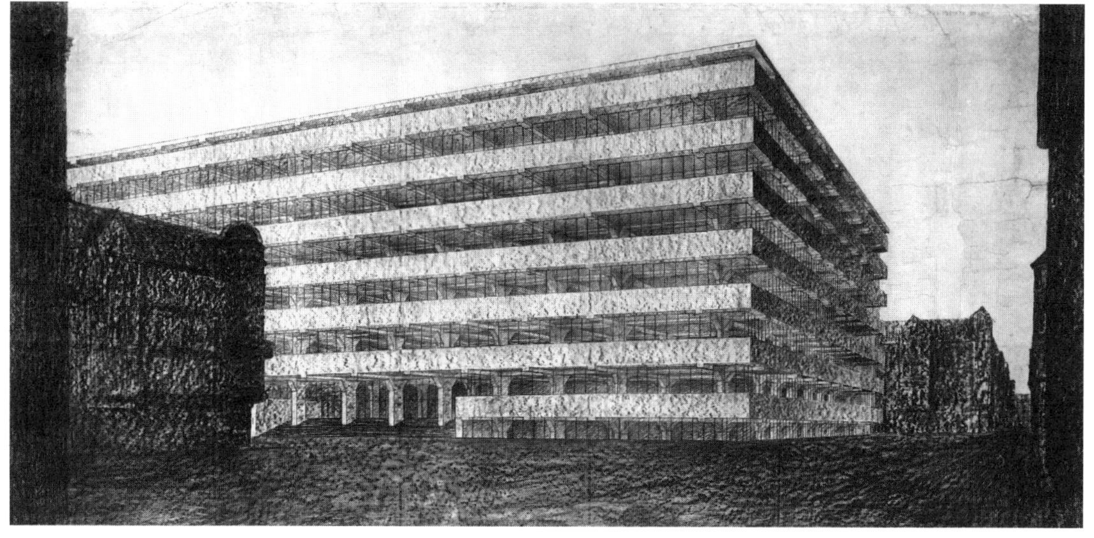

Fig. 47. Walter Gropius
Fagus shoe factory, Alfeld[-an-der-Leine]

Fig. 48. L[udwig] Mies van der Rohe, Berlin
Design for an office building (reinforced concrete)

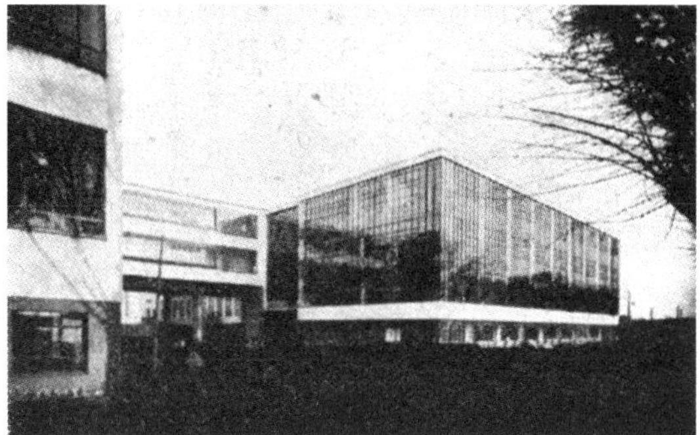

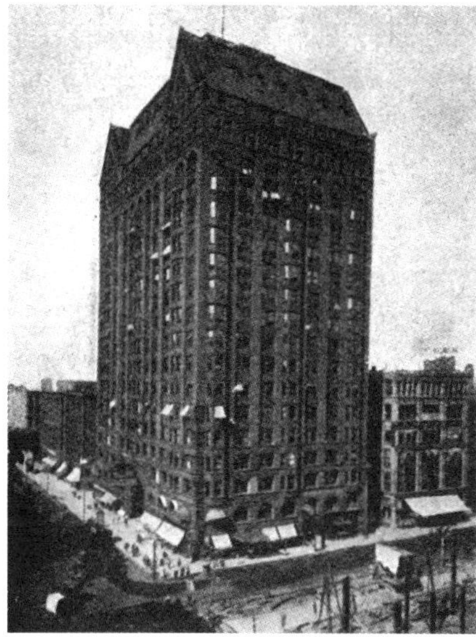

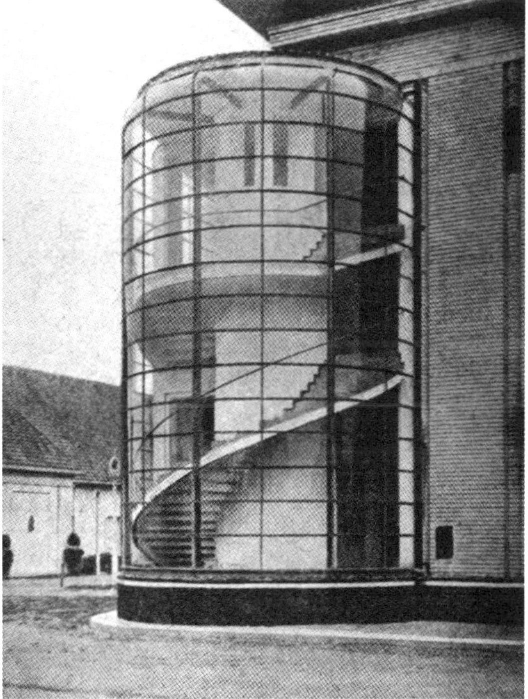

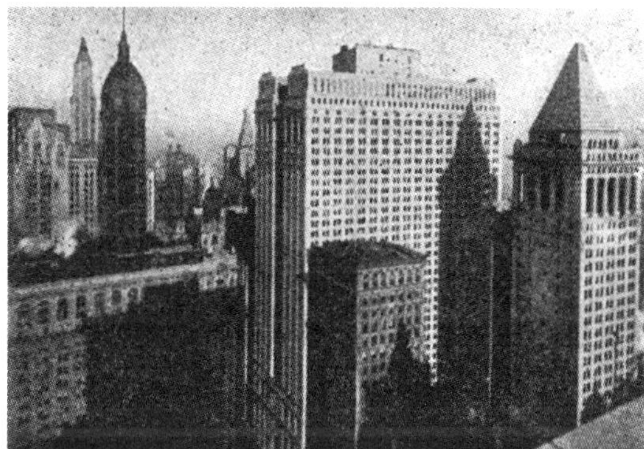

Fig. 49. Walter Gropius
Studio building, Dessau Bauhaus

Fig. 50. Walter Gropius
Staircase, factory building, German Werkbund exhibition
1914, Cologne

Fig. 51. American high-rise of the oldest type

Fig. 52. High-rise building methods, New York

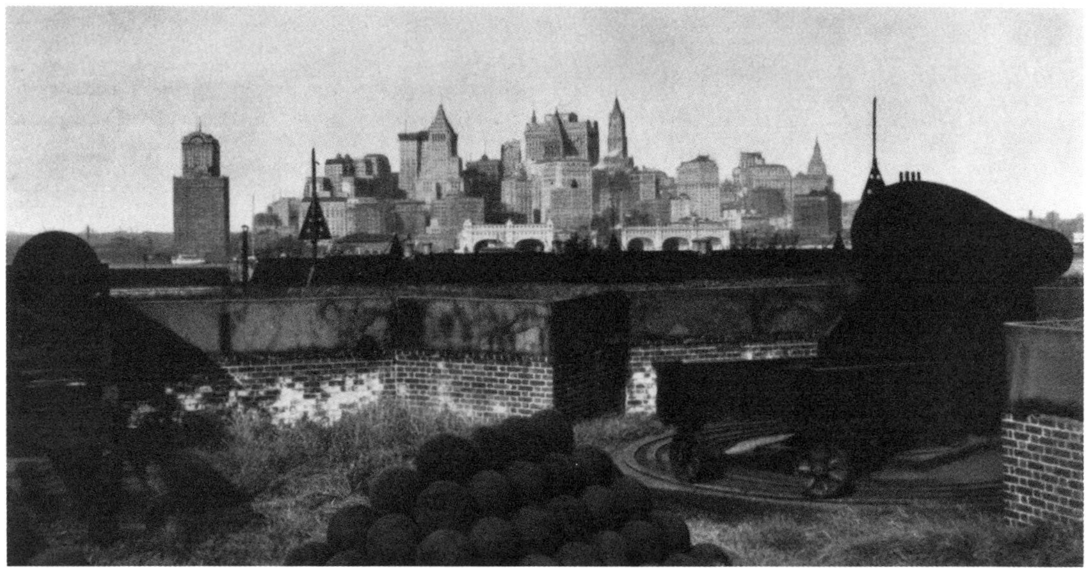

Fig. 53. New York
Southern tip of Manhattan with skyscrapers

started anywhere (but, for practical reasons, usually in the middle). The new building in the background of figure 55 clearly shows that the wall no longer *supports* but *is supported,* that it assumes the character of a skin.

The skyscrapers erected in the last few years take into account this changed building process, and they show a smooth and pronounced, surfacelike treatment of the wall. All floors above the socle are integrated in an architecturally neutral zone, whose smooth surfaces are articulated only by the lively rhythm of numerous rows of windows (fig. 56).

The model in figure 57 by a German architect brings this conception to its logical conclusion. It is a proposal for a high-rise in which the glass wall is treated *unambiguously as a skin.* Whether glass is the right material for this purpose may be debatable, but this formulation of the problem proceeds from correct premises.

Design

Wherever the effort is made to investigate practically and deal honestly with the many formal problems raised by the new realities of our time, it becomes apparent that we cannot tackle them with the conventional forms of "polytechnical architecture." Traditional notions of form—rigid conceptions of form—for the most part even hinder the working out of new forms.

Thus there is no other way than *to start afresh,* abandon the old, invalid

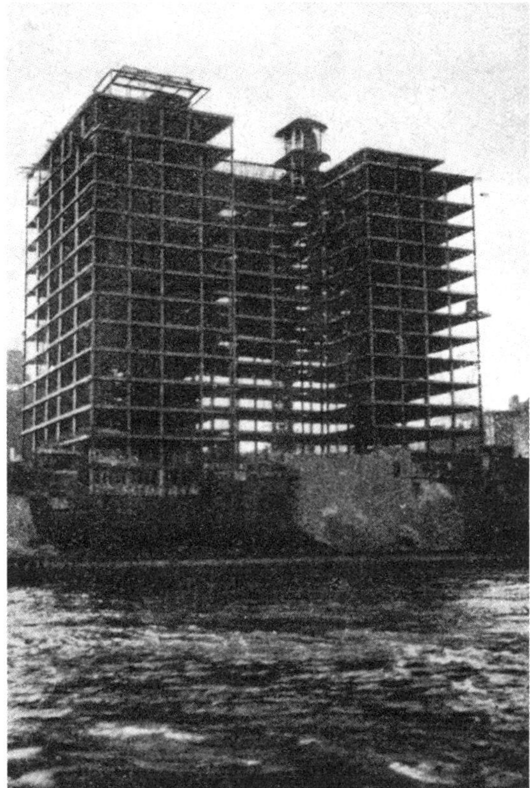

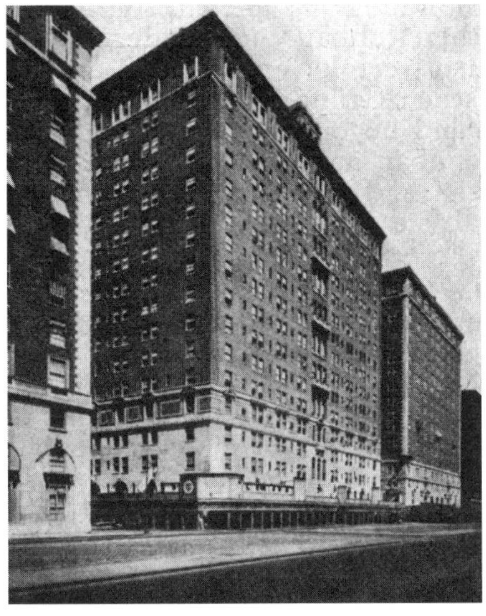

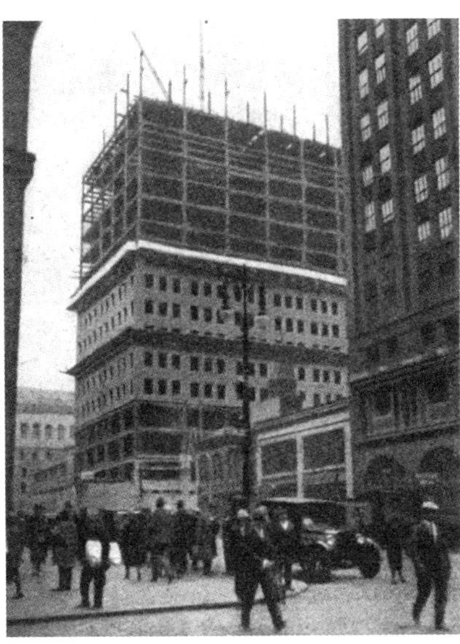

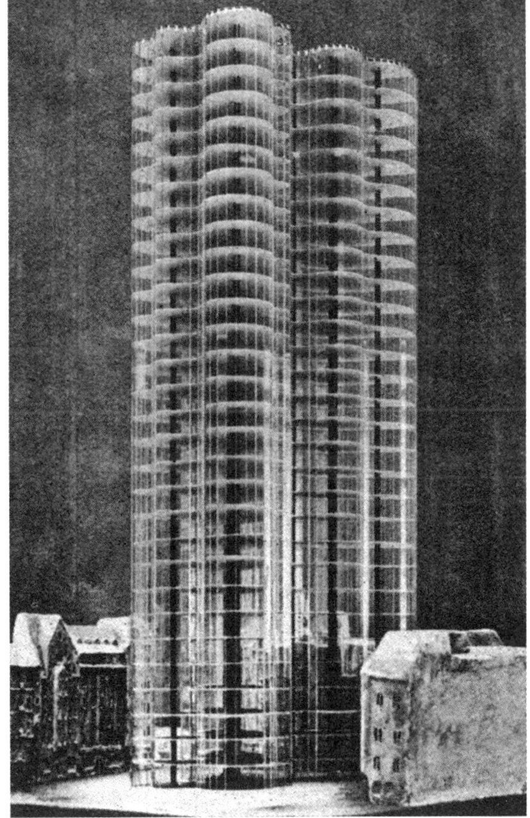

Fig. 54. Steel frame for a high-rise

Fig. 55. High-rise under construction
Enclosing the steel frame

Fig. 56. Skyscraper on Park Avenue, New York

Fig. 57. L[udwig] Mies van der Rohe, Berlin
Model of a high-rise in glass and iron

notions of form, and go to work in one's own independent way *construction-ally, formatively,* and *creatively.*

There is no other way than to conceive anew the *functions* of the building elements, as well as the demands of the new construction processes, and give a unique form to the new *building materials* based on their structural laws and new methods of industrial technology.

There is no other way than to start with the structural framework, make its inner play of forces visible, and thereby produce new aesthetic elements in such a way that the inner tensions of the spatial organism are brought into a pure and harmonious relationship.

The *proportions* thereby adopted will once again achieve their proper and original task: namely, to be the expression, the vital and *truthful* expression, of the *functions* and programmatic requirements of the building and all its parts. Such proportions were always true in classical styles; in classicistic styles they were generally inexact, superficial, and accidental. The whole building will thereby again become a unified organism, whose individual parts entail each other and are held in tension. This way of designing no longer permits chance ornament, superfluous adornment, or applied decoration. One and the same driving force produces forms and proportions altogether integrated, a characteristic that Jacob Burckhardt has described as the most distinctive sign of all original and organic styles.

Let me limit myself here to a single but very striking *example* of this *new way of designing.* Figure 58 depicts the recently completed Chicago Tribune Building. Following the ambitious wishes of its owners, this newspaper palace was to become—as is usually the case in America—"the most beautiful and distinctive office building in the world." To carry out this intention as much as possible, an international competition was announced, whose great appeal elicited participation from architects of almost every country of the world. The building was executed according to the winning design of an American architect. This design portrays a skillful and outwardly impressive, but nevertheless quite trivial imitation of a Gothic spire, specifically, the Antwerp Cathedral. Figure 59 shows the same building under construction with the reinforced concrete ribs of its structural frame. Next to it we see the design that the architects Walter Gropius and Adolf Meyer submitted to the competition (fig. 60). We can observe here how systematically the new formal problems are taken up, how their design has followed the nature of the new construction and the new function of the wall, and we can compare how the structure and proportions of this proposal express the new realities much more clearly and naturally than does the executed design, which misuses the motif of a cathedral tower for a profane purpose and thereby sins irresponsibly against the original.

Color in Architecture

By nature, certain colors accord with the new conception of form. The call for a *colorful architecture* heard so frequently in the last few years only becomes

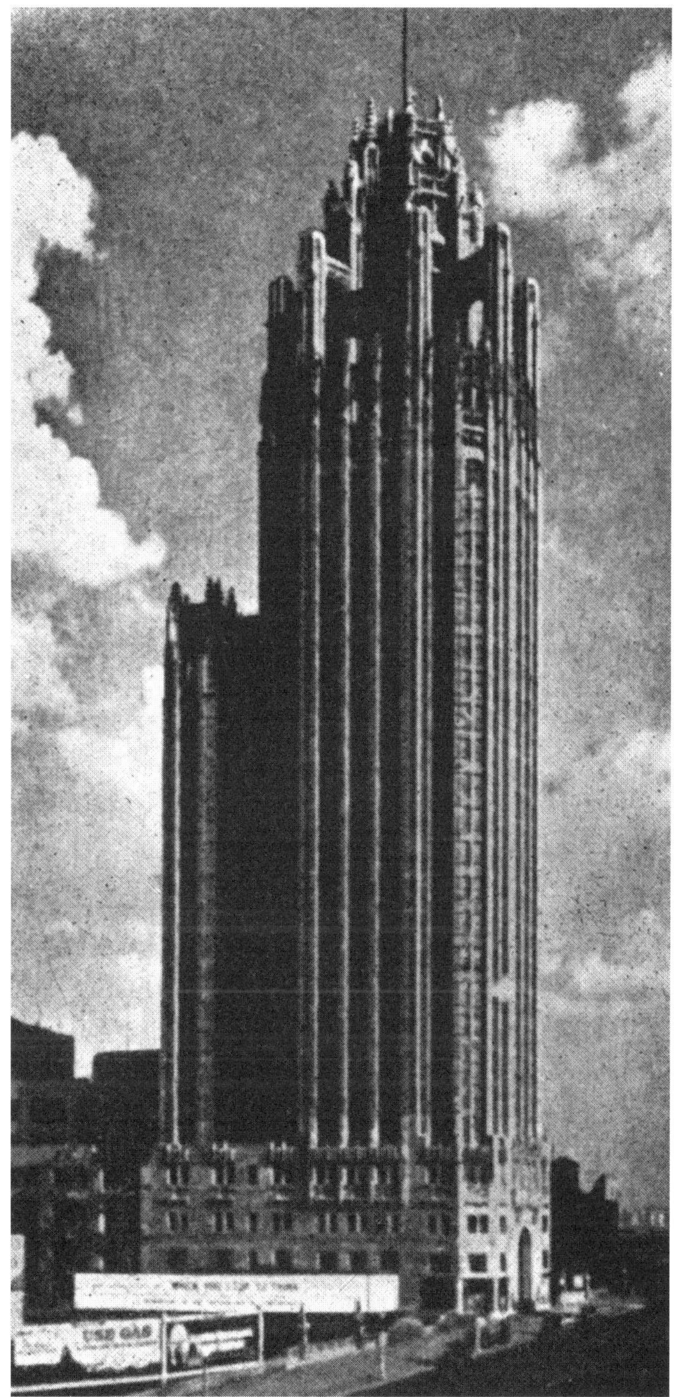

Fig. 58. Chicago Tribune Building, Chicago

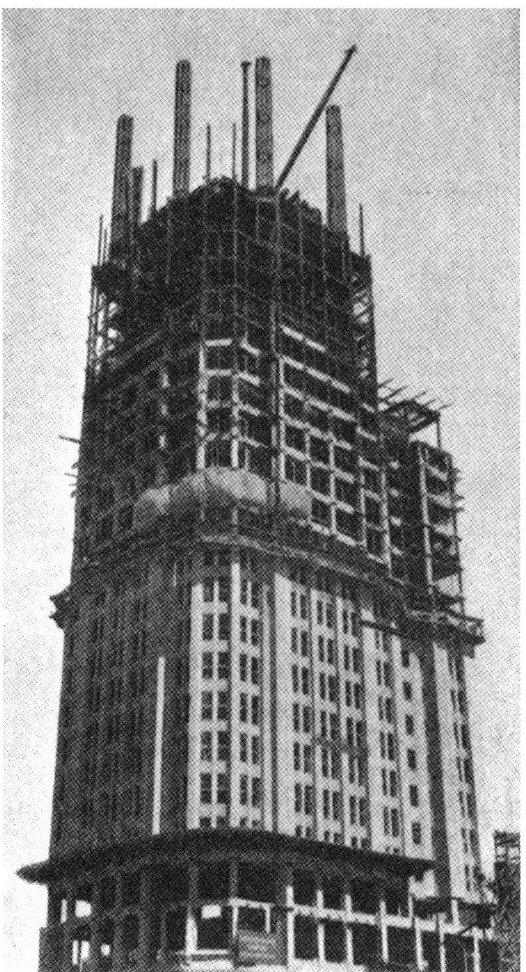

Fig. 59. Chicago Tribune Building under construction

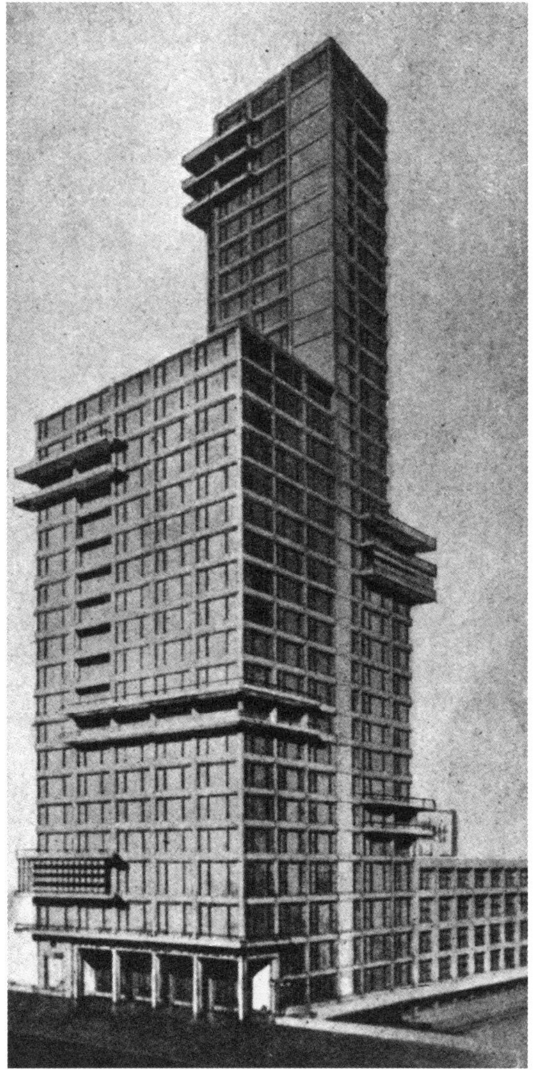

Fig. 60. Competition design of W[alter] Gropius and Adolf Meyer

intelligible in this regard and thereby receives its meaning and justification.

The new architecture needs color; it needs it as a design tool to articulate the smooth surfaces of its walls, and it needs it in a *functional* sense to exploit color's chromatic values and valence and thereby express the tensional relationships of the spatial organism.[2]

The use of color in this new sense can be seen on a coffeehouse in Rotterdam, a temporary building for an empty lot designed by the architect J. J. P. Oud (fig. 61). The colors of the principal surfaces are chromatically distributed as follows: the upper right corner is vermilion; the frame around it to the left is canary yellow; the substructure is ultramarine with black borders; and the front door is gray. The windows above the substructure are yellow, gray, and white with black edges; the firm's large logo has gray letters on a black ground; and the lettering on the illuminated signs is white on a gray ground.

This small building, by the way, is also an excellent example of how the elements by which a shop facade attracts attention—the firm's logo, the illuminated sign, and so on—can be given an organized form.

Color used as a design tool in this way will largely assume the former role of ornament and detailing, which the new architecture lacks and must lack as it has to rely on machine labor and industrial technicians rather than people trained in the arts and crafts. But what the new architecture loses in artistic charm, it will more than compensate by the exactness and precision of its execution, the sharpness and accuracy of its lines, and the smoothness and tension of its forms. One can truly say that the new style is in a very distinct way a *material style,* that is, a style that uses the material—be it steel, glass, ceramics, and so on—for the sake of its materiality or refined material beauty.

Artificial Illumination as a Problem of Form

As attractive as it would be to pursue within the separate technical branches the many problems of design being raised by the new realities of our time, we must be content within the framework of this book to emphasize only the simplest cases. Still, by way of suggestion, we might draw attention to one of these problems, perhaps one of the most interesting and charming facing architecture today, and moreover one that up to now has scarcely been considered, much less tackled in practice. This is the *problem of artificial illumination,* or the problem posed by *using electricity for lighting.*

The introduction of the electric fixture has freed lighting design completely in locating the light fixture, in determining the light intensity, and almost completely in operating the light, because the current can be turned on and off with a switch. Nevertheless, these expanded possibilities have only begun to be exploited. Only the *luminous advertisement* (incidentally, also a new form problem) has until now made extensive use of the new freedom (figs. 62–65). For architecture these new possibilities have been fully exploited with respect to the *materials,* as far as intensification of lighting effects is concerned. In the design of lighting, by contrast, we almost always persist in traditional

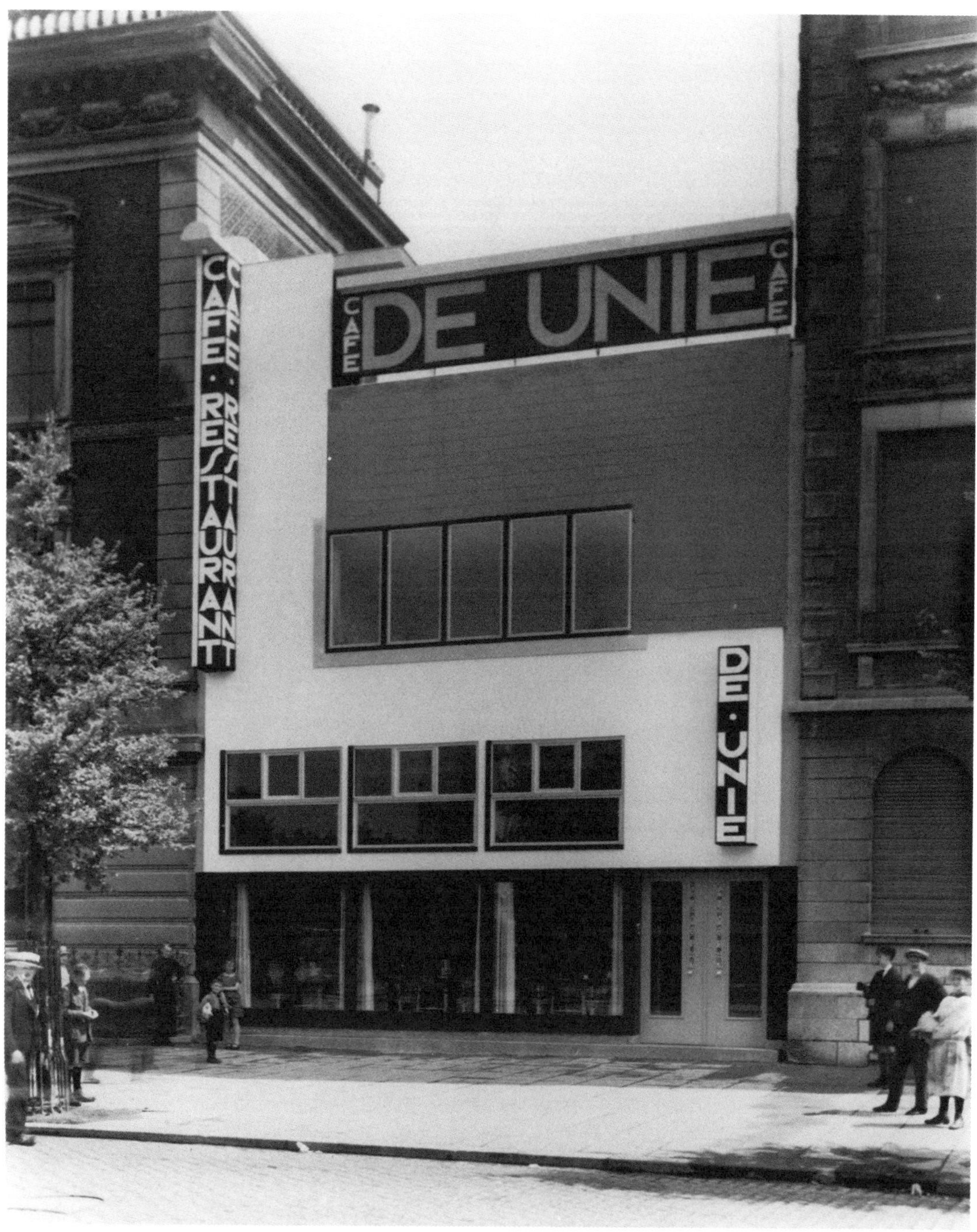

Fig. 61. J. J. P. Oud, Rotterdam
Café de Unie, Rotterdam (temporary building)

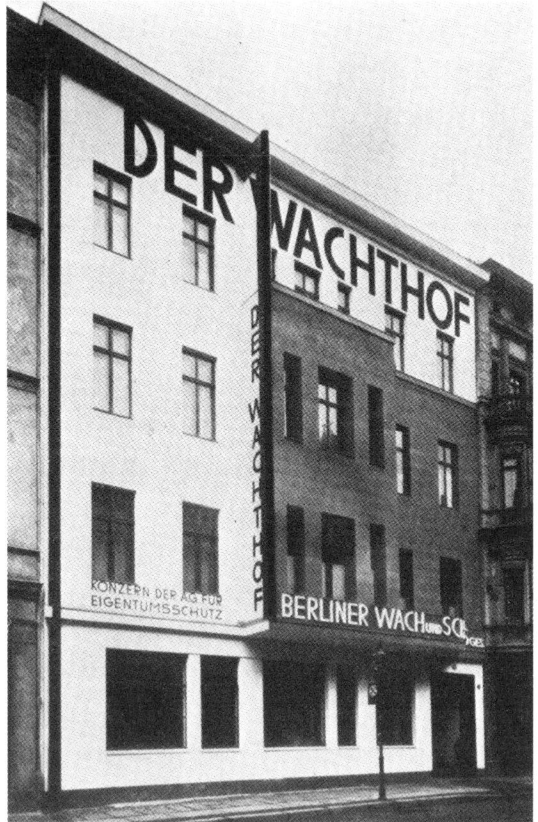
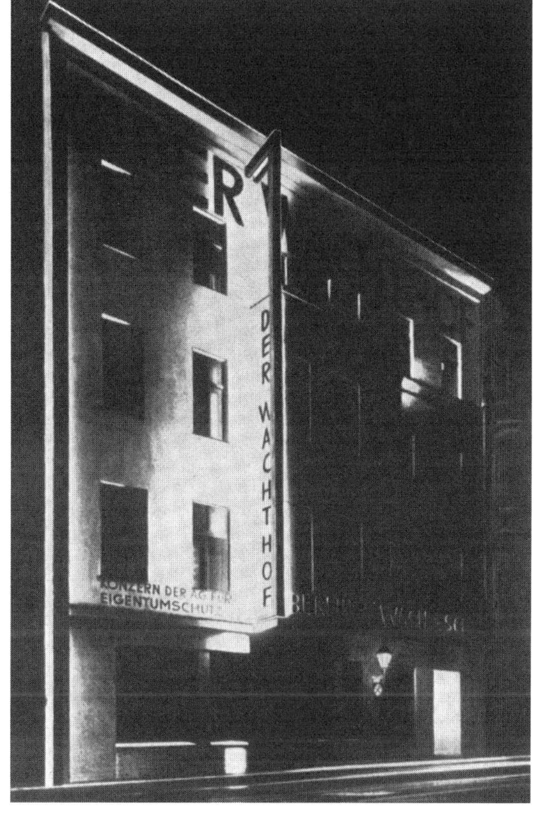

Figs. 62, 63. Arthur Korn, Berlin
Facade with luminous advertising, day and night views

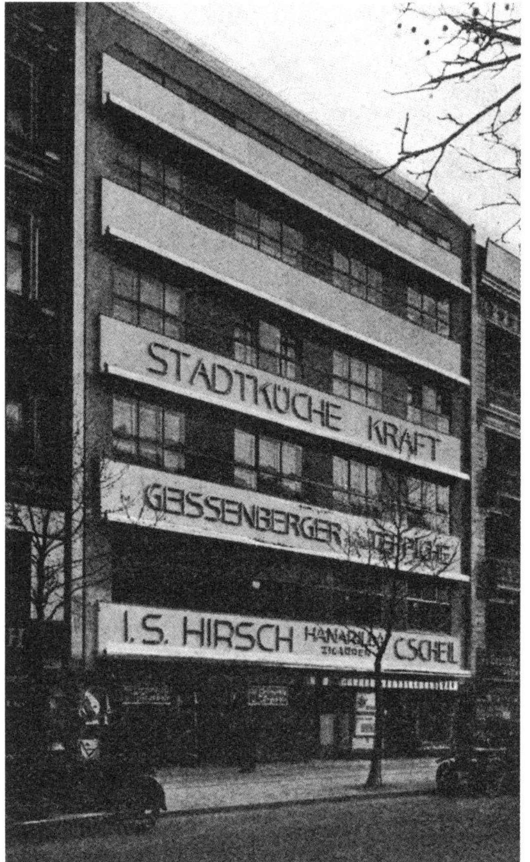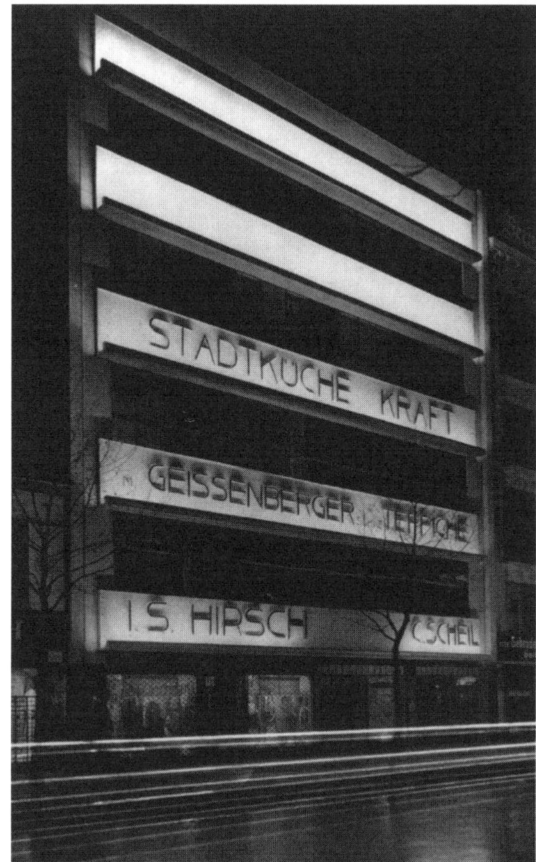

Figs. 64, 65. Luckhardt Brothers, Berlin
Facade with luminous advertising, day and night views

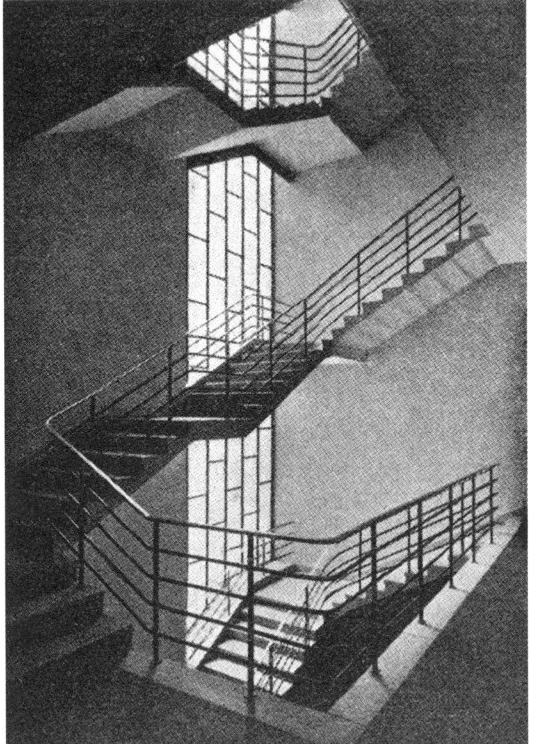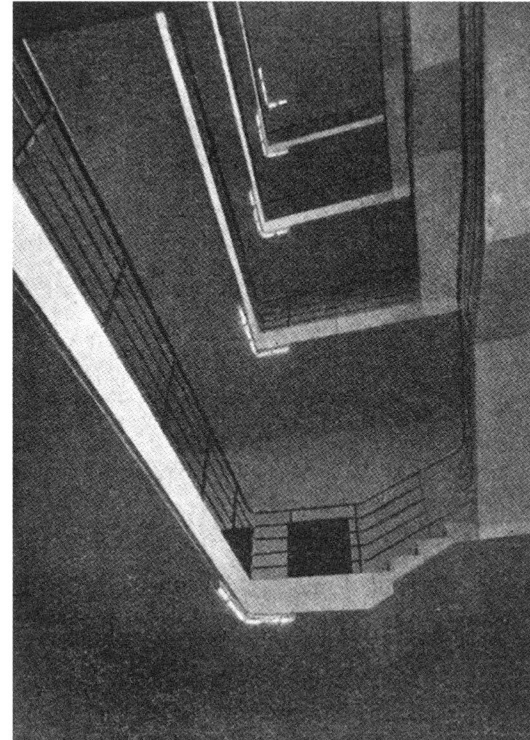

Figs. 66, 67. O[tto] Bartning, Berlin
Stairs in the Red Cross Building, Berlin

notions regarding the shape of the lamp—the candelabra and lightbulbs—that is, in forms developed in response to the technical necessity to concentrate light at particular points.

Where the effort has occasionally been made not only to use these new possibilities but also to design them, illumination is exploited in a functional sense, that is, it becomes an effective tool for designing the space, explaining the spatial function and movement, and accentuating and strengthening the spatial relations and tensions.

This can be seen in the staircase for the Berlin Red Cross Building shown in figures 66 and 67. Here the light fixtures are designed in the shape of angled tubes attached to the bottom of the stair landings, where they underscore both with their form and location the stairs' tendency toward movement.

These very general comments offer nothing more than a few hints regarding the lighting problem, and they are inserted only because they introduce in a vivid way a larger and more important problem, in fact the central problem

133

of all architectural creation: namely, *spatial design*. Notwithstanding its crucial importance, however, it can be treated here only more suggestively than exhaustively.

The Problem of Space

Very generally, this much can be said: the new conception of form is clearly also expressed in *spatial design,* which is directed toward explicating functions and internal tensional forces. Even in the *arrangement of the floor plan,* the intention should be to design the spatial structure as a unified organism that conforms both as a whole and in its parts to the different functions it serves. The individual spaces should thus be designed so that their basic form, sequence, and transition correspond to the various functions they serve: circulation, work, housekeeping, dwelling, and so on. Instead of stringing out spaces along an axis in the usual way and ordering the sequence symmetrically—an idea whose schematic and misunderstood use, following Schinkel's example, has produced so much hypocrisy and tedium—we should now arrange them according to their *functional values* and internal tensional relationships.

This new tendency is logically carried out in the floor plan of an office building (fig. 68). Situated on a busy street, the main facade is inflected not only to increase the number of shop windows but also to create a protected space where one can view the goods on display at leisure, unhindered by street traffic. The shop windows, with their angled placement, are drawn into the visual field of passersby. The traffic areas, the corridors in this floor plan around the staircase, are widest where the traffic flow is greatest; they narrow within the building where the traffic lessens owing to its dispersion into adjacent rooms.

The same intention can be seen in the floor plan of a dwelling (fig. 69), where the rooms of the house wrap themselves around an undulating staircase as around a spinal column, so that all the individual needs of the household operations are most carefully accommodated.

In a freer style, the rooms in the house plan shown in figure 70 almost completely dissolve their borders by flowing into one another, yet they are also bound to one another by the dynamics of their internal tensions.

Formal Problems in City Planning

Finally, it remains to consider how this way of designing also applies to *city planning,* how it conceives the city's formal problems.

It becomes clear that the city can no longer be considered a projected plan whose outlines are to be laid out schematically on a drawing board with a straightedge and triangle, according to the principles of axial symmetry. The city should now be conceived for what it in reality is—namely, *a living organism* whose supporting framework and structure are to be designed to handle as thoroughly and efficiently as possible the many *functions of life* they must fulfill.

The city serves work in all of its aspects; it serves dwelling, traffic, and

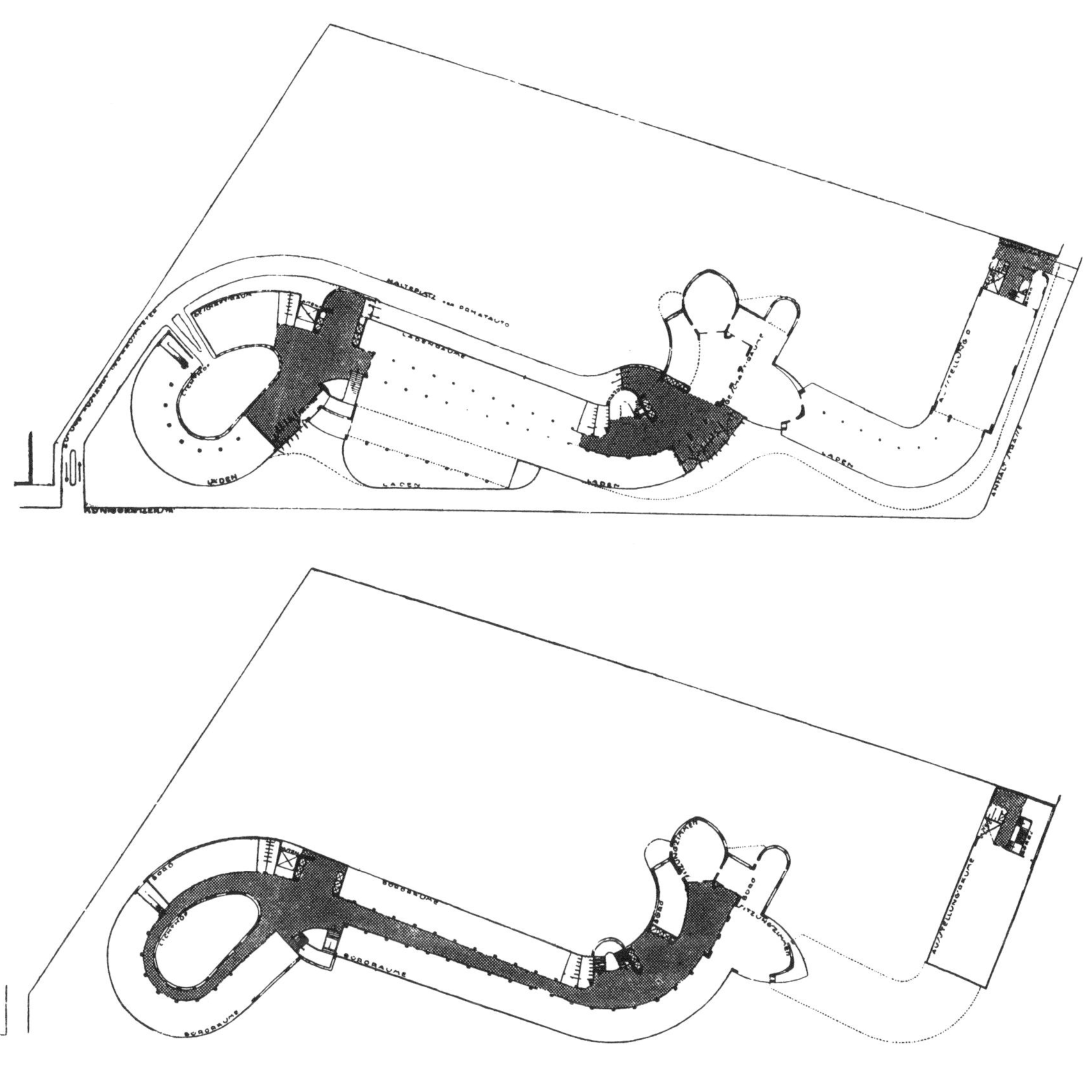

Fig. 68. Hugo Häring, Berlin
Floor plans for an office building

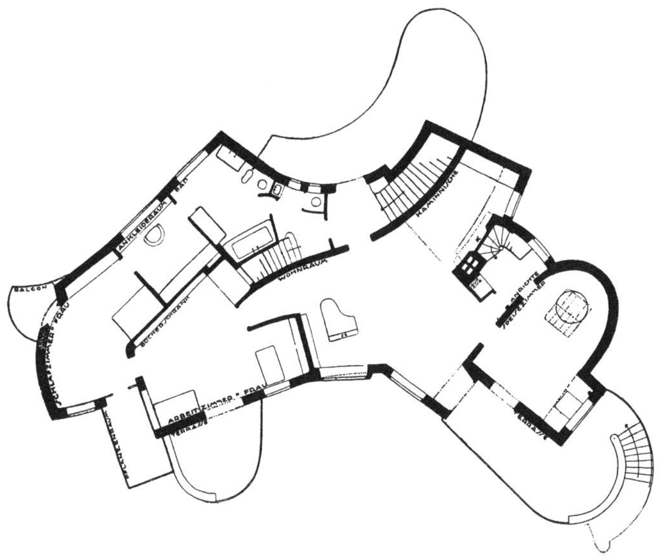

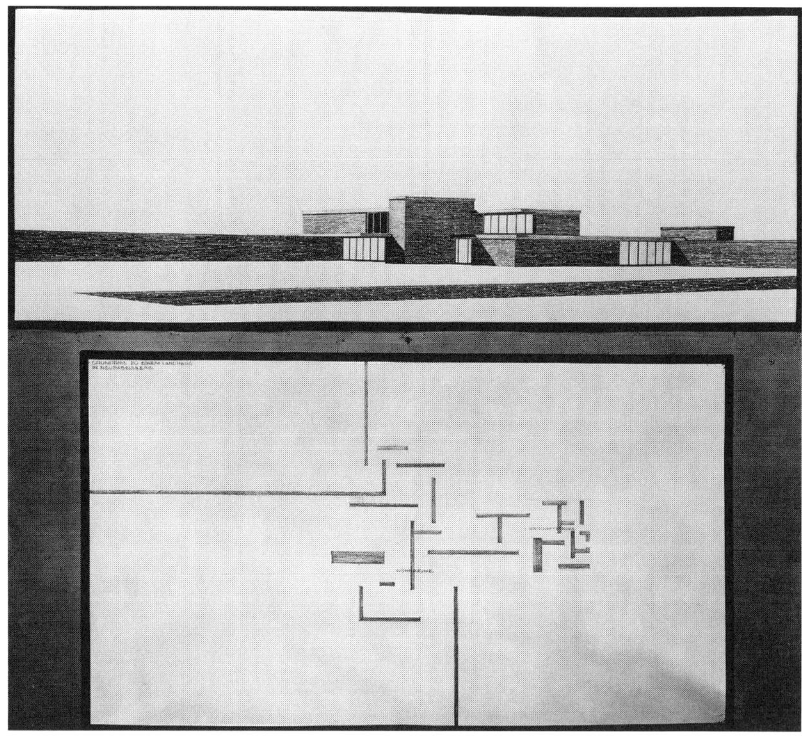

Fig. 69. Hugo Häring, Berlin
Floor plan for a dwelling

Fig. 70. L[udwig] Mies van der Rohe, Berlin
Floor plan for a dwelling

recreation, and as a living organism it carries out these age-old functions with continuous interplay. Therefore, the urban area can be divided into individual living spaces in accordance with the functions of this organism—industrial zones, residential zones, traffic zones, and recreational zones—and these different living spaces are then set in motion and related to one another according to their internal interactions and reciprocal tensions.

These issues elude pictorial representation. Still, the master housing plan for a large central German city (fig. 71) can give a rough idea of it, as the new plan shows how the industrial zones extend along the river, how the residential districts are joined to them, how the green and recreational areas penetrate wedgelike into the inner city, and how the suburbs relate to the urban spaces yet are preserved in themselves as special entities or independent zones.

The new conception goes further. It no longer understands the city as a unity demarcated by politics but sees itself in it; that is, it sees the city as a whole, once again as a living space, whose parts reciprocally relate to other immediate and more remote living spaces in its environment, to the provinces, and to the immediate and more distant spheres of economics and raw materials. It sees it in such a way that the whole country is designed as an integrated organism for dwelling, whose different living spaces and powerful tensions are kept in check and balance.

This understanding of the housing problem holds new and important prospects for the future. In the long run this conception cannot and will not stop at political borders between countries; it must and will eventually lead to the world being planned according to the natural conditions of economic geography, in which the human environment will be developed as an integrated organism serving its peaceful functions according to the principle of human reason, while holding its forces in complete balance.

The Struggle for the New Style

At this point it is appropriate to bring our deliberations to a close. This is not the place to draw a parallel between the new conception of design and other events of our spiritual life, or to relate our changed understanding of form to the general change in our forms of life, economy, and society. Nor is it our task to develop some kind of aesthetic for the new building style, whose primary development we are now experiencing. The style is still not mature enough for such an aesthetic examination; the results achieved up to now are inadequate. Here we have tried only to point out a few selected formal problems of the new style and thus demonstrate the legitimacy of this new way of designing, so that the new forms will be understood as the result of a new formulation of the problem. Still, a few general and summary observations should be added to these remarks.

For several years a growing number of young architects in all countries have concerned themselves with the new formal problems in building. By doing so, they have continued with the problems that the Belgian painter

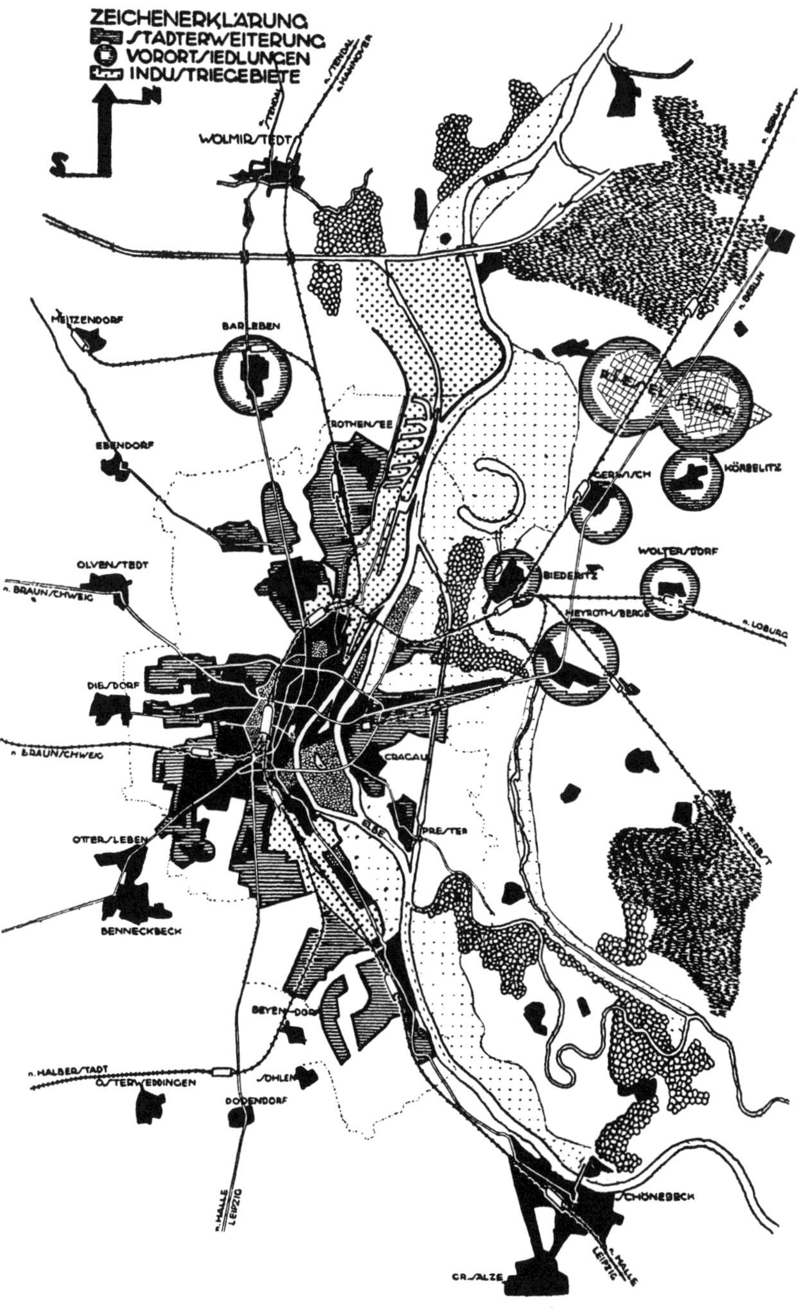

Fig. 71. [Konrad] Rühl, Magdeburg
Master plan for Magdeburg

Henry van de Velde first saw and formulated about three decades ago, problems that he, an outsider and early forerunner, also sought to solve practically in his work, at a time when scarcely anyone sensed or understood the problem. He held in his visionary mind the idea of a new style, whose principle should be, as he himself expressed it, the dogma of rational conception, of Immaculate Conception. He lived up to this idea by always seeking anew to clarify it theoretically and realize it practically: first in the invention of odd functional arabesques, then in the making of furniture, and finally in architecture as well. The new movement that he then called into being in Germany with the explosive force of his idea of a "new style" — the so-called Arts and Crafts movement — has long since receded into decorative tomfoolery, having lost sight of its true goal. His idea of the new style, has remained, however, and has since shown its vitality. The line, wrote van de Velde, the line is a force, and with that he coined the principle of the new style, the principle of a dynamic and functional architecture.

How far he himself was successful in realizing the idea of a functional architecture can be seen in the theater that he built in 1914 for the German Werkbund Exhibition in Cologne — the earliest work of the latest style and in the purity of its intentions also one of its most venerable achievements (fig. 72).

Standing next to van de Velde as the other forefather of the new style is the American Frank Lloyd Wright (fig. 73), the great student of the brilliant Sullivan. His work, which in America is altogether singular and has remained up to now without influence and emulation in his native land, has had a decisive influence, especially on the young Dutch architects. In Holland it has found the soil well tilled through the educational efforts of Berlage, who from the beginning has energetically instructed his students in the value of construction. From Holland, Wright's influence has passed to the other European countries. Among the courageous champions of the new building spirit we should also place in the first rank the Viennese architect Adolf Loos. Early on he intuitively grasped the new formal problems; as a prime mover in both word and deed, he worked for their recognition and solution (fig. 74).

On the shoulders of these men rests the work of the young generation of architects struggling for the new style. No individual talent or personality will decide the issue. It is the spirit of the time that here compels the form.

The works illustrated on these pages as evidence of this struggle should be judged neither as examples of an individual's talent nor as finished results. They were shown here only as examples that in some sense clarify those formal problems that still await solution. All are only preliminary solutions to these problems, stages in the process of design invention, yet all are important and valuable precisely in the way they formulate the problem. For in the end a talented person's importance to his age is also determined by how he himself decides, how he selects his task, and how he prepares himself for it. When young architects who with their work courageously profess their loyalty to

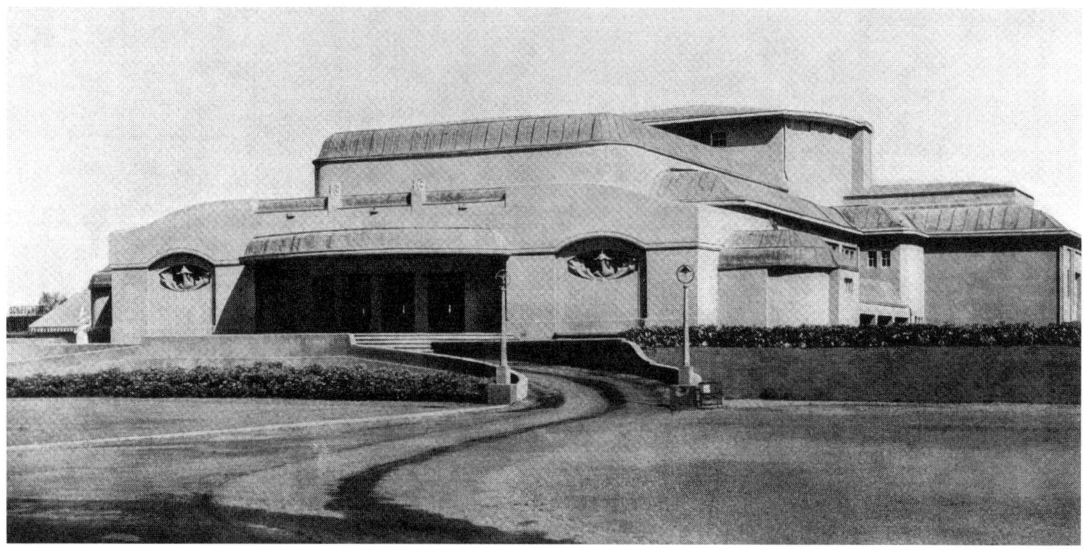

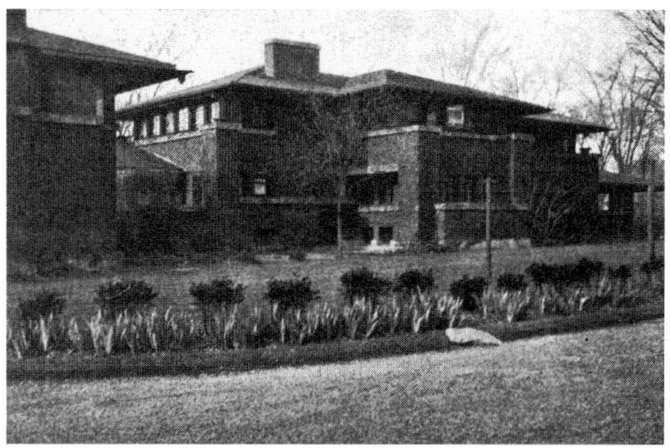

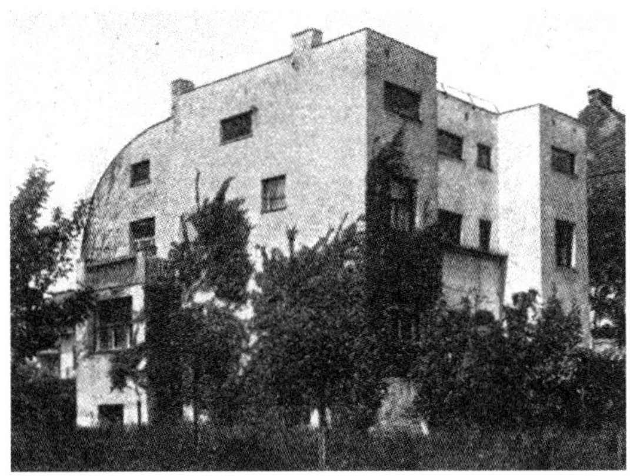

Fig. 72. Henry van de Velde, Brussels
Theater, German Werkbund exhibition, 1914, Cologne

Fig. 73. Frank Lloyd Wright
House in Chicago

Fig. 74. Adolf Loos, Vienna
House in Hitzing near Vienna, 1910

the new problems of the time are rebuked for the incompleteness of their efforts, they can cite the words of Hans von Marées, who, when similarly accused of not finishing his paintings, responded with pride that others had not even begun theirs: "The man who sets out to discover a new land runs the risk of foundering on a reef. It is easy to avoid the reef by letting the land remain undiscovered."

In the end we *must* take up and systematically work out the new building problems of the time that pressure us from every direction, rather than avoiding them again and again, consciously looking the other way, or simply making do, one way or another.

The Technical Colleges

With a few notable exceptions, the *official educational institutions* — the academies and the technical colleges — charged with acquainting the next generation with the new building problems now pay no attention to this present responsibility. Whereas the purely technical departments of these schools, such as the departments of building or mechanical engineering, eagerly see to it that the younger generation is made thoroughly familiar with the new realities of the time so as to prepare them as completely as possible for the practical work of the profession, these things are scarcely considered in the neighboring departments of architecture. Historical styles, however, are discussed all the more. The teaching of style may be necessary, even indispensable, to train one in spatial thinking and to cultivate one's sense of form, just as in higher education instruction in dead languages is continued to train one to think logically and to develop a sense for language. But in the end it is imperative that we learn the syntax of our own *living* language, so that we can correctly construct sentences in which we express our needs and say what disturbs or moves us.

The Clients

Finally, we must say a few words about *clients,* for it is important after all to consider the new architecture from the perspective of consumers as well. It is now apparent that it is precisely they — those who in every respect and for every reason must be the most conscious promoters and most active champions of the new building attitude — who are the most restrained and impeded by false prejudices. In their professional lives these clients (entrepreneurs, factory owners, bankers) are the most unbiased, the most progressive, and the most modern people. They head the most modern companies; they ride to their offices in turbocharged Mercedes automobiles; they travel by plane to their business conferences; they receive their stock reports over the wireless; and now they even place their orders by telephone from a moving express train. In everything pertaining to their profession, they think factually, rationally, and without prejudice. As soon as they speak of art, however, they become sentimental and think of Nuremberg, Venice, or the Petit Trianon. They doggedly persist in the ingrained superstition that art is synonymous with decoration. Thus they dress up their factories like medieval fortresses; they build their banks like sumptuous Renaissance palaces; they build their villas like Baroque castles. Even though they make extensive use of every technical advance everywhere else in their lives, they are surprisingly content to live, work, and dwell in houses in which no trace of the transformed living conditions can be seen.

When will clients finally understand the spiritual discrepancy between their Louis XVI salons and their Rolls Royces? When will they draw the necessary conclusions from such knowledge and bridge this duality in their sense of life? If they eventually succeed in unifying their style of living, the new movement will acquire a powerful burst of energy. This stream of life will lend a powerful impulse to forces in many cases still splintered today by friction and resistance and demoralized by being in flux. And with that, their creations will achieve increased grace and acquire that measure of freedom and sensual richness that their now often cramped and occasionally all-too-doctrinaire architectural works yet lack.

The New Architecture

An architecture that is to be a living component of our time and a true expression of our new sense of life cannot look different, cannot be essentially different than our machines, our mechanical devices, our airplanes, and our automobiles. It can be no more whimsical, no more poetic, no more emotional than our electric motors, turbines, and planetariums. But it can be just as intuitive, just as visionary, and just as creative as the latter—another, no less wonderful emanation of the human spirit.

The new architecture will be clean, exact, and precise in its lines; it will be clear and tense in its forms; it will have an almost classical purity in its proportions. It will, in addition, be imaginative in an unexpected way, that is, in the immaterial gravity of its suspended constructions of glass and iron, in the purity of its colors, in the cultivated beauty of its materials, and in the resplendent wealth of its natural and artificial light. We cannot imagine what richness of expression will unfold when architecture begins for the first time to manipulate freely the elements of the new style that it now seeks to acquire. And we cannot imagine what fanciful creations will arise from the wealth of its new means of expression when it once more happens that, as Hans Poelzig has said, we again build for the good Lord!

Meanwhile, we have only just begun! But in the struggle for the new style that we have so respectfully considered, the architecture has solid ground under its feet now that it has entered on the path that all original creations follow. If it continues along this path, if it goes to work supported by the principles of all original and organic creation and with an objective and suprapersonal dedication to the cause, then the blessing of *art* (that which the "polytechnical style" with all its artistic means has up to now concerned itself in vain) will be bestowed of its own accord on the works of the new style, of the machine style, of—if one wishes to call it thus—the *technical* style.

Notes

1. The growing preference for the *flat roof* is, by the way, not so much a constructional as an aesthetic result of new building design, one that results from the changed elements of the composition. The pitched roof is as little suited to the smooth-walled, sharply angled, and strongly cubic construction of the new house (which is open on all sides and strives for an intimate unity with the world outside) as a steeply pitched gable is to an Italian palace facade, or a smoothly bobbed hairdo is to an amply folded farthingale of the Baroque period. The question debated with such principled fervor—"flat or pitched roofs"—will be settled in the end not by the technical concerns of professional logic but by the creative formative will of the new building spirit. Here, too, building technology will always make available to the formative will the constructional means required to realize its spiritual goals. The construction of the flat roof will come about when the new formative will demands it, as soon as perfected and dependable techniques are made available.

2. See E. Dülberg, "Die Farbe als funktionelles Element der Architektur," in *Der Neubau* (1924): 105 f. and 121 f.

Illustration Credits

Every effort has been made to locate all copyright holders for the images reproduced in this book. The publishers invite any copyright holders they have not been able to reach to contact them so that full acknowledgment may be given in subsequent editions.

The following sources have granted permission to reproduce illustrations in this book:

figs. 1, 2, 9, 14, 42, 71	Stadtarchiv Magdeburg
figs. 4, 23	Fondation Le Corbusier, Paris/Artists Rights Society (ARS), New York
figs. 5, 6, 7, 8, 45, 46	Bildarchiv Foto Marburg
figs. 5, 14, 27, 33, 34, 35, 44, 72	Hans Köster Verlagsbuchhandlung KG, for Walter Müller-Wulckow, *Architektur, 1900–1929 in Deutschland,* 5th ed. (Königstein im Taunus: Karl Robert Langewiesche, 1999) ISBN 3-7845-8041-6
fig. 11	Muzeum Architektury, Wrocław
fig. 13	Estate of Robert Mallet-Stevens/Artists Rights Society (ARS), New York
figs. 15, 30, 31, 36, 47, 49, 50, 60	Bauhaus-Archiv, Museum für Gestaltung, Berlin
fig. 16	SMPK Kunstbibliothek, Berlin
figs. 19, 20	Streekarchief voor het Gooi en de Vechtstreek (SAGV), Fotocollectie Publieke Werken. Photographer: C. A. Deul
figs. 21, 22	Nederlands Architectuurinstituut/Architectenbureau van den Broek en Bakema, Rotterdam. Archive and inv. nos.: Oud ph 200; Oud ph 253. Photographer: Van Ojen, The Hague
figs. 32, 33	Lichtbildverlag für Kunstgeschichte, Meersbusch
fig. 34	AEG Archiv, Frankfurt
fig. 37	Biblioteka Uniwersytecka, Wrocław
figs. 43, 44	Esther Mendelsohn Joseph, San Francisco
figs. 48, 57, 70	Mies van der Rohe Archive, Museum of Modern Art, New York
figs. 58, 59	*Chicago Tribune*
figs. 64, 65, 68, 69	Akademie der Künste, Sammlung Baukunst, Berlin
fig. 72	Bibliothèque Albert I, Brussels
fig. 73	Frank Lloyd Wright Archives, Taliesin West, Scottsdale, Arizona
fig. 74	VBK, Vienna/Artists Rights Society (ARS), New York

Bibliography

Books and Contributions to Books

1911

Alfred Messel. Berlin: Bruno Cassirer.

*Die einheitliche Blockfront als Raumelement im Stadtbau: Ein Beitrag zur Stadt-
baukunst der Gegenwart.* Berlin: Bruno Cassirer.

1919

"Kunst und Technik." In Erwin Gutkind, *Neues Bauen: Grundlagen zur praktischen
Siedlungstätigkeit,* 237–40. Berlin: Verlag der Bauwelt.

Neue Aufgaben der Baukunst. Stuttgart: Deutsche Verlags-Anstalt.

1920

"Einleitung." In Paul Mebes, *Um 1800: Architektur und Handwerk im letzten Jahrhundert ihrer traditionellen Entwicklung,* 7–12. 3d ed. Munich: F. Bruckmann.

Der Kampf um den Stil im Kunstgewerbe und in der Architektur. Stuttgart: Deutsche
Verlags-Anstalt.

1926

*Städtebau und Wohnungswesen in den Vereinigten Staaten: Bericht über eine Studien-
reise.* Berlin: Guido Hackebeil. 2d ed., 1927.

1927

"Hochhäuser in Deutschland." In *Gegenwartsprobleme der Technik.* Edited by Erich
Lasswitz. Frankfurt am Main: Selbstverlag des Messamts Frankfurt am Main.

Der Sieg des neuen Baustils. Stuttgart: Akademischer Verlag Fritz Wedekind & Co.

1928

Die holländische Stadt. Berlin: Bruno Cassirer.

1934

"Post-War Housing in Germany." In *America Can't Have Housing.* Edited by Carol
Aronovici, 37–40. New York: Museum of Modern Art.

1937

Modern Building: Its Nature, Problems, and Forms. New York: Harcourt, Brace &
Company.

1952

"The Example of Frank Lloyd Wright." In *Roots of Contemporary American Architecture,* edited by Lewis Mumford, 396–403. New York: Reinhold. Reprint, New
York: Dover, 1972. Originally published in Behrendt, *Modern Building* (see under
1937).

1984

"Il movimento stilistico" and "La lotta per il nuovo stile," translations of excerpts
from *Der Sieg des neuen Baustils* (see under 1927). In *L'immagine storiografica
dell'architettura contemporanea da Platz a Giedion,* edited and translated by
Maria Luisa Scalvini and Maria Grazia Sandri, 194–97. Rome: Officina Edizioni.

Contributions to Periodicals

1907

"Architektonische Details." *Deutsche Bauhütte* 11:120, 126–27.

"Bauausstellung der kgl. Akademie der Künste zu Berlin." *Neudeutsche Bauzeitung* 3,
no. 50:397–98.

"Die Bauten der Deutschen Armee-, Marine- und Kolonialausstellung Berlin 1907."
Neudeutsche Bauzeitung 3, no. 29:229–30.

"Eine Gedenkfeier für Otto Schmalz im Architekten-Verein zu Berlin." *Deutsche
Bauzeitung* 41, no. 85:597–600.

"Geschäftshausbeispiele: Der Industriepalast an der Warschauer Brücke in Berlin."
Neudeutsche Bauzeitung 3:330–33.

"Haus Siebenstern." *Deutsche Bauhütte* 11:109–10.

"Laden und Schaufenster." Parts 1 and 2. *Deutsche Bauhütte* 11:378–80, 394–95.

"Der moderne Friedhof." *Berliner Architekturwelt* 9:203–5.

"Das Papierhaus zu Berlin." *Neudeutsche Bauzeitung* 3, no. 44:346–49.

"Der Pariser Platz in Berlin." *Deutsche Bauhütte* 11:118, 120.

"Professor Messels Rathaus in Ballenstedt." *Neudeutsche Bauzeitung* 3, no.
37: 289–92.

"Reiseführer." *Neudeutsche Bauzeitung* 3, no. 50:401–2.

"Ueber Backsteinbauweise." *Deutsche Bauhütte* 11:184.

"Vom Weinhaus Rheingold in Berlin." *Deutsche Bauhütte* 11:101–2.

1908

"Althamburgische Bauweise." *Neudeutsche Bauzeitung* 4, no. 7:52–56.

"Architektur und Kunstgewerbe auf der Grossen Berliner Kunstausstellung 1908."
Parts 1 and 2. *Neudeutsche Bauzeitung* 4, no. 35:273–77; no. 36:281.

"Aus unseren Eigenhausbeispielen: Villa Hellwig in Grunewald bei Berlin."
Neudeutsche Bauzeitung 4, no. 25:197.

"Beispiele moderner Backsteinbauten: Der Ritterhof in Berlin." *Neudeutsche Bauzeitung* 4, nos. 1/2:10–12.

"Berliner Architekturspaziergänge." *Neudeutsche Bauzeitung* 4, no. 21:161–63.

"Grabsteinkunst." *Neudeutsche Bauzeitung* 4, no. 40:313–15.

"Das Haus der Allgemeinen Elektrizitäts-Gesellschaft in Berlin." *Neudeutsche Bauzeitung* 4, no. 47:373–76.

"Kleinarchitekturen." Parts 1 and 2. *Neudeutsche Bauzeitung* 4, no. 30:233–35; no. 31:241–44.

"Kleinstadtarchitektur, Schulhaus Hans Spitzner." *Deutsche Bauhütte* 12:27–28.

"Landschaftliche Gartengestaltung." *Neudeutsche Bauzeitung* 4, no. 19:146–49.

"Die Lehren des Klassicismus." *Neudeutsche Bauzeitung* 4, no. 23:177–81.

"Das Münchener Künstlertheater." *Neudeutsche Bauzeitung* 4, no. 39:305–11.

"Neue Backsteinbauten." *Neudeutsche Bauzeitung* 4, no. 47:384–85.

"Neue Grundsätze der Schaufenstergestaltung." *Neudeutsche Bauzeitung* 4, no. 49:393–95.

"Die neuen Bahnhöfe der Berliner Untergrundbahn." Parts 1 and 2. *Neudeutsche Bauzeitung* 4, no. 26:201–4, 209–12.

"Eine neue Schaufenster-Anordnung." *Deutsche Bauhütte* 12:10.

Review of *Die Schönheit der grossen Stadt,* by August Endell. *Neudeutsche Bauzeitung* 4, no. 49:396.

"Sommer- und Ferienhäuser." *Neudeutsche Bauzeitung* 4, no. 19:151.

"Villenkolonie und Landhausbau." *Neudeutsche Bauzeitung* 4, no. 38:297–300.

"Vom neuen Stil." *Neudeutsche Bauzeitung* 4, no. 3:17–20.

"Vorbildliche Entwürfe für Vorortbauten." *Neudeutsche Bauzeitung* 4, no. 43:340–43.

"Wettbewerb zur Ausschmückung des Pappelplatzes in Berlin N." *Neudeutsche Bauzeitung* 4, no. 25:199–200.

1909

"Alfred Messel." *Neudeutsche Bauzeitung* 5, no. 20:225–33.

"Die Architektur auf der Grossen Berliner Kunstausstellung 1909." *Neudeutsche Bauzeitung* 5, no. 33:381–85, 388; no. 34:394–96.

"Ludwig Hoffmann." *Neudeutsche Bauzeitung* 5, no. 46:539–53.

"Neubauten des Beamten-Wohnungs-Vereins zu Berlin." *Neudeutsche Bauzeitung* 5, no. 1:6–8.

"Das Problem des Einküchenhauses." *Neudeutsche Bauzeitung* 5, no. 40:465–74.

1910

"Alfred Messels Museumspläne." *Kunst und Künstler* 8:366–69.

Architectural report on the aesthetics of bridges in Berlin. *Kunst und Künstler* 8:282.

"Bauten von Martin Elsässer." *Der Baumeister* 8:109–15.

Report on the results of contest to expand the A. Wertheim building. *Kunst und Künstler* 8:327–28.

Review of Keller & Reiner gallery opening. *Kunst und Künstler* 8:325–26.

1911

"Für die stadtbaukünstlerische Einheit von Gross-Berlin." *Die Bauwelt* 2, no. 123:15–16.

"Ludwig Hoffmanns Bebauungspläne für die Stadt Athen." *Moderne Bauformen* 10:426–28.

"Neubauten des Architekten (B.D.A.) Hans Bernoulli, Berlin." *Moderne Bauformen* 10:229–46.

Report on August Endell's construction of a sanatorium in Berlin-Westend. *Kunst und Künstler* 9:158–59.

Report on land development in the municipality of Schöneberg. *Kunst und Künstler* 9:454–55.

Report on the Joseph Olbrich exhibition at the Königliche Akademie der Künste. *Kunst und Künstler* 9:111.

"Zu den Arbeiten des Architekten Paul Baumgarten, Berlin." *Moderne Bauformen* 10:589–90, 598–600.

1912

Architectural report on expansion of A. Wertheim building. *Kunst und Künstler* 10:616–17.

"Das Berliner Stadthaus." *Kunst und Künstler* 10:145–52.

"Julius Habicht." *Moderne Bauformen* 11:105–13.

"Julius Habicht." *Zeitschrift des Verbandes Deutscher Architekten- und Ingenieur-Vereine* 1:425–26.

"Messels Nachfolge." *Kunst und Künstler* 10:354–66.

Report on art exhibition planned for the 1913 jubilee of the emperor's reign. *Kunst und Künstler* 10:172.

"Zu den Arbeiten des Architekten J. Theede in Kiel." *Moderne Bauformen* 11:445–64.

1913

"Arbeiten der Architekten Jürgensen und Bachmann, B.D.A., Berlin." *Der Profanbau* 9, no. 12:361–62, 392–94.

"Die Bauten der Jahrhundertausstellung in Breslau." *Zentralblatt der Bauverwaltung* 33:433–36, 437.

"Gedächtnisausstellung für Julius Habicht in Berlin." *Kunst und Künstler* 11:481.

"Hans Poelzig." *Kunst und Künstler* 12:55–61. Reprinted in *Hans Poelzig: Gesammelte Schriften und Werke*, edited by Julius Posener, 63–65. Berlin: Gebr. Mann, 1970.

"Julius Habicht." *Berliner Architekturwelt* 15:387–98.

"Der Neubau der Königlichen Oper in Berlin." *Bau-Rundschau* 4:229–34.

"Neue Bücher: Über Baukunst." *Kunst und Künstler* 11:484.

"Neuere Baukunst in Schlesien." *Architektonische Rundschau* 29:49–60.

"Paul Wallot." *Kunst und Künstler* 11:54–56.

Review of *Frank Lloyd Wright, Chicago*, by Charles Robert Ashbee. *Kunst und Künstler* 11:484–88.

"Schloss Rheinsberg." *Kunst und Künstler* 11:560–69.

1914

"Architektur und Kunstgewerbe in Alt-Dänemark." *Wasmuths Monatshefte für Baukunst* 1:269–71.

"Die deutsche Werkbundausstellung in Köln." *Kunst und Künstler* 12:615–26.

"Malmö: Die baltische Ausstellung." *Kunst und Künstler* 12:650.

"Über die deutsche Baukunst der Gegenwart I–III." *Kunst und Künstler* 12:263–76, 328–36, 373–83.

"Die Wiederaufbau im Osten." *Wasmuths Monatshefte für Baukunst. Wochenkorrespondenz,* 9:65–67.

1915

"Neue Reichsbankbauten." *Der Profanbau* 11, no. 13:185–216.

"Der nordische Geist in der französischen Architektur." *Kunst und Künstler* 13:241–49.

"Warschau." *Kunst und Künstler* 13:267–68.

1916

"Ausstellung von Kriegergräbern." *Kunst und Künstler* 14:416.

"Berliner Kirchenbaukunst von 1840–1870." *Kunst und Künstler* 14:535–54.

"Das Freiluftsmuseum in Hadersleben." *Bau-Rundschau* 7, no. 22–24:89–104.

"Hans Grisebach." *Kunst und Künstler* 14:297–307.

"Kleinsiedlungen." *Die Kunst: Monatshefte für freie und angewandte Kunst* 19:205–28.

1919

"Alt-Gent." *Kunst und Künstler* 17:51–64.

"Der Meister des Bebauungsplanes: Hermann Jansens zum 50. Geburtstag am 28. Mai 1919." *Die Volkswohnung* 1, no. 10:132–34.

"Die Normenbewegung im Bauwesen." *Die Volkswohnung* 1, no. 5:57–59.

"Zur Einführung." *Die Volkswohnung* 1, no. 1:1–2.

1920

"Der Aufbau einer kriegszerstörten Stadt in Ostpreussen." *Kunst und Künstler* 18:301–9.

"Grundrisskunst." *Das Werk* 7:260–66.

"Rückblick und Ausblick." *Die Volkswohnung* 2, no. 1:1–4.

"Stuttgart: Zur Tagung des deutschen Werkbundes." *Kunst und Künstler* 18:90–91.

1921

"Das Einküchenhaus." *Die Volkswohnung* 3, no. 6:81–83.

"Die Organisierung der Künstler." *Die Volkswohnung* 3, no. 7:93–95.

"Der Sinn der Siedlungsbewegung." *Die Volkswohnung* 3, no. 1:1–3.

"Schloss Sanssouci." Parts 1 and 2. *Kunst und Künstler* 19:399–407, 423–34.

"Wohnungs- und Siedlungsbauten in Lübeck." *Die Volkswohnung* 3, no. 16:213–17.

1922

"Das erste Turmhaus in Berlin." *Die Woche* 9:193–94. Reprinted in *Der Schrei nach dem Turmhaus*, 312. Exh. cat. Bauhaus-Archiv and Museum für Gestaltung. Berlin: Argon, 1988.

"Das Schicksal des Handwerks." *Die Volkswohnung* 4, no. 23:317–18.

"Weg und Ziel." *Die Volkswohnung* 4, no. 1:1–3.

"Die Wohnungsfrage in New York." *Die Volkswohnung* 4, no. 22:308–13.

1923

"Architektenerziehung." *Die Volkswohnung* 5, nos. 17/18:209–11.

"Deutsche Gewerbeschau München 1922." *Kunst und Künstler* 21:55–60.

"Die internationale Siedlungs- und Stadtbaukonferenz in Gothenburg, 1923." *Die Volkswohnung* 5, no. 16:197–202.

"Das neue englische Wohnungsgesetz." *Die Volkswohnung* 5, no. 10:125–28.

"Praktische Baupflege." *Die Volkswohnung* 5, no. 21:257–59.

"Skyscrapers in Germany." *Journal of the American Institute of Architects* 11, no. 9:365–70. See also responses to Behrendt: George C. Nimmons, "Skyscrapers in America," 370–72; William Stanley Parker, "Skyscrapers Anywhere," 372.

"Das Stadtbauproblem." *Kunst und Künstler* 21:171–79.

1924

"Die Architekten gegen den Berliner Magistrat." *Der Neubau* 6, no. 10:114.

"Die Architektur auf der Grossen Berliner Kunstausstellung 1924." *Kunst und Künstler* 22:347–52.

"Das Ehrenmal der Gefallenen in Berlin?" *Das Werk* 1, no. 7:7–8.

"Das Hochhaus." *Kunst und Künstler* 22:175–81.

"Industrialisierung des Wohnungsbaues." *Der Neubau* 6, no. 5:41–43.

"Das Industriegut." *Der Neubau* 6, no. 16:195–99.

"Die Internationale Städtebautagung Amsterdam 1924." *Der Neubau* 6, no. 15:177–79.

"Die Jahrhundertausstellung des Architekten-Vereins zu Berlin." *Der Neubau* 6, no. 17:210.

"Unsere Aufgabe." *Der Neubau* 6, no. 1:1.

1925

"Berliner Kaleidoskop." *Die Form* 1, no. 3:59–60.

"Geleitwort." *Die Form* 1, no. 1:1–2.

Review of *Der neue Stil in Frankreich*, by Henry van de Velde. *Die Form* 1, no. 3:60.

Review of *Vom Blockhaus zum Wolkenkratzer* (translation of *Sticks and Stones*), by Lewis Mumford. *Die Form* 1, no. 2:34.

"Die Situation des Kunstgewerbes." *Die Form* 1, no. 3:37–41.

"Zum Bauprobleme der Zeit." *Der Neubau* 7, no. 1:1–4.

1926

"Aus dem Tagebuch einer Amerikareise." Parts 1–3. *Kunst und Künstler* "Das Schiff,"
 24:18–23; "Das Herz der Welt oder die Stadt des Teufels," 24:61–66; "Kulturlandschaft," 24:97–99.

Review of *Kommende Baukunst* (translation of *Vers une architecture*), by Le Corbusier. *Die Form* 1, no. 10:228.

Review of *Probleme der angewandeten Kunst*, edited by Alfred Rohde and Hans
 Dorén. *Die Form* 1, no. 10:228.

"Tradition: Schlusswort der Schriftleitung." *Die Form* 1, no. 10:227.

"Wohnbauten der Stadtgemeinde Wien." *Die Form* 1, no. 8:167–71.

"Zum Formproblem der Zeit." *Die Form* 1, no. 9:187–94.

1927

"Formprobleme der werdenden Weltstadt." *Kunst und Künstler* 25:438–39.

"Geschäftshaus- und Ladenbau." *Zentralblatt der Bauverwaltung* 47:589–94.

"Haus Otto Rudolf Salvisberg, Berlin-Südende." *Moderne Bauformen* 26:453–60.

"Holländische Grachten." *Kunst und Künstler* 25:16–22.

"Landesplanung in den Vereinigten Staaten." *Der Neubau* 9, no. 3:25–32.

"Neue Wohnhausgruppen der Architekten Paul Mebes und Paul Emmerich, Berlin."
 Der Neubau 9:10–12.

Review of *Handbuch der Architektur*, by Herman Sörgel. *Zentralblatt der Bauverwaltung* 47:601.

Review of *Junge Baukunst in Deutschland*, by Heinrich de Fries. *Frankfurter Zeitung*,
 6 February, *Literaturblatt*, 6.

1928

"Geschäftshaus- und Ladenbau." *Frankfurter Zeitung*, 6 January, evening ed., 1–2.

"Vom neuen Bauen." *Zentralblatt der Bauverwaltung* 48:657–62.

"Vom neuen Bauen." Part 1, "Akademische Baukunst," *Kunst und Künstler*
 26:347–53; part 2, "Die Stilbewegung," *Kunst und Künstler* 26:420–26.

1929

"Die Bebauung des Scheunenviertels in Berlin." *Zentralblatt der Bauverwaltung*
 49:281–86.

"Hans Poelzig zum 60. Geburtstag." *Frankfurter Zeitung*, 30 April, 1st morning ed.,
 1–2.

"Hans Poelzig zum 60. Geburtstage." *Kunst und Künstler* 27:301–9.

"Karl Scheffler und die moderne Architektur." *Frankfurter Zeitung*, 28 February, 1st
 morning ed., 1.

"Neues Bauen in der Welt." *Kunst und Künstler* 27:494–98.

"Paul Schultze-Naumburg: Gelegentlich seines 60. Geburtstages." *Frankfurter
 Zeitung*, 10 June, evening ed., 1.

"Platz der Republik." *Frankfurter Zeitung*, 14 December, evening ed., 1–2.

1930

"Eine Gedächtnisstätte für die Gefallenen des Weltkrieges: Zum Umbau der Neuen Wache in Berlin." *Zentralblatt der Bauverwaltung* 50:513–18.

"Vom Bauherrn." *Frankfurter Zeitung*, 17 April, 1st morning ed., 1–2.

"Walter Gropius: Bemerkungen zu einer Gesamtausstellung." *Frankfurter Zeitung*, 14 April, evening ed., 1.

1931

"Anfang und Ende." *Frankfurter Zeitung*, 15 March, *Reiseblatt*, 1.

"Die Ausstellung der Staatshochbauverwaltung auf der deutschen Bauaustellung Berlin 1931." *Zentralblatt der Bauverwaltung* 51:341–46.

"Frank Lloyd Wright: Zur Ausstellung in der Akademie der Künste in Berlin." *Frankfurter Zeitung*, 30 June, 1st morning ed., 1–2.

"Le Corbusier." *Kunst und Künstler* 30:53–58.

"Vom neuen Bauen in Berlin." *Frankfurter Zeitung*, 22 November, *Literaturblatt*, 6.

"Das zeitgenössische Gebrauchsgerät." *Frankfurter Zeitung*, 16 December, evening ed., 3–4.

1932

"Architekt P. Mebes." *Frankfurter Zeitung*, 24 January, evening ed., 3.

"Carl Ferdinand Busse: Ein preussischer Baubeamter." *Zentralblatt der Bauverwaltung* 52, no. 53:628–36.

"Sonne, Luft und Haus für Alle." *Kunst und Künstler* 31:262–66.

"Theodor Fischer: Zu seinem siebzigsten Geburtstag." *Frankfurter Zeitung*, 27 May, evening ed., 1.

1933

"Neuer protestantischer Kirchenbau," review of *Protestantischer Kirchenbau seit 1900 in Deutschland*, by Walter Distel. *Frankfurter Zeitung*, 18 June, *Literaturblatt*, 3.

"Das Polstermöbel," review of *Das Polstermöbel*, by Adolf G. Schneck. *Frankfurter Zeitung*, 12 November, *Literaturblatt*, 6.

"Der Wandel der Raumgestalt: Zu dem Buche von Gustav Adolf Platz, *Wohnräume der Gegenwart*." *Frankfurter Zeitung*, 14 July, evening ed., 1.

1937

"A City Planner Looks at Buffalo." *City Planning* 13, no. 4:1–4.

Archival Collections

Letters from Behrendt to Lewis Mumford, 1925–1945. Lewis Mumford Papers. Folders 362–66. Special Collections. Van Pelt-Dietrich Library Center. University of Pennsylvania.

Reviews of "Der Sieg des neuen Baustils"

Compiled by Kai Gutschow

1927

Düttmann. *Rheinische Blätter für Wohnungswesen und Bauberatung* 22:105.

Hallbaum, Franz. "Rückblick auf Stuttgart." *Die Gartenkunst* 40:195–96.

Das Kunstblatt 11, no. 12 (December): 413.

L[ampann], G[ustav]. *Zentralblatt der Bauverwaltung* 47, no. 46:601.

V[ölter], [Ernst]. *Die Baugilde* 9, no. 23:1436.

1928

Adler, Leo. *Die literarische Welt* 4, no. 10:6.

Behne, Adolf. *Reclams Universum* 44.2, no. 32:732.

Dexel, [Walter]. *Frankfurter Zeitung*, 26 February, *Literaturblatt*, 5.

Herrmann, Wolfgang. "Alte und Neue Baukunst." *Kunst und Künstler* 26, no.
    1:480–82.

Der Neubau 10, no. 5:63.

Wohnungswirtschaft 5, nos. 9/10:109.

1929

Hartmann, Karl von. *Deutsche Bauzeitung* 63.1, no. 70 (31 August): suppl., 7–8.

H[ellwig], R. *Schlesisches Heim* 10, no. 2:42.

Selected Articles on Behrendt

"Behrendt, Walter Curt." *Who Was Who in America*. Vol. 2 (1943–50), 56. Chicago:
    A. N. Marquis Co., 1950.

"Behrendt, Walter Curt. (12/26/1884–4/26/1945)." *Biographical Dictionary of Ameri-
    can Architects (Deceased)*. Edited by Henry F. Withey and Elsie Rathburn Withey,
    48. Los Angeles: Hennessey & Ingalls, 1970.

"Behrendt, Walter Curt (1884–1945)." *Roots of Contemporary American Architec-
    ture*. Edited by Lewis Mumford, 421–22. New York: Reinhold, 1952.

"Behrendt, Walter Curt, 1884–1945." *Zwischen Kunst und Industrie: Der Deutsche
    Werkbund*, exh. cat. Edited by Wend Fischer, 594. Munich: Die Neue Sammlung,
    Staatliches Museum für Angewandte Kunst, 1975; reprint, Stuttgart: Deutsche
    Verlags-Anstalt, 1987.

Heiligenthal. Review of *Städtebau und Wohnungswesen in den Vereinigten Staaten*,
    by Behrendt. *Der Neubau* 9, no. 4 (1927): 100.

"In Norwich, Vermont...: Walter Curt Behrendt, architect; John Spaeth Jr., Associ-
    ated" *Pencil Points (Progressive Architecture)*, no. 2:55–59.

Isaacs, Reginald R. "Walter Curt Behrendt." *Macmillan Encyclopedia of Architects*.
    Vol. 1, 164–65. New York: Free Press, 1982.

M[üller]-W[ulckow], Walter. "Neue Aufgaben der Baukunst." *Frankfurter Zeitung*,
    12 November 1919, evening ed., 1.

Neumeyer, Fritz. "Alfred Messel, Der grosse Unbekannte" In Behrendt, *Alfred Messel.* Berlin: Gebr. Mann Verlag, 1998.

R[eifenberg], B[enno]. Review of *Die holländische Stadt,* by Behrendt. *Literaturblatt,* supplement to *Frankfurter Zeitung,* 11 November 1928.

Samson, M. David. "'Unser Newyorker Mitarbeiter': Lewis Mumford, Walter Curt Behrendt, and the Modern Movement in Germany." *Journal of the Society of Architectural Historians* 55, no. 2:126–39.

Scalvini, Maria Luisa, and Maria Grazia Sandri. "Walter Curt Behrendt, *Modern Building: Its Nature, Problems, and Forms.*" Chapter 4 in *L'immagine storiografica dell'architettura contemporanea da Platz a Giedion,* 98–125; includes biography, 156–57. Rome: Officina Edizioni, 1984.

"Das Wasser im Stadtbild." Review of *Die holländische Stadt,* by Behrendt. *Frankfurter Zeitung,* 3 December 1927, 1–2.

Obituary

"Dr. W. C. Behrendt, City Plans Expert." *New York Times,* 27 April 1945, 19.

Periodicals Edited

Neudeutsche Bauzeitung 6, 1910.

Die Volkswohnung 1–5, 1919–1923.

Der Neubau 6, 1924.

Die Form 1, nos. 1–15 (October 1925–December 1926).

The Victory of the New Building Style
Introduction by Detlef Mertins
Translation by Harry Francis Mallgrave

Detlef Mertins is associate professor of architecture at the University of Toronto, where he has been teaching since 1991. He received his doctorate from Princeton University in 1996, having practiced architecture for ten years after completing his professional degree at the University of Toronto. He is editor of *The Presence of Mies* (1994) and *Metropolitan Mutations* (1988). His essays on German modernism in architecture and art have appeared in the anthologies *Architecture and Cubism* (1998) and *Architecture and Ideology* (1997), in the journals *Assemblage, ANY, AA Files, A+U, ARCH+,* and *History of Photography,* and in *The Encyclopedia of Aesthetics* (1998). Mertins has taught at Harvard University, Columbia University, Rice University, and the Architectural Association. He was visiting scholar at the Canadian Centre for Architecture in 1998 and is currently completing a catalog essay for the CCA's upcoming exhibition, *Mies in America* (2001).

Harry Francis Mallgrave received his doctorate from the University of Pennsylvania in 1983 with a dissertation on Gottfried Semper. Between 1986 and 1988 he was a Research Fellow and Associate at the Getty Center for the History of Art and the Humanities. His translation of Otto Wagner's *Modern Architecture* inaugurated the Research Institute's Texts & Documents series. Since the series's inception, he has served as a consultant and editor for architecture and aesthetics. His most recent publication is the personal and intellectual biography *Gottfried Semper: Architect of the Nineteenth Century*. With Eleftherios Ikonomou, he translated *Empathy, Form, and Space: Problems in German Aesthetics, 1873–1893* and is currently at work on Johann Joachim Winckelmann, *The History of Ancient Art*.

Sigfried Giedion, *Building in France, Building in Iron, Building in Ferroconcrete* (1928)
Introduction by Sokratis Georgiadis
ISBN 0-89236-319-3 (hardcover), ISBN 0-89236-320-7 (paper)

Hendrik Petrus Berlage: Thoughts on Style, 1886–1909
Introduction by Iain Boyd Whyte
ISBN 0-89236-334-7 (paper)

Adolf Behne, *The Modern Functional Building* (1926)
Introduction by Rosemarie Haag Bletter
ISBN 0-89236-364-9 (paper)

Aby Warburg, *The Renewal of Pagan Antiquity* (1932)
Introduction by Kurt W. Forster
ISBN 0-89236-537-4 (hardcover)

Alois Riegl, *The Group Portraiture of Holland* (1902)
Introduction by Wolfgang Kemp
ISBN 0-89236-548-X (paper)

In Preparation
Jean-Nicolas-Louis Durand, *Précis of the Lectures on Architecture* (1802–1805) and *Graphic Portion of the Lectures on Architecture* (1821)
Introduction by Antoine Picon

Gottfried Semper, *Style in the Technical and Tectonic Arts; or, Practical Aesthetics* (1860–1861)
Introduction by Harry Francis Mallgrave

Designed by Bruce Mau Design Inc.,
Bruce Mau with Chris Rowat and Catherine Rix
Coordinated by Stacy Miyagawa
Type composed by Archetype in Sabon and News Gothic
Printed and bound by Thomson-Shore on Cougar Opaque
Cover printed by Phoenix Color

Texts & Documents
Series designed by Bruce Mau Design Inc., Toronto, Canada